There You Have It

San Diego Christian College
2100 Greenfield Drive
El Cajon, CA 92019

THE LIFE, LEGACY,

AND LEGEND OF

HOWARD COSELL

070.449796
C834H
B655t

There You Have It

JOHN BLOOM

UNIVERSITY OF MASSACHUSETTS PRESS *Amherst & Boston*

Copyright © 2010 by University of Massachusetts Press
All rights reserved
Printed in the United States of America

LC 2010037284
ISBN 978-1-55849-837-2 (paper); 836-5 (library cloth)

Designed by Richard Hendel
Set in ITC Charter and Aller by Westchester Book
Printed and bound by Thomson-Shore, Inc.

Library of Congress Cataloging-in-Publication Data

Bloom, John, 1962–
    There you have it : the life, legacy, and legend of
Howard Cosell / John Bloom.
        p. cm.
    Includes bibliographical references and index.
    ISBN 978-1-55849-837-2 (pbk. : alk. paper)—
    ISBN 978-1-55849-836-5 (library cloth : alk. paper)
1. Cosell, Howard, 1918–1995.   2. Sportscasters—United
States—Biography.   I. Title.
    GV742.42C67   B56   2010
    070.449796092—dc22
    [B]

                        2010037284

British Library Cataloguing in Publication data are
available.

Title page photo courtesy Mitchell Seidel.

To Catherine and Nick,
who have led their family to
explore its Jewish identity.

Contents

Illustrations

In addition to issues surrounding ethnicity, Cosell was distinctive in the way he publicly expressed an overarching critique of the very medium that employed him. I call this the "Cosell critique." Cosell routinely expressed this critique when he would succinctly label the practitioners of his profession, and the networks that employed them, as shills. *Shill* was the perfect word for Cosell to use. It describes a person who is secretly paid to voice enthusiasm for something being sold. Shills receive compensation for looking honest and sincere while actually having put their integrity up for sale. Although Cosell would use this term with increasing frequency toward the end of his life, throughout his career he saw sports institutions and broadcasters in an "unholy alliance" with each other. He sharply criticized the fact that networks were clients of sports institutions yet were also charged with covering sporting events objectively.

As revealing as Cosell's identities, principles, and political stands were, this book is also about the cultural contradictions that he embodied, which were equally revealing of the times in which he lived. He was a product of Jewish Brooklyn who could not hide his ethnicity or background, but who downplayed this identity throughout his career. He had a deep fascination with sports and athletes, and risked almost everything that was dear to him for a career in sports broadcasting, but he expressed contempt for individuals and institutions that constituted the sports establishment. He took courageous stands for causes like civil rights without fear of a confrontation, but at other times in his life shied away from controversy. As much as he criticized the relationships between sports and corporate America, he was fiercely loyal to the company that employed him. As much as he was driven by causes of social justice, he also loved fame and the power and wealth it gave him. My book is about these contradictions.

The origins of this book go back to my days in graduate school at the University of Minnesota. Up until that time I had developed a kind of knee-jerk dislike for Cosell, a reaction rooted in my earliest memories of the man. From the time I was eight years old, whenever I turned on *Monday Night Football,* I have to admit to yelling "Shut up, Howard!" at the television set, just at the sound of his voice, not listening to the content of what he was actually saying. By the time I was in graduate school in the mid-to-late 1980s, Cosell was gone from *Monday Night Football.* In fact, although I had not really noticed it at

Preface

What is the significance of a man like Howard Cosell: a sportscaster, a media figure, a celebrity? In an unpublished oral history interview, Cosell once said that only a few years after his death, nobody would remember who he was, that celebrity is fleeting. In some ways he was right. Many reading this book might have no, or very little, idea who Howard Cosell was. From the outset, then, I want to tell those readers the story of Howard Cosell, a very unlikely person to have become one of the biggest media figures of his time. For those who remember Cosell, I want to remind them about a sportscaster who was a product of his times, whose intellect and political commitment made him a unique celebrity, and who became one of the principal public figures who helped define his era.

This is a biography of Howard Cosell, but even more than that, it is a critical biography. It seeks to show why Cosell rose to fame, and how historical trends and conditions allowed for such an unlikely figure to develop into one of the most widely recognized people of his generation. What did Cosell mean to people? Why and how did he resonate with audiences?

Cosell's ethnic identity is central to this book. To put it more directly, Cosell was Jewish. Even though he almost never mentioned this on the air, it was a core aspect of his expressive public personality, mentioned often in print if not over the air. In addition to his being Jewish, Cosell's career was marked in large part by his relationships with African Americans. From an early point in his career, when he presided over the production of a documentary about the Grambling College football team in the early 1960s, to his support for Jackie Robinson, to his defense of baseball player Curt Flood (who sought to fight the game's "reserve clause"), to his defense of Tommie Smith and John Carlos, who registered their protest against the U.S. government from the medal stand at the 1968 Mexico City Olympic Games, to his highly publicized defense of Muhammad Ali, Cosell championed the causes of African American athletes who asserted themselves forcefully in public debates.

the time, he was gone from television entirely. He was not yet, however, entirely out of the public eye.

It was also at this time that I was becoming interested in popular culture as a key component of the language shared by citizens of the United States and the world. I had taken an anthropology course on the cultural meanings of Hollywood film, taught by a very traditional neo-Marxist. His thesis was that American popular culture cannot allow any social analysis to enter into its narrative structures. Instead, Americans are fed stories about individuals: heroes, villains, antiheroes, and so on. Even films that tackle social problems, such as labor rights, end up blinding audiences to a consciousness of themselves as social subjects and instead offer only individual action as a solution.

It was not long after taking this course that I was reading the sports page one day. Howard Cosell had a syndicated column, and this particular one dealt with Joe Paterno, coach of the Penn State University football team. At the time Paterno had a reputation for supporting high academic standards for scholar-athletes, and Cosell expressed admiration for this. His larger argument, however, had to do with the broader corruption that was endemic in the way scholarship athletics operate in the United States, where athletes are exploited not only by universities for what they can bring in publicity and student interest, but also by a myriad of other economic interests for which they generate advertising revenue, concession sales, parking receipts, beer sales, and the like.

I was stunned. Here was the sportscaster whom I had derided all these years providing a cogent social analysis. His point was actually that the problem of corruption within college athletics was part of its very structure, and that the intervention of a heroic individual like Paterno did nothing to change the situation. Indeed, Cosell argued, it made matters worse by allowing more people to accept the system as fundamentally fair and in need of only minor reforms and virtuous saviors.

I brought up this article with a different professor, one who was more up-to-date on the complexities of popular culture: the "polysemous" and "multivocal" resonances that characterize public utterances, emancipatory possibilities, hegemonic ruptures, and so on. Look at this, I said. Does not this column show that in fact there are people out there who tell alternative stories, people who are part of, even at the center of, popular culture who actually do provide social analysis? I must have been expecting to be laughed at, and having studied Cosell closely for quite some time, I am pretty certain that it would have given him a great deal of pleasure if I had been. This professor took me seriously, however, and said that while he had not read the article to which I was referring, he did know that Cosell was very good to Muhammad Ali.

Let me stop here and make it clear from the outset that I do not argue in this book that Howard Cosell was a radical or a leftist. Those who knew him well describe him as a liberal. But when given an opportunity to stand up for progressive causes, Cosell usually took the moderate road, and sometimes even aligned himself with the Right. He was, however, someone who loudly professed his principles, and who at times had a keen eye that could see right through the obfuscation of corporate self-congratulation, media hype, and pompous self-importance. He said that the National Football League and the television networks were in an unholy alliance, and he was right. He said that sports franchises held cities hostage in ways that robbed communities of valuable resources, and he was right. He said that the International Olympic Committee was a group of pompous, arrogant, medieval-minded men, and once again he was right.

I have grown to like Cosell, but that is not always an easy thing to do. The great sportswriter Red Smith once wrote that he had tried to like Cosell but had failed miserably. Cosell could at one moment extol a principle as unassailable and set in stone, and then turn around and argue against that principle out of vindictive spite toward an individual he did not like. Cosell was all too human, but to his credit, he never hid his human frailties. Cosell's vanity, his insecurities, his temper, and his bombastic temperament were as exposed to the public as his keen intellect and his analytical mind.

This book is not what one might expect in a typical biography of a celebrity. I do not treat with much depth issues pertinent to Cosell's personal life that others have explored, his often excessive drinking being one. Instead I look at Cosell's unlikely rise to stardom in American culture within a number of historical and social contexts: historical trends like the Red Scare and the civil rights movement, the development of mass media and consumer culture, the formation of mass media institutions, and the gender politics surrounding sports and broadcasting.

This may be a book that Cosell would have enjoyed, but I imagine there are many passages that he would not have liked. In fact I have a vision of him storming into the Almighty's office waving a copy of this book in the air and screaming, "Did you read what he wrote about me?!" Of course, if the Almighty is all-knowing, She will not have to read it. So I hope that She will grant mercy upon me for any transgressions I may have committed in the course of writing this volume. And if Cosell's spirit is still alive out there, I hope he will understand that this is a book about a most remarkable public figure in the history of American media, someone who managed to reach the very highest heights of celebrity and fame yet made a social vision the central component of his life's work.

Acknowledgments

Like all authors, I have a lot of people to thank for helping me write this book. I began the process of preparing this project in 2004 and early 2005. Jeff Pearlman and Farley Chase were two of my earliest contacts and provided valuable suggestions and encouragement. Each steered me in the right direction for interviews. I also owe the title of the book to a suggestion from Farley. At University of Massachusetts Press I have had the privilege of working with Clark Dougan, who is everything a sports scholar could want in an acquisitions editor. He has overseen some of the finest books on sports history in publication, and I hope that mine lives up to the standard that he has set. The anonymous readers who reviewed the manuscript for University of Massachusetts Press provided detailed comments that were essential to my revision of this book. I would particularly like to thank Amanda Heller for her close reading of my manuscript and her thoughtful and careful copyediting.

Dave Kindred was another very early and generous supporter. Dave provided me with some valuable contact information while he was on tour promoting his own Cosell-Ali biography. Paul Buhle was very generous with his time and offered contacts and information regarding the 1950s blacklist era, which was important to Cosell's early career. Not only is my brother, Jim Bloom, a supportive family member, but also he drew on knowledge developed through a career in sports public relations to provide contact information and interview suggestions that proved invaluable.

I especially thank all of those who generously permitted me to interview them about Howard Cosell. These are (in alphabetical order) Jill Cosell, Justin Cosell, Frank Deford, Harry Edwards, Frank Gifford, Keith Jackson, Peter Mehlman, Jimmy Roberts, Joan Scott, Jim Spence, Bert Randolph Sugar, and Joe Valerio. All allowed me to conduct recorded interviews with them even though none knew who I was or anything about my book. Sugar and Spence offered particularly helpful comments. Although I am extremely grateful to all of my narrators for their participation in this project, I want to single out Howard Cosell's daughter Jill and grandson Justin for their help and

ACKNOWLEDGMENTS

for allowing me to question them about someone whom they hold very dear.

I am particularly lucky to be conducting scholarship on sports and popular culture among a strong community of scholars. The works of José Alamillo, Amy Bass, Adrian Burgos Jr., Susan Cahn, Gena Caponi-Taberi, George Lipsitz, Sharon O'Brien, and Mike Willard have provided me with immense intellectual inspiration. I also thank the faculty and staff of the History/Philosophy Department at Shippensburg University for their support and encouragement as I have worked on this project: Kwabena Akurang-Parry, Douglas Birsch, Steve Burg, Catherine Clay, Betty Dessants, Allen Dieterich-Ward, Jim Edwards, David Godshalk, Kim Klein, Chandrika Paul, John Quist, Susan Rimby, Christine Senecal, Robert Shaffer, Jon Skaff, Mark Spicka, and Allan Tulchin. Department secretary Janice Reed's diligence, organization, and efficiency allow faculty members like me to have the time during the summer to complete projects like this one. Christopher Gwinn, my graduate assistant in Shippensburg University's Applied History program, transcribed numerous interviews, as did my son, Nick Bloom. I thank both of them for their contributions to this book.

Finally, I thank my family, both extended and immediate. In particular, I want to acknowledge the love and support of my parents, Maxine and Sidney Bloom; my brother and sister-in-law, Kristina Lucky-Bloom and Jim Bloom; and my in-laws Lois and Jim Farrell. My daughter Catherine makes me proud and has been an enjoyable partner with whom I have watched many a Howard Cosell clip on YouTube. My son Nick, who entered college as I was writing this book, was a terrific research partner in New York as we tracked down Cosell sources early in this project. And, finally, I thank my wife, Amy Farrell, who is finishing her own book as I write this. As those who know Amy are already aware, she is beautiful, brilliant, witty, wise, and as I like to say, delightfully grounded. Without her, this book would not have been possible.

There You Have It

Introduction

Cosell can be seen in the dressing rooms of fighters, both before and after every major bout, at the ballparks and just about every other place sports news is likely to develop. "I try to get my guests to think out loud," explains Cosell. "My approach to sports coverage is three-dimensional. Being on the scene where news of dramatic impact is being made, going beyond the news story itself by asking searching questions and maintaining a spirit of friendship with sports personalities."
—ABC Radio Network press release, August 29, 1958

In 1976 Yale University refused to allow radical historian Herbert Aptheker to teach a seminar on his friend and colleague W. E. B. Du Bois as part of a one-semester student-organized program for undergraduates. The course would have paid Aptheker very little. It was a class that offered lecturers from outside the university an opportunity to teach, and gave students the chance to work with emeritus faculty and nonacademics who had built interesting careers. Aptheker was a historian whose work in the 1940s on the history of slavery in the United States had broken new ground. He seemed to be ideally suited for such a program, except for one thing: he was a communist.

The same semester that Aptheker was denied a seminar position at Yale, sportscaster Howard Cosell was allowed to teach a class titled "Big Time Sports and Contemporary America" in the very same program. To the leftist historian and Yale Ph.D. Jesse Lemisch, this was an irony that symbolized a larger corruption which he saw historically characterizing Yale, an irony he drew upon in the title of an article he had published in the *Newsletter of the Radical Historians Caucus,* "If Howard Cosell Can Teach at Yale, Why Can't Herbert Aptheker?"[1]

For Lemisch, it seemed that Yale was far more fascinated by the glow of media celebrity than it was by the ideas of a scholar who could teach from firsthand experience about one of the most significant historical figures of the twentieth century. What is more, Yale's blacklisting of Aptheker was for Lemisch a manifestation of what he had seen as the institution's long-standing racism and anti-Semitism. Yet if he had looked more closely at Cosell's biography, Lemisch might have been able to add yet another ironic twist. Just a little over twenty years earlier Cosell had himself been in danger of being blacklisted for having represented a union whose West Coast secretary had been called before the House Un-American Activities Committee. Just fifteen years earlier he had been kept off the air for reasons that he felt had to do with anti-Semitism. And just eight years earlier he had put his career on the line as one of the few broadcasters to have defended loudly and publicly the political actions of African American athletes such as Curt Flood, Tommie Smith, John Carlos, and Muhammad Ali.

While Howard Cosell may not have been a Trojan horse for the Left when he arrived at Yale for the 1975–76 academic year, neither was he simply a talking head. By 1976 Cosell may have been a relatively benign—if not, for many, annoying—popular entertainer and sportscaster, but he was also a remarkably unlikely person to emerge as perhaps the most universally recognized figure in sports broadcasting. He was a sportscaster, yet the flickering screens of the country's television sets had rarely projected before viewers the image of a less athletic physical specimen. He was respected for bringing journalistic integrity to sports reporting, yet he had very little training in professional journalism before he entered broadcasting. He excelled in a medium that, by the mid-1960s, rewarded banality and homogeneity, yet he thrived on controversy, forcefully expressed strong opinions, and spoke with an accent seasoned by his Brooklyn upbringing. He entered broadcasting in the wake of the McCarthy era during the 1950s, yet he excelled in part because of his outspoken support for the controversial cause of civil rights.

Understanding who Howard Cosell was and why he became such a central figure in the media culture of the United States is part of the mystery that I explore in this book (but do not promise to solve). When I asked media insiders their opinions, they often explained the Cosell phenomenon with a single word: "storyline." The term refers to the ability of a media commentator to connect individual human

2

events to some larger story that is meaningful to audiences. Those interested in the study of language might use the term "narrative" to refer to the same thing. Without narrative or storyline, the events of the day's news, or the actions of very fit people running around on a field, are random and meaningless. Storylines connect these actions to ideas, ethics, and emotions through narratives that audiences recognize and to which they respond.

Howard Cosell was a master of this kind of storytelling, but he did not introduce storyline to sports coverage. As a case in point, long before Cosell, Grantland Rice connected college football to epic storylines, such as when he termed the Notre Dame backfield the "Four Horsemen." As Rice's biblical reference suggests, sports journalists have long employed narratives that are familiar to a culture, and that evoke strong emotional responses. Such narratives have a universal quality, connecting victories on the field to broad heroic cultural themes. For example, in the 1970s, NFL Films framed the success of the Dallas Cowboys during the decade by pronouncing them "America's Team," evoking a myth of American exceptionalism and western grit that extended even beyond the famous thesis of Frederick Jackson Turner.

Roone Arledge, Cosell's boss in the sports department at the American Broadcasting Company, consciously applied narrative storylines to event coverage, making it a signature of ABC's sports programming. Cosell was in fact very good at this, but he was also something of a rebel within the traditions of sports storytelling. He liked to frame sports not just within universal themes but within topical ones that were relevant to his times. He not only celebrated those whose actions conformed to conventional plotlines (Cosell loved portraying almost any successful athlete as someone who had faced the adversity typical of the hero of a Horatio Alger story), but also enjoyed telling the stories of those who did not conform to conventions, those whose lives away from the athletic field or basketball court or boxing ring generated controversy. While Cosell entered a profession that celebrated the hero, he often exalted the antihero.

Perhaps this made Cosell a particularly well suited spokesman for the generation following the racial integration of American sports. During this period a number of African American athletes such as Curt Flood, John Carlos, Tommie Smith, Bill Russell, and Muhammad Ali upset a complacent sports-watching public by calling attention to their country's racist history and legacy. They were successful athletes, but their victories did not translate easily into models of athletic heroism that had been crafted a generation earlier, when major league sports were racially segregated and open only to whites. Cosell's most compelling storylines, like those he followed with Muhammad Ali, were not ones that led to an uncomplicated triumphant conclusion but instead were characterized by tensions left unresolved.

In this sense Howard Cosell was a political figure. He and others have written that he seriously contemplated running for the United States Senate late in his career. My understanding of Cosell's political significance, however, is broader than any desire that he might have had to hold political office. Cosell would likely have found the mainstream political arena far too confining. Instead, his political role can be discerned in the meanings that emerged from his career as a sports broadcaster. On the most obvious level, he used his platform on the national stage to advocate for social justice and to relate sports to larger issues that were particularly relevant to life in late-twentieth-century America. This was probably most true during the first half of his career, as he was rising within the ranks of ABC and its famed sports programming division. Even more than this, however, Cosell was a popular figure who took the perspective of someone who, in an earlier era, would have been marginal to American society and brought it into the very center of cultural life in this country. His own storyline was that of the underdog. As is often true, however, the closer Cosell got to the center of cultural production, the more diluted his critical perspective became.

In fact, as Cosell emerged as an increasingly ubiquitous presence within sports broadcasting and the mass media during the 1970s and early 1980s, his style was transformed into a caricature, as fans and detractors increasingly identified all of his critical ideas as mere accessories of a boorish egomaniac. Yet at the same time, it was during this era, when he appeared weekly on *Monday Night Football,* that Cosell also had the greatest access to the public. It is at the time of his greatest banality that Cosell may also have had the greatest impact, simply because his very presence—his accent, his opinions, and his use of language—all connoted a history, one that could not be erased, even within a medium that erases history better than any other.

In his memoir *Cosell* he wrote: "Arrogant, pompous, obnoxious, vain, cruel, persecuting, distasteful, verbose, a show-off. I have been called all of these. Of course, I am."[2] Cosell was a television personality who placed his human frailties before viewers as few others have done before or since. His remarkable rise to a central place in American culture from such modest origins, and his subsequent decline as a network sports analyst, might be attributed to his complex personality traits. Cosell was indeed ambitious, extremely intelligent, hardworking, opinionated, self-centered, and all of the other things for which he was famous. Some might write a book about a man like Cosell that places the analysis of his psychological traits and personality profile at the center of his biography.

This book, however, draws primarily on three categories of information. First, I look at the story of Cosell's own life. His upbringing typified the experiences of many second-generation Americans whose parents immigrated to the United States from Europe during the early years of the twentieth century. As the child of Jewish immigrants from Poland, Cosell grew up in the ethnically divided world of Brooklyn during the 1920s and 1930s. From an early age he exhibited a strong drive to succeed—a driving ambition to propel himself to a higher station in life. Upward mobility plays a leading role in his accounts of his own life story, and so does assimilation, or at least the desire to escape the expectations of his parents. While the degree of his ambition was exceptional, his desire to assimilate was not. He characterizes his move into broadcasting as a symbolic break from his family, his community, and his background. For Cosell, this seems to mark the trajectory of his life until the 1972 Olympics, when the terrorist killings of the Israeli team embittered him and led him to focus more on his Jewish identity.

Second, this book explores the media and culture apparatus that developed from the 1940s through the 1960s, which provided Cosell with the opportunity to reach a mass audience and to achieve a central position in American cultural life. Although Cosell was an unlikely celebrity, he grew up in the right place at the right time. New York was the center of the commercial broadcasting establishment in the early years of its formation, and particularly the sports and news broadcasting establishment. Getting a foot in the door was not easy for Cosell; his broadcasting career would not begin until he was thirty-six years old, and he did not appear regularly on network television until ten years after that. Yet by working in New York, first as a lawyer, then as a local sports broadcaster and freelance radio sports reporter, he was able to gain access to a national television audience. He also had the good fortune to have begun his television career working for an affiliate of ABC, a fledgling third commercial network that was the severed limb of the National Broadcasting Company, grafted from the old NBC network in the 1950s when antitrust infringements forced the split. Undercapitalized and in search of an audience hook, ABC invested in sports and was more willing than other networks to take a risk on a personality like Cosell.

Not only was Cosell lucky to be able to gain access to network television, but also he did so at a time when the three major broadcasting networks—the Columbia Broadcasting System along with ABC and NBC—dominated national television. In most U.S. television markets between 1960 and 1980, viewers had far fewer channels to choose from than they would later with the advent of cable, satellite, and digital television. There were only these three network stations (if that many), and perhaps a public television station and two or three independent stations, all of which broadcast over the airwaves for free, and all but public broadcasting gaining their revenue from commercial advertising. In fact, during most of Cosell's career, viewers would not even have owned videocassette recorders. This meant that network television personalities commanded far more attention than they would in later years, and the few stars who emerged, such as Ed Sullivan, Walter Cronkite, or Howard Cosell, became almost universally recognized throughout the country.

Finally, and perhaps most important, I locate Cosell's life and career within the historical, social, and political contexts that made it meaningful. Howard Cosell grew up a product of working-class, ethnic New York City. Although there is little indication that his own family was especially political, he lived in an environment where political action—union activism, workplace agitation, and social protest—was commonplace. Many of those who, like Cosell, migrated from the Jewish neighborhoods of Brooklyn to the soundstages and production rooms of television—and there were many who did so—came from politically active backgrounds. Some had been active themselves during the 1930s in the Popular Front, some in the Communist Party, and some were simply liberals who felt a commitment toward using their careers to advance causes such as civil rights.

Many of these writers and performers had their careers unceremoniously ended during the years of the 1950s Red Scare, when anticommunist witch-hunts led corporate executives to purge such people from their staffs. Others were able to salvage their careers, working behind the scenes as writers or negotiating with the advertising wing of networks that had a direct hand in program censorship. As I show, Cosell's own commitment to civil rights, and particularly to the rights of African Americans, came from his background. What is more, he benefited from the fact that he was involved not in the writing or creation of entertainment programming but in sports. While the conventions of sports broadcasting might seem to offer little opportunity for a committed liberal to espouse his political opinions, the emergence of an assertive, political, and militant consciousness among African American athletes during the 1960s would do just that. Unlike the majority of white sports reporters (and on 1960s network television there were only white sports reporters), Cosell was uniquely prepared to address and understand the Black Power movement that would rock the world of sports.

Chapter 1 details the early years of Cosell's life, focusing on the environment of Jewish Brooklyn that nurtured him into adulthood. Much of the discussion focuses on Cosell's own memories and the emphasis he placed on his experiences with anti-Semitism in his formative years. His background situates Cosell ideologically within the frame of what cultural historian Michael Denning calls the "cultural front," a community of writers and artists who came from working-class backgrounds and adopted the egalitarian values of radical movements during the 1930s.

Chapter 2 begins with Cosell's transition into cultural work as he left a stable career as a lawyer and went into broadcasting. As for many during the 1950s this move was not an easy one, carrying him into the torrential waters of the Red Scare.

In chapter 3 we find Cosell entering his first rocky years as a broadcaster. Starting on radio, he slowly shifted into television, but only on the local level, for the president of ABC made sure that Cosell stayed off the air. In this chapter we see the development of Cosell's career as not only a function of his own ambitions but also the product of factors peculiar to the broadcasting industry, and more specifically a fledgling network within that industry. I show how Cosell's career at ABC took off when a talented young network executive, Roone Arledge, decided to take a chance by bringing Cosell onto the network. Arledge gambled that the controversy Cosell brought with him would pay off in the end by attracting viewers. He turned out to be right. Cosell's franchise as a network television star had begun.

Chapter 4 shows how Cosell's early career was defined by his interest in and commitment to athletes who promoted civil rights for African Americans. The centrality of his relationship to African American causes was important not only because it made Cosell distinctive, and in some ways helped him to advance his career, but also because it was linked to a tradition of liberal Jewish writers and cultural workers in other realms of entertainment who also took an interest in civil rights. For a sportscaster, the late 1960s were a particularly important period in which to embrace such issues, for this was a time when African American athletes were taking bold, empowering political stances. Unlike many other white commentators, Cosell did not condemn black athletes for doing so but instead allowed them to state their case and took their positions seriously.

I begin chapter 5 with what was probably the most important development in Cosell's career other than his decision to enter broadcasting: his appointment as a broadcaster for ABC's new experiment with sports, *Monday Night Football*. It was on this program that Cosell not only stepped away from his more serious work of exploring the connections between sports and society but also created a character type for his audiences. In many respects Cosell became the same kind of "shill" on *Monday Night Football* that had been at the center of his critique of the medium. He was being paid by a network with a vested interest in a corporation (the National Football League) to cover that same corporation. He strove to do so objectively, openly criticizing the games that he broadcast when he felt they deserved criticism. Yet as the resident crank in the broadcast booth, he was often not taken very seriously, and instead became the object of ridicule. This chapter also addresses one of the key events in Cosell's life, the 1972 Olympics, when eleven members of the Israeli Olympic team were taken hostage and killed by Palestinian terrorists. Cosell wrote after this event that it had brought him to a new awareness of being Jewish, and indeed his written recollections about his Jewish background did not appear until after Munich.

Chapter 6 recounts the emotional decline that many of Cosell's friends observed in him during the mid-to-late 1970s. Cosell was tiring of his work on *Monday Night Football*. He increasingly sought to take on work that was more serious and important than sports broadcasting—

flirting with a run for the United States Senate, teaching adjunct courses at Yale and New York University, and angling for a position as anchor on ABC's evening news broadcast, *World News Tonight*. At the same time, Cosell was called upon to cover the major TV spectacles of the decade, such as the "Battle of the Sexes" tennis match between Billy Jean King and Bobby Riggs.

Even though his mood was in decline, his star had never shone brighter. As I show in chapter 7, however, his stardom would come to an end by the early 1980s, when Cosell pulled himself out of broadcasting—or, in the eyes of some, self-destructed. As Cosell's career on *Monday Night Football* and boxing coverage was drawing to a close, however, he put together a program that he saw as his crowning achievement, a sports journalism magazine show called *SportsBeat*. The series was a critical success, yet its ratings were low, and by 1985, when Cosell published a scathing tell-all book about ABC Sports, his career at the network was over.

I conclude the book by addressing the final years of Cosell's life and his significance as a sportscaster and a cultural figure.

1 Poor, Jewish, and from Brooklyn

He died thinking he was poor and Jewish.
—Jill Cosell on her father, Howard Cosell

It should be no surprise to anybody who remembers Howard Cosell that even the date of his birth is a matter of controversy. In his first autobiography, *Cosell,* he writes that he
was born on March 25, 1920.[1] Other biographical references,
however, list the year of his birth as 1918.[2] A U.S. Census record taken in January 1920 only slightly clarifies the matter.
Listed beneath Isadore M. and Nellie Cohen are sons Hilton
and Howard. This is clearly the record for Cosell and his
family, as the information corresponds with Cosell's own
published recollections—the names of his parents, the place
of his birth, and his family name before he changed it to
Cosell in the 1940s. Howard's age appears to read "2 1/12,"
but the handwriting is smudged and unclear; it could also
say "1 11/12."[3]

Beyond these vague census records, it is difficult to obtain
any primary information about Cosell's early life. Most of
what can be learned about his youth comes from interviews
with his family and with Cosell, a few scattered newspaper
and tabloid articles, and, most voluminously, Cosell's own
published memoirs. These memoirs are revealing in the ways
they illustrate not only Cosell's perspective on his own life
but also themes that are common to the children of what social historians describe as the "second wave" of immigrants
to the United States. Cosell's mode of writing about his childhood is invariably nostalgic, but it reveals an individual who
was extremely conscious of his own past and its relationship
to dramatic historical transformations: the trans-Atlantic immigration during the late nineteenth and early twentieth
centuries of Jews fleeing persecution in Europe; the gradual
assimilation and acceptance of "white" ethnic groups such as

Jews, Irish, and Italians; the rise of a mass media consumer society; the disintegration of urban European-ethnic communities; and the great migration of African Americans to cities and neighborhoods like the Brooklyn of Cosell's youth.

While Cosell almost never mentioned his ethnicity while on the air as a sports broadcaster, his Jewish identity is central to his published memoirs and to a narrative tension that he presents consistently. Cosell's Jewishness was not about the practice of religion. Although his autobiographical writings frequently reflect on his Jewish background, he almost never mentions any religious ritual, learning, or belief, except to point out that he never had a bar mitzvah. In one of the few oral history interviews conducted with Cosell, he speaks slightly more extensively about the role of religion in his life, but only with impatience and an air of dismissal. Yet being Jewish is clearly something that was important to Cosell. It was about neighborhood boundaries; about being the target of bullying by Irish Catholic street thugs; about limitations placed on expectations for his own life by his parents; about a street culture of kosher foods, stickball games, and gossip; about belonging to a people who were the target of international prejudice and genocide; and about something in his own speech and style that audiences could clearly identify, and that could be used against him and his career.

In *Cosell,* he first mentions his Jewish identity to explain his characteristic ambition. Noting that he is often asked about his "drive," he writes: "Surely a lot of my drive stems from the way I grew up—in Brooklyn, during the Depression, Jewish, fighting a group of Studs Lonigans and running away from them, to get to school safely; to get home safely. That was part of life then."[4] Here we can see a core tension in the way he represents his being Jewish. On the one hand, he identifies it as the motivation for his later success. Yet on the other hand, there is very little that is positive in the way Cosell addresses his Jewishness. It is a hardship like the Great Depression, and a source of stigma and humiliation. This tension is not unique to Cosell. It is a common theme in the experiences of Jewish writers, actors, comedians, journalists, and television personalities who, during the 1930s, 1940s, and 1950s, became central figures in American culture in a way that Jews had never been before. They were a new generation who gained unprecedented access to public culture in the United States thanks to the opportunities provided by the emerging media outlets of film, radio, and television. Within the forms of entertainment they helped to create, they brought perspectives that were new to, and often critical of, mainstream American culture. Cosell would be no exception, even as he turned his critical eye on a world that had long represented the values of conformity in American life: the world of athletic competition.

———

Howard Cosell was born Howard Cohen in Winston-Salem, North Carolina, most likely on March 25, 1918. His father was an accountant who traveled up and down the eastern seaboard working for a credit clothing chain. In the same book in which Cosell incorrectly reported his birth date, he writes that he moved to Brooklyn shortly before he was three years old. The January 1920 census record gives the Cohen family's place of residence as Brooklyn, which means that when the survey was taken, the family must have moved north quite recently. Despite his father's continued travels for work, Brooklyn would remain Cosell's home until his broadcasting career began to take shape in the late 1950s.[5]

Cosell's father, Isadore Martin Cohen, was a first-generation immigrant to the United States, having arrived with his family at the age of two in 1890.[6] Cosell writes that his father was from Poland, and recalled in an oral history interview conducted in 1981 that Isadore Cohen was born in the city of Lodz.[7] Cosell's mother's parents, the Rosenthals, arrived in the United States from Russia in 1880 and 1882. Eventually they moved to Worcester, Massachusetts where Cosell's maternal grandfather, Jacob, worked as a clothier. It is here that Cosell's mother, Nellie Rosenthal, was born.[8] Sportswriter Dave Kindred describes the union of Nellie and Isadore Cohen as an " 'arranged marriage,' meaning not so much a union of lovers as a merger of class, heritage, and fortune."[9]

Cosell's memory of his father's family history was never clear, but during interviews he did recall that they lived in a number of Brooklyn neighborhoods, including Williamsburg and East New York.[10] In his 1974 biography *Like It Is,* Cosell also recalled that his paternal grandparents lived in the Brownsville section of the city, a ghetto known for being extremely poor, a magnet for Jewish immigrants, and a center of radical politics between 1910 and 1930.[11] Whether this tradition rubbed off on Howard is not altogether clear, but it at least suggests that Cosell grew up in an environment of dynamic politics closely tied to an ethnic identity that was rooted in neighborhoods.

Cosell's own parents were not particularly political. Instead they struggled to make a living and support their family. According to Cosell, his father was seldom home, having to travel frequently to make ends meet, especially during the depression. Often his income was not enough to pay the family's bills. "I remember the electricity being turned off in our house for nonpayment of rent and my dad fighting with the janitor to try and get it turned back on," writes Cosell. He portrays his mother, who was left alone to take care of the family, as a hypochondriac who was "either sick, on the verge of being sick or thinking about being sick."[12] Perhaps the greatest health crisis that the family faced, however, was when Cosell's brother Hilton, four years his senior, contracted tuberculosis. In order to save money to pay for a doctor's care, the Cohens moved into a two-family house on President Street between Franklin and Bedford avenues, in the Crown Heights neighborhood. Cosell recalls that the doctors needed to collapse Hilton's infected lung, and allowed it to expand back only after the infection had been killed. Hilton convalesced in bed and on the balcony of the house for months, but ultimately he survived. In his book *Like It Is* Cosell recalls: "I could see those empty boxes of cough drops—Smith Brothers and Luden's—that we had found in Hilton's pockets when he emptied out his suits. There would be no more cough drops. Somehow Dad got the money to pay [the doctor]. . . . [M]y mother has never gotten the nursing award of the year which she earned."[13] Not surprisingly, Cosell remembered that his own home life and his parents' marriage were "unhappy."[14]

Cosell went to P.S. 9 for elementary school, where he reports that he finished second in the city's standing broad jump competition.[15] He went on to attend Alexander Hamilton High School, a boys' secondary school in Brooklyn. Throughout his childhood he was an avid sports fan, and particularly a fan of the Brooklyn Dodgers. In high school he gained his first opportunity to use sports journalism as an outlet for his passion when he became the sports editor of the school paper, the *Ledger*. He remembers that the football coach, who had been an important mentor, told him, "You may be doing this the rest of your life."[16] According to a 1987 résumé, he also ran track and had an "outstanding scholastic record."[17]

After leaving high school, Cosell enrolled at New York University. His father had to take out a loan every three months to enable him to attend. The year he entered is unclear, but he made his first appearance in the NYU yearbook, the *Violet,* in 1936 as a member of the Pi Lambda Phi fraternity, which means that his freshman year was likely 1935–36. He also appears in the 1937 yearbook, where he is identified as a sophomore, and in the 1939 edition. He does not appear in the 1938 *Violet,* however, and there is no record that he ever completed a B.A., although his résumé states that he completed this degree in 1937. Instead, an Alumni Records Office document suggests that he transferred to the university's law school in 1937 after earning sixty-six credits in the University College. Cosell's résumé also states that he was elected to the Phi Beta Kappa honor society, but there is no record of this in the university yearbooks between 1937 and 1940 or at the national office of Phi Beta Kappa. In any case, he did graduate with a Bachelor of Laws degree and was admitted to the New York State Bar in 1941 at the age of twenty-three.[18]

Cosell enlisted in the United States Army as a private on February 2, 1942, and was assigned to a post in Brooklyn, only a trolley ride from his home. He rose to the rank of technical sergeant in less than two years, at which point, hoping to be sent overseas, he applied to the Officer Candidate Battalion (Provisional), and was accepted. He was discharged as an enlisted man on February 1, 1943, and sent to the Transportation Corps School at Mississippi State University, where he was appointed to a position as a second lieutenant and eventually assigned, once again, to Brooklyn and the headquarters of the New York Port of Embarkation. Surviving army records (most from that era were destroyed in a fire at the National Personnel Records Center in St. Louis) show that he was a procedures control officer and personnel staff officer. Cosell long maintained that he eventually rose to the rank of major, and in fact in the résumé he submitted to New York University, Cosell states that he was "the youngest major in the Army during World War II." His military record confirms that he did attain the rank of major but cannot confirm whether he was actually the youngest to achieve this rank.[19]

In *Cosell* he writes that his duties in the army included managing a 65,000-person combined workforce of civilians and military personnel. He remembers negotiating in that capacity with the International Longshoremen's Association, an experience that provided expertise

Photo of Pi Lambda Phi fraternity from the 1936 New York University yearbook, *The Violet*. Cosell is in the second row from the top at the far right. New York University Archives, Photographic Collection.

in labor issues that would partially frame his brief legal career. As important as these professional experiences were, Cosell also met his future wife, Mary Edith "Emmy" Abrams, while in the military. She was a private in the Women's Army Corps (or WACs), and Cosell recalls that he had to break military rules in order to date her, since military law barred officers from going out with enlisted personnel. Overcoming these barriers, however, would be relatively easy compared to surmounting those of ethnicity and class. Emmy Abrams came from a prominent Philadelphia Protestant family that was not receptive to her marrying a Brooklyn Jew. And Cosell's parents had no easier a time accepting Emmy. In 1977 Emmy Cosell told *Family Circle* magazine:

Back at the time Howard and I were starting to get serious about each other, when two people obviously wanted a sexual relationship, the only alternative was marriage. I felt an enormous sexual attraction to Howard, but for a long while, my parents opposed the marriage on religious grounds. That kind of situation is so absurd, because the God they're calling on in such instances has to be a very bigoted, narrow-minded God. In my father's case, God happened to belong to a very nice little country club, and Howard didn't. Marrying amid all this ill feeling, into a totally different culture, was really a gamble for a sheltered little Emmy, I can tell you.[20]

The two were married on June 23, 1944. The ceremony took place at City Hall in New York. Only the Abramses attended. Despite the adversity of its beginnings, their marriage would remain intact until Emmy's death in 1990.[21]

After being discharged from the army on May 28, 1946, Cosell faced the same job and housing shortages that plagued most veterans returning from World War II. "We went heavily into debt," Cosell remembers. "It has long been paid back, every cent, but we struggled. I was a lawyer, living and working within a few miles, a few minutes, of the neighborhood where I had spent most of my years. Was this all there is?"[22] He had hoped to begin a career in radio sports broadcasting immediately after leaving the army, but he was quickly turned down after an audition at the New York City radio station WOR.

Indeed, in the early years of their marriage, Emmy garnered far more public recognition than Howard. The woman whom local newspapers called "Mrs. Howard Cosell," noting that she could be "remembered as Edith Abrams formerly of Prospect Park," often appeared in the society pages of the *Chester Times* back in Pennsylvania. Announcements of her attending weddings, hosting friends, and visiting local families show that she maintained a connection to Philadelphia society throughout the early years of her marriage.[23] Her father, Norman R. Abrams, had risen from his job as a production worker in a floor-covering factory after returning from World War I to become a vice president of the company. In 1953 Arthur Summerfield, the postmaster general under President Dwight D. Eisenhower, appointed Abrams assistant postmaster general.[24]

After leaving the army, Cosell went into private law practice, eventually becoming a junior partner in the law firm of Marro, Pomper, and Cosell at 25 Broad Street in Manhattan.[25] Lewis Pomper, the founder of the firm, had made his name before the war as a specialist in immigration law, aiding refugees attempting to enter the United States from Nazi Germany.[26] Cosell was now working in a high-powered legal practice near Wall Street, earning, as he recalls, over $30,000 a year.[27] He made his mark by representing athletes, most notably Willie Mays and Monte Irvin, who needed a license for their Brooklyn liquor store. In 1953 Cosell represented Little League Baseball when it applied for a charter in New York City. He would parlay this experience into his first broadcasting job, a Saturday morning radio show in which Little League players asked questions of their major league idols. Cosell was the emcee.[28]

In writing about his past, as well as in interviews, Cosell identified his Jewish background as central to his development as an adult. Yet religion was not important to his life as he was growing up. When asked in 1981 how much religious training he'd received, he responded: "Virtually no formal religious training. I was never bar mitzvahed. My brother was. My mother's father was a rabbi," Cosell told the interviewer, but added, laughing: "He was a funny guy, nice guy. I'd be playing ball on Lincoln Place in Brooklyn or wherever and he'd come trudging up the street to give me a Hebrew lesson and I really don't think either he or I ever took it seriously. I had virtually no religious training."[29] Although his father did attend shul on holidays, only occasionally would Howard "trudge along," and only into his early teens. "I never paid much attention to it," he said. When asked if he regretted not having had a bar mitzvah, Cosell responded: "No. I've never even thought about it. Never even thought about it. I don't have much truck with religious ritual." Cosell did recall his grandfather fondly, but more for his role as a Jewish ethnic elder than for his religious expertise.[30] "He wasn't that serious a rabbi," said Cosell, again laughing. "I related to him as a grandfather very much. He was very funny. He used to drink beer and put sugar in it, stir it, and then play me rummy and he would cheat. I loved him. I let him think he was beating me all the time."[31]

The last three chapters of Cosell's autobiography *Like It Is* contain recollections illustrating some important perspectives on his ethnic identity which he decided to share with readers and fans. In these episodes he remembers his childhood as he travels back to Brooklyn with his wife, Emmy, in the mid-1970s. The premise of these chapters is itself revealing. The mood is nostalgic, even though the nostalgia is often painful. He paints a vivid picture of places like his elementary school, P.S. 9, where he won second place in the broad jump competition, or Radin's delicatessen, the "'Stage Delicatessen' of Brooklyn, the eatery for ballplayers." Cosell describes Radin's as a place where "hot dogs (crisp, all-beef ones) were always ready on the grill. The hot pastrami was unfailingly lean. You never had to ask, the tongue would be cut from the center."[32]

Cosell writes of his return to his home as an epic journey back to a place he had not visited in years, and it may well have been. The geographic distance between Brooklyn and his Manhattan apartment, or even his home in suburban Pound Ridge, New York, may not have been great, but the social distance was tremendous. Cosell's narrative is not only about the dramatic changes that had taken place in his life as he elevated himself from an ethnic neighborhood and poverty to fame and wealth, but also about the racial transformations and economic decline that characterized Brooklyn in the 1970s.

In his narrative Cosell discusses his Jewish identity as something that often made him feel victimized, not just by the anti-Semitic street thugs he ran from but even by fellow Jews from whom he felt separated by class. Shortly after Howard left elementary school, the Cohens moved to Classon Avenue in a neighborhood where they were surrounded by the elite of Brooklyn's Jewish society. Recalling their new apartment house, he writes:

> It was surrounded by the fine, modern, doorman-attended, elevator-equipped, six-story buildings of Eastern Parkway. Eastern Parkway was for rich people. We were not that. Eastern Parkway had the rich Jews, the successful merchants of the garment center, the kings of the textile industry, the fabric merchants. I used to think about how much the heads of the families would bring home each week. Maybe as much as $400. "Who would be my friends?" I began to wonder. "With whom could I play? Would I be accepted as one who lived on Classon Avenue in a four-story walk-up?"[33]

In the next chapter, titled "Eastern Parkway All-Stars," Cosell writes about his sense of exclusion from Union Temple, one of the finest Jewish institutions in the area. "I always dreamed of someday belonging to it," he wrote. "But that never happened. My folks just couldn't afford it." Union Temple offered the kinds of sports facilities that Cosell craved—a swimming pool, basketball courts, and a gymnasium. He was lucky to have a friend who would bring him in as a guest, and Cosell would take advantage of this opportunity, going to basketball games on Sunday nights. He recalls the vibrant ethnic amateur basketball leagues of the era, before the rise of the National Collegiate Athletic Association and professional basketball: "The club game was the thing. The Crescent Athletic Club was tough, so was the 92nd Street YMHA [Young Men's Hebrew Association]. Eighth Avenue Temple of Brooklyn had some very good players."[34]

According to the common stereotype, Jewish Brooklyn would not seem a likely breeding ground for a budding sportscaster such as Cosell to emerge from. Jews have been long characterized as cerebral, physically weak, and not interested in sports. Jewish studies scholar Stephen Whitfield argues that the stereotype of Jewish non-athleticism is actually closer to the truth than most Jews who write about sports would like to admit. Nevertheless, many Jews embraced sports in the urban world of Cosell's childhood and young adulthood. Contrary to perceptions of Jews as being concerned only with the life of the mind, Jews excelled in sports such as boxing and basketball during the 1930s. Gena Caponi-Tabery has found that by some estimates, almost 50 percent of players in the American Basketball League during the Great Depression were Jewish. She writes that "Jews dominated the sport," and that YMHAs fielded strong teams from cities such as Pittsburgh and Philadelphia, as well as from New York.[35]

As much as Cosell fondly remembered the sports world of his childhood, he continues to remind readers of his exclusion and marginalization even within the Jewish world of Brooklyn. He recalls how some residents of Eastern Parkway would rent lockers for the season at Manhattan Beach. But Cosell "could never get one because of the cost," until a wealthy uncle leased one for him for the summer.[36]

Cosell tended to present the traditions of his family, though not specifically Jewish in nature, as ones that held him back, or at least obliged him to make decisions in life that limited him. His choice of high school was the first example. In *Like It Is,* Cosell writes that he and his brother Hilton went to Alexander Hamilton High School, an all-boys' institution. "I don't know if Hilton really wanted to go to Hamilton, but I don't believe he had a choice. My mother did not believe in coeducation. . . . Mother was fixed in her conviction that a boy could not possibly pay attention to school work if there were girls around."[37] In an oral history interview Cosell repeats this theme, applying it more directly to his own high school experience. He refers to Erasmus Hall High School as "the glamour school of Brooklyn" in his day but adds, "It was coed and my mother wouldn't let me go there." Asked why, he replies: "She didn't want me in a coed school. She thought I'd not concentrate on studies. It was a different era then. All my friends went to Erasmus."[38]

A second area in which Cosell discusses the limitations imposed by his background (albeit only indirectly related to his Jewish identity) has to do with the expectations of his parents. His first career as a lawyer, like his "choice" of high school, was actually determined for him by his parents. In his oral history Cosell says, "I went to law school because my parents wanted a son who'd be a lawyer and sacrificed for me to go through law school and I didn't have any objection, I didn't know what I wanted to be and I felt that a legal education would be as good as any."[39] In *Cosell* he writes in greater detail about attending New York University in the late 1930s and graduating with a law degree, and he acknowledges how important his education in law was to developing the interviewing and critical skills that would mark his career as a sports journalist. He is less positive, however, in describing his experiences as a lawyer, and paints his law career as a time when he earned a lucrative paycheck but led a constrained life. For example, Cosell remembers that immediately after World War II, "the future seemed to offer little excitement. I was in law, in debt and in the home of my parents. Living with them was a disaster, but apartments were scarce and beyond our budget."[40] When he decided to go into radio work full-time in the 1950s, he writes, "my own father never recovered from his disappointment at my decision to abandon the law."[41]

Further underscoring the uneasy relationship between his Jewish identity and his broadcasting career, writers and sports fans have often accused Cosell of changing his name from Cohen in an attempt to downplay his background. According to Kindred, however, his reasons were not quite this simple. In fact, Howard's brother Hilton was the first in the family to change his name, and claimed that he did so at the request of his grandfather. Kindred quotes Hilton as saying: "When I was an accountant in a firm where there were a million Cohens, my grandfather came to *me* and said 'Listen, "Cohen" means priest, and we're not priests. Our name should be Cosell.' So I changed it. After a while, so did Howard."[42] Cosell often claimed that "Cosell" or "Kassell" was the original family name in Europe. In the oral history interview archived at the New York Public Library, he says: "Arthur Cosell, my cousin, who was in my class in law school, who's the leading furniture dealer in High Point, North Carolina, spells it with a 'C.' I've got relatives in Trenton who spell it with a 'K.' You know how those things, during the great immigration waves, became diffused."[43] At the same time, many Jewish entertainers and others during the 1940s and 1950s did change their names in an effort to fit in with mainstream society.

Kindred, in fact, asserts that the name change was a form of "rebellion" against a Jewish world that Cosell found suffocating, and writes that marrying "a *shikse*," as Cosell's Jewish family derisively called Emmy, a gentile, was a similar act.[44] Indeed, Cosell observes, "My folks recoiled at the thought of their son marrying a *shikse*." Even more significantly, however, he compares his marriage—a happy one—to his parents' purgatorial relationship, of which the best he can say is that "when people suffer together something does develop between them."[45] The fact that he, a Brooklyn Jew, married the Protestant "daughter of a very well-known industrialist who wound up in the Eisenhower administration" left both of them alienated from their families. In *Cosell* the reader is presented with sketchy details of family tensions resulting from their marriage. Emmy and her father did not speak for two years; Cosell recalls that his father-in-law (an "Old World Republican . . . distinguished family, a mixture of Pennsylvania Dutch and Welsh") was "coldly indifferent" in the years after the war, when he and Emmy would visit; Cosell's mother-in-law had to sneak up to Brooklyn for visits.[46]

In *Like It Is,* Cosell provides more details of this period in his life, describing his first meeting with the Abrams family and Emmy's first meeting with his. On the way up to his parents' apartment they bumped into a notorious gossip, who "smiled and eyed Emmy with the look of a jeweler using his spy glass to appraise a diamond." He recalls a tense conversation over cocktails of gin and pineapple juice ("you know, all *shikses* drink," Cosell records his mother saying).[47] The next day his mother's "worst suspicions were confirmed" when she "bumped into the gossip." He reports the conversation:

> "I saw Howard bringing a girl up to your apartment yesterday. He looked serious, and she's good looking. But is she Jewish?"
>
> "No," my mother gulped, and then added defensively, "but she's a lovely girl."[48]

Cosell's memories of visiting Emmy's family are equally uncomfortable. Most striking is his recollection of saying good-bye to Norman Abrams after his first dinner at their house. "I had the urge to tell him then and there that I loved his daughter, and was going to marry her. But I chickened out."[49] Those who remember Cosell's on-air persona might find it hard to imagine an instance in which he would have been so intimidated. The incident nevertheless highlights how important Cosell's Jewish identity was in his early life, and how ethnicity and class threatened to cleave his family.

Cosell's daughter Jill recalls that, after the family moved into Peter Cooper Village, a middle-class housing development in Manhattan built just after World War II, her mother was in the minority, "ostracized" by the Jewish social world of the community. The few non-Jewish acquaintances she had were Puerto Ricans, who also shared very little socially with her mother, and Emmy constantly faced the gossip of neighbors. Jill remembers having to ask her parents if she could stay home from school on Jewish holidays so that she would not feel the scorn of her childhood friends. Raised in close proximity to her father's parents, Jill remembers her mother's family as being more "laid back" about Cosell's Jewish background, although there were times when anti-Semitic prejudice emerged in the Abrams family gatherings. Jill recalled: "[Norman Abrams] asked me if I thought that Jesus was the son of God at dinner. . . . I was a little child of [about] five, and I knew even then that was a loaded question . . . a terrible position to put a child in, by the way, on my grandfather's part." Sometimes she would visit her Abrams grandparents with only her mother. But at times Cosell was present, and at remarks like this, says Jill, "he became stiff. I was a child. . . . I knew it was uncomfortable, and I adored my daddy.[50]

Intermarriage was one of the most difficult issues facing Jews and all European immigrants during the first half of the twentieth century. At issue was not only one's individual family dynamic or structure but also the maintenance of ethnic communities, the acceptance of American norms and values, and one's personal mobility into a new class position. Riv-Ellen Prell's study of relationships between Jewish women and men during the early decades of the twentieth century reveals that Jews intermarried much less frequently than other immigrant groups. While roughly 30 percent of New York–born, second-generation non-Jewish immigrants married out of their ethnic group, fewer than 3.5 percent of second-generation Jews did the same.[51] In contrast to these findings, Prell's survey of popular culture from the same period shows that films, plays, and fiction portrayed the intermarriage of European ethnic groups, including Jews, as extremely common and desirable. Indeed, in plays such as *The Melting Pot* (1908) by Israel Zangwill, intermarriage was portrayed as the cornerstone of Americanization. While much of the Yiddish and Jewish press scorned such representations as potentially leading to the erasure of the Jewish community, films, novels, and magazine articles commonly represented intermarriage as a key to class mobility and success in America.[52]

In fact Cosell refers to the romantic imagery of World War II films to frame his romance with Emmy. Introducing their relationship in *Cosell*, he writes: "This may sound like the scenario for one of those World War II movies they turned out like sausages in the early Forties, starring June Allyson (whom Emmy resembles). It so happens that we met—and courted—in the Army."[53] In many respects World War II provided an opportunity for Cosell to expand beyond the expectations and constraints that he associated with his family and community. Ironically, even though his commission never moved him outside his native Brooklyn, it allowed him to achieve the rank of a military officer, a position of authority and power in mainstream American society that even his WASP father-in-law was forced to respect.

Even more than he portrays his Jewish family as a barrier to his social mobility, Cosell highlights the deep-seated anti-Semitism that characterized the social environment of his youth. In a reference he would often repeat in interviews, Cosell writes: "I grew up on *Studs Lonigan* by James T. Farrell. It was light reading—until the age of

Hitler. And then, *then* you began to take it seriously. As young as you were you knew, by God, that you were Jewish, and you knew every restrictive boundary and every thoughtless slight."[54] Here Cosell refers to Farrell's famous trilogy, *Young Lonigan* (1932), *The Young Manhood of Studs Lonigan* (1934), and *Judgment Day* (1935). In 1960 the novels were made into a film titled *Studs Lonigan* (directed by the blacklisted documentary filmmaker Irving Lerner). That such a set of books would have a great influence on Cosell is significant, as we will see in the next chapter. Farrell was what historian Michael Denning calls an "anti-bureaucratic Marxist," a follower of Trotsky who was both championed by and later viciously critical of the popular front of radical writers, actors, and other workers in radio and film. In fact, Farrell's criticisms of radio and Hollywood film almost directly mirror the diatribes against commercialized sports that Cosell would give voice to in the late 1970s and 1980s.[55] Drawing upon concrete settings, and based on the experiences of Farrell's early years, the Studs Lonigan novels explore the perpetuation of gang violence and anti-Semitism among youths in Irish Catholic Chicago. Along with Richard Wright's *Native Son,* they were among the first works of fiction to address directly the causes and consequences of racism in American urban life.[56] That Cosell would refer to them often in writing and in interviews suggests that they not only influenced him but also provided a meaningful framework within which he could understand his own experiences. In the same passage, Cosell goes on to describe his own experiences with Farrell-like realistic detail. He recalls growing up "together with the Catholic kids from Saint Theresa's parish. . . . Running from them, hiding from them; they were always after the little sheenie." Some years later he and Emmy were in a restaurant on Franklin Avenue in Brooklyn.

> I was now a major, and there at another table was the very kid who had been at me again and again and again, in that same restaurant, in a private's uniform. . . . And you know what? I began to sweat with fear because I didn't want to make a scene while I was wearing the uniform of a field-grade officer. And then the fear turned around. Maybe he's still going to come at me and he's only a private. Then what do I do? Because now I was a grown man and I was six-one and a half, and do you know how big he was? Five-seven. He was a runt, a midget. I could have killed him.

But it all ran through me, the whole background, all of it, sitting in that restaurant in Brooklyn. I won't ever forget it.[57]

Once again, it is surely hard for most who remember Howard Cosell, the reporter who asked fearless questions of Muhammad Ali, to imagine him intimidated by a five-foot-seven army private. As with his first meeting with his future father-in-law, however, this incident illustrates the degree to which anti-Semitism structured not only Cosell's life but also the lives of Jews all over the United States during the first half of the twentieth century. Prell notes that during the 1940s, between 15 and 24 percent of Americans polled stated that Jews were a "menace to America." Even during World War II, more Americans had negative feelings against Jews than they did toward either German or Japanese Americans. Between 1938 and 1945, Prell writes, almost 45 percent of those polled agreed with the statement that Jews had "too much power" in finance, commerce, and business. In 1944, 43 percent of Americans went so far as to state their support for "a campaign against Jews." In this particular survey, Jews fared worse than nearly every other group, including "foreigners, Negroes, or Catholics," except for "Radicals"— and as Prell points out, the term "Jew" and "radical" were interchangeable in the minds of many.[58]

In all of his writings, Cosell's most positive memories are of popular culture—the movies, radio programs, and sports that were part of life in New York, and that allowed him to imagine a different reality from the one that he lived. He credits his mother with allowing him to go into Manhattan alone when he was only twelve years old, and recalls bragging to his friends about the shows that he was able to see there. He remembers the vaudeville productions that came to Brooklyn with performers like Eddie Cantor, comedians like Milton Berle, Jack Benny, and Jack Oakie, entertainment palaces like the Brooklyn Paramount, the Brooklyn Fox, the Brooklyn Strand, Loew's Metropolitan, Minsky's Burlesque House, and Werba's Brooklyn Theater.[59] But of all the popular entertainment that Cosell remembers so warmly, none compares to the sports that he grew up with in Brooklyn, which extended from the most local amateur basketball team competing out of Union Temple, to the revered Brooklyn Dodgers. In *Cosell* he writes, "Sports was the one luxury you had." He recalls the track and field team from his elementary school, P.S. 9, and the roar of the crowd from Ebbets Field that he could hear all the way down Eastern Parkway.[60]

For Cosell, the Dodgers were foremost among all the experiences of popular culture that Brooklyn had to offer, the one entity that could unite all the different ethnic groups in the borough. "All that mattered was that they belonged to Brooklyn; that they gave Brooklyn an identity separate and apart from Manhattan. They made Brooklyn big league." In short, "the Dodgers were a civic enterprise. The ground of Ebbets Field was as hallowed as Gettysburg."[61] Curiously, this is precisely the kind of sentiment toward sports that Cosell would grandly criticize later in his life. In his critical writings about sports, he would mock the notion that any professional sports team might be worshiped in such a manner. He would come to argue that no professional team could ever be considered a "civic enterprise" but rather should be seen only as a crass business that cynically sells its stupefied audience the illusion of community that is otherwise missing from their lives.

His later arguments notwithstanding, his comments about the Dodgers of his youth perhaps accurately describe Cosell's sentiments when he was younger and suggest the importance that sports, and popular culture more generally, held for him while he was growing up in Brooklyn. Seen in relation to the struggles that he faced as an adolescent and a young man—and to his ethnic identity and the prejudice that he confronted while growing up—sports and popular culture became significant in two ways. First, they were a refuge from ethnic strife, economic struggle, and restrictive family expectations. Peering under the fence or sneaking through the turnstiles of Ebbets Field, Cosell didn't simply escape; he became part of a world that was bigger and more central to the larger American story than the one he perceived to be his own. Cultural scholar George Lipsitz remembers that his own parents had a similar relationship to popular culture. He connects this with the "cultural front," a term coined by historian Michael Denning to describe the democratic, working-class-oriented cultural movements that emerged out of the artistic and cultural movements of the 1930s.[62] Lipsitz recalls: "They listened and danced to swing music, loved motion pictures, and played and followed sports. The celebratory 'America' of the New Deal 'cultural front' turned immigrants and their children from unwanted aliens into redemptive insiders. Like millions of other ethnic Americans, my parents secured a measure of cultural and political inclusion for themselves through the populism and celebrations of regional and ethnic specificity that fueled the New Deal 'culture of unity.'"[63]

This is not to say that children of the second wave of immigrants had an easy relationship with popular culture. In fact, as important as Cosell's attachment to sports is, he always took a very critical stance toward the sports establishment in the United States. Sports certainly provided a popular world of fantasy, fun, and escape for Cosell, but the civic culture of Brooklyn also provided him with a kind of access to "high" culture from which his parents had been excluded. He writes in *Like It Is* of marveling at the beauty of buildings like the Brooklyn Public Library and Brooklyn Museum, and the splendor of Brooklyn landmarks such as the Botanical Gardens and Grand Army Plaza.[64] Of particular importance to Cosell was his education: English teachers who introduced him to Shakespeare, Keats, Byron, Shelley, and Milton. He writes, "Forty years later, I still read Keats and he remains my favorite poet."[65] He remembers his history teacher fondly for teaching him European history: "When we studied the Sinn Fein Rebellion in Ireland, by the time she was done, I felt a sense of having lived through Victor McLaglen's performance in John Ford's classic film, *The Informer*." Despite wishing that he had attended Erasmus Hall High School, Cosell concedes that his education allowed him to score a 98 on the New York State Regents exam in geometry, and provided him with his first opportunity to work in sports journalism, as sports editor of the Hamilton High School *Ledger*.[66] It is curious that Cosell would still take pride in his 98 on the Regents exam (even remembering that the grade was a 97 before it was adjusted). For Cosell, it seems that tests in such standard areas of culture and knowledge served as a proving ground on which he could demonstrate his worth in a way that knowledge of sports could not equal.

Ironically, Lipsitz argues that the opportunities that public education offered someone like Cosell often left people of his generation dismissive of the popular culture that was so central to their lives. Lipsitz writes of his own parents:

> As children of working-class immigrant parents, they viewed education, ideas, and culture with reverence. All the humiliation and subordination that they and their parents faced for being

foreigners, for being Jews, for being working class conflicted with the self-esteem and self-respect they felt for themselves and for their community. The public schools offered them an opportunity to demonstrate their merit, to display their talents and abilities, to prove that they could master all the prestigious cultural forms that were considered the private preserve of more privileged groups. They read the great books, listened to classical music, and became knowledgeable about sculpture and painting. This created in them a disposition against popular culture, a fear that common tastes might make them appear undiscerning and unworthy.[67]

Lipsitz's observations may help us understand Cosell's ambivalence toward sports in American society, an attitude that would sour into outright scorn and contempt by the end of his career. To use a Lipsitz term, popular culture was a dangerous crossroads. On the one hand, it offered pleasure, glamour, and fantasy that helped someone like Cosell imagine a life outside the poverty and humiliation he often faced. On the other hand, for Jews trying to prove themselves worthy citizens, too much of an investment in popular culture might threaten to associate them with the common masses. We can see this tension extending into the second way in which popular culture and sports became important to Cosell: as a vocation that allowed him mobility beyond the expectations of class, community, and ethnicity. This was obviously something that was very important to Cosell. As a lawyer in New York, he strove to represent athletes and entertainers in order to bring attention to his firm, and thus gain the inside track on any opportunities that might arise in the field of entertainment. Magazine writer Ray Robinson, who became friendly with Cosell, noted his persistent drive to become part of the expanding media world taking shape in the 1950s. Robinson "thought Cosell obsessively ambitious, smart, difficult, and strident," writes Dave Kindred. He was dumbfounded that a lawyer like Cosell, with a nasal Brooklyn Jewish accent, would even dream of becoming a sportscaster, and considered it a "mad ambition" when Cosell told him, "I'm going to be the most famous sports broadcaster there is."[68] Cosell sacrificed a $30,000-a-year position as a partner in a law firm to do fewer than a dozen radio spots for ABC, at $25 a show, when he began his broadcasting career in 1955. "My own father," recalls Cosell, "never recovered from his disappointment at my decision to abandon the law" for the "freakish radio opportunity."[69]

Almost from the start of his career, Cosell was one of the few sports broadcasters to understand sports as entertainment. In many respects this makes sense, given his background. In Brooklyn sports were just one aspect of a larger world of popular entertainment, with all of the perils and promises that popular culture entailed. Likewise, Cosell's ambivalence toward the world of entertainment, where he would one day gain employment, is not unusual. In fact it is typical of many other Jews who, like Cosell, would not only seek fame and fortune in show business but also attempt to interject a sense of social consciousness into their work. Yet his transition from Brooklyn Jewish lawyer to sports broadcaster would prove to be a rocky one. His early experiences in sports and entertainment would reveal the dangerous fault lines that had emerged as the cultural front of the 1930s, which ushered young Jews like himself into the world of popular entertainment, began to fragment under the weight of anticommunism.

2 From the Law Office to the Broadcast Booth

Sports is human life in microcosm.
—Howard Cosell

Reflecting on the era in which he became a sportscaster, Cosell wrote: "Great changes in technology were coming; an increase of leisure time; the exodus to the suburbs to escape from the great cities. The whole pattern of society was changing, and sports would become even more important." In these changes he saw an opportunity to inject himself into radio and television. Noting how the integration of African Americans into white-dominated sports had changed the way those sports would be experienced, he added: "A whole new set of smoldering problems would emerge. Could we keep giving the country line scores as news?"[1]

Here are encapsulated the dual forces that would shape the character of Howard Cosell's career as a broadcaster. On the one hand, Cosell, like nobody else in sports broadcasting before or since, had an understanding of the relationship between sports and the larger social forces shaping the late twentieth century: the rise of commercial culture, transformations in the nature of work and leisure, revolutions in racial politics, even the feminist movement and the challenges it posed to the gendered status quo (though this last only occasionally, and in spite of his own significant sexism). So keen was his understanding, in fact, that he often belittled athletes, team owners, franchise-hungry municipal governments, and any other individual or institution that, to Cosell's mind, overemphasized sports. What is more, he had a social conscience, and was willing to stand up for causes that were of no immediate benefit to himself or his social class—most notably civil rights for African Americans.

On the other hand, this same passage from *Cosell* also hints at another force that would propel Howard Cosell to fame: an almost insatiable ambition. Here, and in many other places as well, he not only connected sports to important social forces but also claimed to have a unique ability to understand, and fearlessly report, these connections to a public that was not always ready for the truth. This lack of modesty is vintage Cosell, but it also underscores a level of determination that kept him pursuing a broadcasting career long after most would likely have decided to quit.

Even in his earliest years as a sports reporter, these two aspects of Cosell's character—social conscience and ambition—would come into conflict with each other. More than defining a personal story of tortured conflict, however, they reveal the political and social turmoil that surrounded the early decades of television. During the 1960s, producers and executives struggled to create and air programming that fulfilled an advertising and entertainment function but that also addressed the often violent social transformations and conflicts that were covered on their networks' evening news programs. The tension between Cosell's political ideals and his professional ambitions, between his insightful reporting and his rhetoric, as well as his quest for fame and adoration, parallel the larger tensions within the medium of television itself.

I focus in this chapter not only on Cosell's early career but also on the political and social contexts it which it developed—most notably the "culture of unity" that was part of the "cultural front" of the 1930s and 1940s; the emerging opportunities for urban working-class European ethnics within the new culture industries that emerged with broadcasting after World War II; and the "Red Scare" of the 1950s. In many respects, such experiences were common among young Jewish writers, directors, actors, and entertainers of Cosell's time. What made him special was the way he brought these to the world of sports broadcasting.

———

Interviewed by Baltimore area radio sports broadcaster Ted Patterson in 1968, Howard Cosell pontificated in the third person about what made him a unique, and sometimes disliked, figure among televised sport announcers:

> The public has very mixed views about Howard Cosell, and the public always will because the public grows up the way you grew

up [speaking to Patterson], and the way you are now and the task that you're pursuing here, and the research you're doing. Sports is something very dear and very special for you, very much apart from real life. . . . You see, the big things in sport today, because of the nature of the civilization in which we live, are not the events. They're the things that transcend sport, they're the things that relate to the economy, the sociology, the politics of this nation. The things that matter in sport today are the things that the play-by-play announcers and those who read wire copy can't even talk about.[2]

In this interview Cosell conveys ideas that he expressed many times throughout his career: about the serious critical insight that he brought to the coverage of sports, about his difference from (and sense of superiority to) other sports reporters, and about the immaturity and folly of sports fandom. Cosell was in fact different from what he liked to call the "rip-and-read" radio sports reporter, who provided box scores and little more. It would be this difference, this edginess, that would eventually propel him into the national spotlight. That Cosell brought an intense brand of social commentary to sports broadcasting was indeed new, and since his retirement, no one else has truly repeated this feat. But the idea of making entertainment and broadcasting socially relevant was not completely novel. One has only to look at the social cohort with which Cosell associated himself during the early years of his career to recognize the vibrant intellectual environment in which his career in entertainment developed.

As Cosell's writings make clear, he was not particularly happy with pursuing a career in law after he left the army. In his interview with Patterson he presents his entry into sports broadcasting as an accident, something he just stumbled into: "In 1954 the American Broadcasting Company called me [as the attorney for Little League Baseball] in reference to using the name 'Little League' on a network radio show they were preparing to initiate. I gave them permission on a noncommercial basis. They then asked me if I would host the show, and I said yes, more as a lark than [from] having any desire to broadcast. But I found out I liked broadcasting very much, primarily because of its immediacy. I am, in my opinion, a born reporter."[3] Cosell's recollections here are somewhat apocryphal. In fact, he reports in

Cosell, "a radio career had been on my mind the moment I got out of the Army."[4] While Cosell's association with Little League Baseball in Manhattan did provide him with his first opportunity to enter sports broadcasting, this was an opportunity that he had been working to create throughout his years as a lawyer.

After becoming a law partner, Cosell would take baseball stars such as Phil Rizzuto and Mickey Mantle to lunch, using these outings to build a clientele among athletes.[5] In 1955 the *New Yorker* ran a feature on Cosell's legal practice. At a table over lunch at a restaurant owned by Bob Olin, a former light-heavyweight champion boxer, Cosell characterized himself as a "*voorloper,* or vanguard, guiding [athletes] through the veldt of agents constantly besieging them with questionable propositions." The article characterizes Cosell as a "busy, erudite man of thirty-five who handles legal problems that come up to harass Monte Irvin and Willie Mays, of the New York Giants, and Wally Moon and Alex Grammas, of the St. Louis Cardinals, and has given business advice to Bobby Thomson, of the Milwaukee Braves, and Gil Hodges and Don Hoak, of the Dodgers." The legal services that Cosell provided are ones that have become requisite in the contemporary marketplace of highly paid athletes. At the time, however, they were noteworthy enough to require an explanation from Cosell. "Ballplayers are apt to approach business propositions *à bouche ouverte,*" he is quoted as saying, using the French term for "with an open mouth." He continued: "Because they're gregarious, if an agent sells one player something he can generally sell the entire team. The result is players are apt to fall victims to horn-swoggling and pettifoggery on a huge scale." Hornswoggling and pettifoggery aside, at the end of the article Cosell notes that, in addition to giving legal advice, he "conducts two sports-interview shows for the American Broadcasting Company."[6]

The first of these was a six-week trial program called *All-League Clubhouse,* in which young fans came into the radio studio and asked questions (written by Cosell) of major league athletes and coaches. The show debuted on May 16, 1953, after Cosell pitched the idea to network executives. It remained on the air for five years.[7] Cosell called it "a combination of *Meet the Press* and *Juvenile Jury.*"[8] Shortly after it premiered, ABC offered him a second show, a daily commentary called *Speaking of Sports,* which Cosell would continue to broadcast until the end of his career.[9] In June 1956 Cosell began a third show for WABC radio, *Sports Close-Up,* a fifteen-minute program that featured interviews he conducted with players on the field and in the locker room.[10]

During the time that Cosell hosted the children's interview show, he was still a practicing lawyer (as evidenced by the *New Yorker* article). His big break came after he developed a friendship with Ed Silverman, a radio producer and magazine sportswriter who had connections with all three networks. It was when ABC offered him *Speaking of Sports* for $25 per show in 1956 that Cosell went to Emmy and proposed that he give up his law practice for a risky new career in broadcasting. According to sportswriter Dave Kindred, her answer was, "Go ahead."[11] Cosell recalled: "My father was horrified. Right down to the day he died, in 1957, he would say to Emmy, 'Please, dear, have him go back to the profession.' It meant so much to him for his son to be a professional man, a lawyer."[12]

However much Cosell may have gambled his future livelihood and steady income on this decision, he could never be accused of not working hard to succeed. Even before Cosell pioneered the interjection of social commentary into sports reporting, during his earliest years as a reporter in the 1950s he introduced an even more fundamental innovation that radio listeners have come to take for granted: the recorded locker room interview "actuality" or "sound bite." Up until the time Cosell became involved in radio, print reporters were the only ones who routinely conducted spontaneous interviews in offices and locker rooms. Radio sports reporters might do live interviews with athletes in the studio or before a game, but they rarely dragged around what were then large, heavy, expensive tape recorders to interview players immediately after games. This is precisely what Cosell did every day. According to Kindred, he spent $350 (or, according to Cosell, $480) of his own money to purchase a seventeen-pound (or, according to Cosell, thirty-pound) Magnemite, the elite recorder at the time. Using three 1.5-volt A batteries and one 90-volt B, it was nearly a foot wide, eight inches tall, and five inches deep.[13] Cosell would strap it to his back and carry it with him for postgame interviews. A tall man at six feet, one inch, hunched over, Cosell became quite a spectacle in team clubhouses. Frank Gifford, while playing as a running back for the New York Giants in the 1950s, first met Cosell when the latter approached him for a recorded interview in the locker room. "The first thing I remember about him was his schlepping around with that big tape recorder that he had," says Gifford. "That was before the days of little tape recorders."[14]

Recalling his use of recording technology, Cosell writes:

> I was infected with my desire, my resolve, to make it in broadcasting. I knew exactly what I wanted to do, and how. Not having a name or a reputation, I knew that I had to have the biggest names I could get. I needed name value. I intended to bring to radio the actuality of sport—people in the news, as they were making it, explaining it. . . . I was probably the first reporter to carry his own tape recorder everywhere he went. . . . I must have looked like Edmund Hillary [the first mountain climber recorded to have scaled Mount Everest] carrying his knapsack.[15]

He was constantly working and recording, bringing his interviews to his radio programs and adding the dimension of recorded actualities to sport reporting as no other broadcaster had done before. So overwhelming was Cosell's presence that Yankee catcher Ralph Houk would tell him, "You're like shit, you're everywhere." Cosell later would write, "That line, I can say with certain mixed feelings, has survived to this day."[16] Gifford remembers the novelty of Cosell's approach to his work, and recalls that athletes treated him with a degree of reserve.

> Nobody knew much about him, and he'd stick that mike in front of your face and then start asking you questions. I do remember one of the first times that he wanted to ask me some questions. I had heard that you'd better watch that guy. People said, "He's really treacherous," or something like that. At that time in sports, there weren't as many cutthroat people as there are now. If I remember, the first time he came up to me I said, "Where are you going to go with this?" He said, "Just a couple of questions if you don't mind." I said, "Nothing that's going to get me in trouble."[17]

During spring training in 1956, Cosell traveled to Florida with his tape recorder for a new program he planned to do called *Baseball Sportstacular.* Silverman, who was his writer and producer, discovered, according to Kindred, that Cosell worked under a constant sense of insecurity. Before their first show Cosell paced back and forth in the production room while Silverman edited and reedited the program, mixing in music, replaying it constantly for Cosell, who in turn chain-smoked, muttering: "It's not going to work, I just know it. I made a terrible mistake. I shouldn't have done this. . . . I don't know, Eddie, I just don't know, but it's not your fault, it's mine." The show went on the air at eight o'clock that evening. The next morning the show business newspaper *Variety* gave it a rave review, and Cosell was jubilant, showing the article to every ABC network executive he could find.[18]

Regardless of its success, Cosell had reason to be insecure about his decision to become a broadcaster. He had risked a great deal as the male salary earner in a post–World War II middle-class household. He had been a pioneer in many respects, breaking away from family, community, and ethnic expectations, but this also left him vulnerable should he fail. That would mean more than a loss of income; it would bring humiliation. In fact, entering broadcasting in the 1950s as a Jew from New York who *sounded* like a Jew from New York was hard enough. Cosell, however, was also a liberal, a lawyer who had represented African American athletes in the newly integrated major leagues, and a sports reporter whose hook would later be his critical understanding of social justice and politics. For this kind of person, the waters of the entertainment world were treacherous ones in the 1950s, and Cosell had come to learn this in his path toward a broadcasting career.

––––––––

On January 15, 1954, buried on page twenty-seven of the *New York Times,* a brief article appeared about an incident involving a union called the Television Writers of America (TWA). The union was split between two regional centers, East and West. The executive secretary for the Western Region, a woman named Joan LaCour (a pseudonym that she used at the time for her own writing, as well as for ghostwriting that she did for blacklisted writers), had been called to testify before a subcommittee of the House Un-American Activities Committee. When asked if she had any former association with the Communist Party, LaCour refused to testify, invoking her right against self-incrimination guaranteed under the Fifth Amendment of the U.S. Constitution. In response, ten members of the Eastern Region's executive board, including its president, Irve Tunick, resigned from the union, citing "a complete difference of opinion on basic union principles." The last sentence of the article reads, "Howard W. Cosell, an attorney of 25 Broad Street, has withdrawn as counsel for the Eastern Region."[19]

Very little information about Cosell's involvement with the TWA exists. LaCour, who still remembers Cosell as being hostile toward her at the time, does not remember the details of his counsel to the union, and it is unclear whether Cosell advised the executive board members to resign. Information does exist, however, about the brief life of the TWA, LaCour's testimony before HUAC, and the relationship of the union to the blistering anticommunist crusades of the era. These are all windows into a past that provides historical depth to the development of Cosell's social consciousness later in his career.

Cultural historian Michael Denning has noted that during the 1930s, a new commercial entertainment apparatus was taking shape around film, recorded music, and radio. As a central component of cultural discourse, it became notable on two accounts. First, those who owned the productive capacity of the industry were not the typical cultural elites of the past century, but were often people who had prior experience "in the less respectable urban amusements," such as nickelodeon theaters or the vaudeville stage. They tended to recruit and seek creative talent from the urban centers from which they themselves originated, "giving a plebeian, ethnic accent to mass entertainment."[20] What is more, those who were hired as "cultural workers" in these new industries—the writers, actors, directors, set designers, illustrators, musicians, technicians, and so on—"began to organize themselves into culture industry unions and guilds."[21] It was within these traditions and contexts that the Television Writers of America was born.

Like much else in television (including Howard Cosell himself), the TWA had its origins in radio. During the 1940s, in the wake of World War II, advertising agencies loosened their grip on radio content just a bit to allow for patriotic—and sometimes social-critical—themes to emerge in programs. Some writers of these programs organized into a collective bargaining organization called the Radio Writers Union (RWU). Many of these writers were among the founders of the TWA, including its first president, Dick Powell (no relation to the actor), and Frank Tarloff, Carl Reiner, Norman Lear, and Larry Gelbart.[22]

Led by Sam Moore, a progressive former communist who would later be blacklisted, the RWU was a closed shop and represented almost all the writers who worked in radio. The progressive forces within the RWU were largely those who joined together to form the TWA.[23] In 1953 Joan LaCour became involved with the union as executive secretary of its West Coast branch, and she campaigned to have the union represent television writers as a bargaining unit. An election on affiliating with the TWA was set to be held in May 1953 (though it was later postponed to the fall), and LaCour went to New York along with Dick Powell to drum up support for the TWA.[24] One example of how they went about promoting their union is an advertisement sent to potential members for a television writing school featuring lessons in the craft from some of its most successful members. In addition, the union advertised itself as a democratic one that included freelance as well as full-time staff writers.[25]

According to LaCour, rival unions such as the Screen Writers Guild underestimated the Television Writers of America. After a tough and contentious election battle, the TWA won approval from the writers' bargaining unit. It is easy to see why a young, ambitious lawyer like Cosell, looking to gain a foothold in the entertainment industry, would have been attracted to the job of representing this union. Among those supporting the TWA were some of the most talented writers in television, working on some of the most popular shows, including *I Love Lucy, Four Star Theatre,* and *Dick Tracy,* and for stars such as Burns and Allen, Martin and Lewis, Bing Crosby, Jack Benny, Bob Hope, Red Skelton, and Jimmy Durante.[26] Indeed, Lacour recalls that in the beginning, "it looked like the TWA had a bright future." By the late summer and early fall of 1953, however, its main rival, the Screen Writers Guild, along with the networks, had found an effective means of weakening the TWA in the run-up to the election, what LaCour describes as "a carefully orchestrated red-baiting."[27]

LaCour was already familiar with the entertainment industry blacklist. Her entry into the field of television and radio writing had been as a ghostwriter for Adrian Scott, a member of the Hollywood Ten who went to jail for refusing to cooperate with HUAC, and whom LaCour would eventually marry. An example of this Red-baiting against the TWA is an August 1953 article by Martin Berkeley that appeared in *American Mercury,* titled "Reds in Your Living Room." Berkeley was a film screenwriter who had become well known for providing over one hundred names to HUAC.[28] Claiming that communists had once controlled Hollywood but had since been "crushed,"

Berkeley wrote that "Reds" had now figured out how to make new inroads into the hearts and minds of Americans: through radio and television. The Trojan horse by which the Communist Party was soon to gain access to these powerful broadcasting media, according to Berkeley, was none other than the Television Writers of America, "a potent weapon to assail you—*right in your own living room!*"[29] The article strove to establish that the TWA was a subversive organization by linking it with board members of the RWU who had been identified as communists by friendly witnesses who had testified before HUAC. (Among those mentioned is Studs Terkel.) The article sharply singles out LaCour as someone who "has long played house with the comrades" and who had a role in creating a "Thought Control Congress" in Los Angeles. It paints her as a communist for having supported left-wing and progressive causes, such as the Independent Progressive Party in 1948 (which Berkeley describes as "red controlled"). In contrast, Berkeley depicts the rival Screen Writers Guild as a democratic organization that, if pitted against the TWA in a national election, would win easily.[30]

After the election, LaCour remembers, network lawyers in Hollywood refused to negotiate with her because she was a "known communist." They were eventually forced to do so by the National Labor Relations Board official assigned to handle negotiations between the TWA and the networks, but because of the negative publicity, LaCour wanted to resign as executive secretary. It was only after Powell urged her to stay that she changed her mind. "The big, successful comedy and drama writers in the TWA knew what had happened to the Ten," she recalled. "But they wanted to stick it out. There weren't even that many of us, but some of the struggle was wonderful, just the feeling of fighting back against McCarthyism."[31]

Eventually HUAC came looking for LaCour with a subpoena, and she was forced to go into hiding. The union eventually agreed that LaCour should testify, however, and Morris Cohn, a colleague from the union, sat down with Lacour to prepare her for what she would experience. He told her, "Of course, you'll deny that you've ever been a Communist." LaCour responded, "No, I can't Morris." She had been a member of the Communist Party, though "a long time ago and only for a short time." LaCour told him, "I'm not ashamed of it, but I won't admit it, because that would open the door for them to demand that I 'name names.'"[32] LaCour ended up refusing to testify, pleading her

Fifth Amendment rights against self-incrimination before a subcommittee of HUAC. Reporters snapped photos of her, asking her to pose crossing her legs and powdering her nose. "I felt marked with a scarlet 'C,'" she recalled. "Naked. You never lose the feeling."[33]

Asked what she remembered of Cosell during this time, LaCour answered, "Certainly my memories are all negative and hostile." Cosell attacked her but did not inform on her. "I don't know if he would have turned anyone in," she said. "You pretty much had to have access to the committee to do that, and there were a lot of people who did." Her memories were unclear as to the forum in which Cosell engaged in his attacks. Although she stated during an interview that he did radio commentaries and wrote newspaper columns criticizing her,[34] this seems unlikely, since his career as a journalist in the winter of 1954 still consisted mainly of his job as host of *All League Clubhouse*. This does not mean, of course, that LaCour's recollections are entirely inaccurate.

A statement issued by Irve Tunick explaining the reason for his resignation from Television Writers of America certainly expresses very pointed criticism of LaCour. The day before it reported the resignation of the TWA East Region executive board, the *New York Times* published an article that focused on Tunick's individual resignation from the TWA in protest of LaCour's lack of cooperation with the subcommittee. He declared: "The action of the Western Region in retaining in its employ an executive secretary who has refused to answer questions put to her by a legally constituted Government body places the union in an untenable position at the bargaining table. Further, it involves the entire membership in an area not properly a union concern: the individual political or philosophical convictions of a paid employee."[35]

The tone of this letter—which would certainly have been made available to Cosell as the lawyer for the TWA East—is consistent with Cosell's resignation as counsel in the wake of LaCour's testimony. Cosell was in fact extremely concerned by the anticommunist witch-hunts of the 1950s, especially with regard to their potential for jeopardizing his future career in broadcasting. The only argument Jill Cosell can remember her parents ever having occurred when her mother signed a petition to have a traffic light installed at an intersection near the family's apartment in Peter Cooper Village. "My father went ballistic. 'You must never sign any kind of petition,'" he told Emmy. "My career could be ruined."[36]

Yet any cooperation with or avoidance of Red-baiting politics on Co-sell's part during this period was certainly not an endorsement of the tactics that HUAC employed. According to Jill Cosell, some of her father's sharpest private criticisms of any public figure were aimed at Joseph McCarthy. She recalls that when McCarthy died, Cosell watched the funeral on television. "My father said, 'Look, Jill, see, no one came to his funeral. He's evil.' . . . He said, 'Everybody hates him. He's evil. He's ruined lives.'"[37] Ultimately the actions by TWA East, HUAC, and the Screen Writers Guild proved fatal to the TWA. According to Powell, most of the writers named in Berkeley's *American Mercury* article were soon forced by their employers to leave the TWA. The defection of the Eastern Region board was in many respects the final blow. The TWA folded in 1954, and the Screen Writers Guild merged with the Radio Writers Union to form the Writers Guild of America (East and West); in essence, the Red-baiting was a success.[38] "A lot of people in the East just jumped overboard," LaCour remembers. "It was kind of a mass panic." Joan LaCour landed on the blacklist. For the remainder of the 1950s her career in the United States was over. She and Adrian Scott were forced to leave the country and move to England, where they worked as television writers for seven years.[39]

Cosell's behavior as the TWA East's attorney with regard to this incident constitutes something of a paradox. On the one hand, he was a critic of Joseph McCarthy and a future champion of civil liberties and individual rights. Yet on the other, when the time came to stand up for an individual who was being persecuted by HUAC, the best one can say about Cosell's actions is that he withdrew his professional support and left LaCour to defend herself. However one might feel about how this reflects on his individual character or moral choices, Cosell's actions at the time reveal a great deal about his ideological perspective, which would serve as a kind of bridge between the politics of the 1930s and those of the 1960s. In fact, Cosell was not alone in this kind of ambivalence toward the Red-baiting of the 1950s. Others who cooperated with, or at least refused to resist, HUAC were at the same time bitter critics of the entertainment industry, which imposed increasingly rigid rules of conformity and permitted explicit censorship by advertisers and often engaged in bizarre meddling into their creative processes. Among these critics were people who had relationships with Cosell.

Irve Tunick, president of TWA East who resigned and signed the letter pointedly attacking LaCour, is a good example. In addition to leaving the union in the early 1950s, Tunick signed a petition mentioned in the Berkeley article titled "We the Undersigned." Berkeley described the petitioners as a group of "intelligent, informed anti-Communists" who "have freely acknowledged their beliefs and identities, [and] have tried to wrest control of RWU from the Party."[40] Yet as a television writer, Tunick also chafed under the censorship of advertising agencies. One example involves the work he did in the 1950s on a special dramatic program on the Dead Sea Scrolls for a live television series called *Armstrong Circle Theatre.* The script was originally to center on a Jewish family in Israel, with the protagonist, a professor, as the leading character, and his wife and sons in supporting roles. For the initial reading before the network and ad agencies sponsoring the program, Tunick brought in the Israeli actor Joseph Yadin. "The main fear of the agency people was that it was going to be a Jewish show," Tunick recalled. To compensate, the network and ad agency hired an actress who was best known for playing an Irish mother on a soap opera at the time, and a blond-haired boy with a "Norwegian cast" to play the youngest son. There was a moment in the script in which the mother was to say to her son, Tunick recalls, "a typical Jewish line, and it had to be said by a nice Jewish mother. When I heard that line come out with a Gaelic intonation, I don't have much hair on my head but the little I had stood up and waved."[41]

Robert Alan Aurthur was another TWA East board member who resigned after LaCour's testimony. In 1960, however, he also complained of censorship and advertising agency interference during the preceding decade. He once quipped that while writers in film often fight to have their names included in credits at the end of a motion picture, writers for television programs are usually so ashamed of the final product that they fight to have their names removed.[42] He remembered writing a program for *Philco Playhouse* based on his short story "On the Docks," about a time before World War II when he had worked as a stevedore alongside an African American laborer. In order to have the script accepted, however, he needed to conceal the fact that one of the leading characters would be African American. He wanted Sidney Poitier to play the role, but this created problems with regard to the blacklist, since Poitier "had signed certain petitions," said Aurthur. "He had belonged at one time to organizations which, on the face of them, had no meaning at all except that he was a Negro and interested in Negro civil rights." Ultimately Poitier was called to a meeting before the attorneys for NBC and was asked to defend his past political associations. "It was a dreadful meeting," remembered Aurthur, because at one point Poitier was asked why he had lived with Canada Lee, a pioneering African American actor who died shortly before being called before HUAC, when the two actors were filming *Cry, the Beloved Country* in South Africa in the late 1940s. Poitier ran from the room very upset and had to be consoled at length before he was willing to return and take part in the program. Ultimately, Aurthur remembered, "there were serious repercussions from the show in that there were editorials in Southern papers accusing everyone concerned of being a Communist."[43]

Rod Serling, who, according to Jill Cosell, was a close friend and a second cousin of her father's, accepted that advertisers had the right to change his scripts and claimed that he never objected to or challenged their decisions.[44] He also claimed never to have been personally affected by the blacklist. Nevertheless, he often attempted to "probe current social problems" in an effort to provide depth to his scripts. After the lynching of the African American teenager Emmett Till in Mississippi was exposed in *Look* magazine (following a prior exposé in *Jet*), Serling wrote a script for a teleplay based roughly on the event. Since, as he later put it, it was "unacceptable" to write such a play about African Americans for fear of upsetting advertisers concerned with offending southern markets, he changed the event to one involving a white mob attacking a white Jewish victim. After word leaked out that he was writing a script loosely based on Emmett Till's murder, ad agencies and the network were threatened with boycotts by southern white citizens' groups. As a result, the network allowed advertising agencies to edit the program thoroughly, transplanting the setting to a New England village and removing all references— even mention of Coca-Cola—that might conceivably identify the setting as southern.[45]

The stories of Aurthur and Serling are particularly telling in that it was common for Jewish entertainers, writers, musicians, and others in the industry to express a special empathy with African Americans. As Paul Buhle puts it: "Most participants at any point in the creation of popular culture, Jewish, black, or otherwise, simply went (as they continue to go) along resistless with individual opportunities, following whatever prospect has led to the most personal success. . . . But many Jews of the first, second, third, and fourth generation had, and have, an impulse to swim upstream, looking for allies along the way."[46] Michael Denning locates much of the empathy between Jews and African Americans in the era of the popular front of the 1930s, when the democratic working-class culture of the Congress of Industrial Organizations sought to create alliances between workers on the one hand and urban professionals and the middle classes on the other. "Under the sign of the 'people,' this popular front public culture sought to forge ethnic and racial alliances, mediating between Anglo American culture, in part by reclaiming the figure of 'America' itself, imagining an Americanism that would provide a usable past for ethnic workers, who were thought of as foreigners, in terms of a series of ethnic slurs."[47]

The career of film producer and director Stanley Kramer, a friend and former fraternity brother of Cosell's, illustrates the connection between Jews and African Americans, and the kind of cultural alliances that Denning describes. In his autobiography *Cosell,* Howard Cosell describes an encounter with Kramer after World War II, when both men had just been discharged from the military. The two had traveled to Philadelphia to watch a basketball game between NYU and Temple. During dinner on the first night of the trip, Kramer told Cosell that he was going to make movies: "I'm gonna make *Home of the Brave,*" said Kramer, a war film that probed the issue of anti-Semitism, "but I'll make the Jewish boy black and I'm gonna deal with the great problem of America to come. The black problem."[48] Cosell notes: "The 'Jewish Problem' was the major social trauma in this country up to and through World War II. And then it was supplanted by the 'Black Problem,' as Stanley Kramer so astutely foresaw."[49]

While we do not have to accept the grandiose narrative into which Cosell manipulates twentieth-century American history, it is worthwhile to look at the conversation itself. The most striking feature of Cosell and Kramer's discussion about their career plans is their urgent desire to make socially relevant entertainment linking the experiences of African Americans and Jews. In *Like it Is,* Cosell provides a more detailed and complex discussion of race as he saw it in 1974 on his return to the Brooklyn of his youth:

> It is when you leave Eastern Parkway and walk down
> Washington or Underhill Avenues that you come upon the new

scene in this part of Brooklyn. You enter a whole new world—a black world. In the 1930's and 1940's, the blacks were carefully contained. They could not move beyond Fulton Street. But, as new sociological forces swept the United States in the 1950's and the 1960's, Brooklyn was not to be excluded. [It was feared that] the blacks and the islanders from Puerto Rico, Jamaica and Haiti would "transgress." They would climb the wall of Fulton Street, and they have. According to my mother, who only moved out of Brooklyn two years ago, even Eastern Parkway has been forced to open its doors to our citizens of dark skin. The fact that decent housing for black people is long overdue doesn't alter the hideous reality that white people scurry like a horde of lemmings out of the neighborhood when the blacks approach it. And despite denials by landlords, they permit the buildings to run down as their black tenancies increase. In the meantime, they continue to raise the rents. In net effect, what has happened to this part of Brooklyn is a tragic commentary on the wretched racial problem that continues to haunt our nation.[50]

Much has been made of Howard Cosell's relationship with Muhammad Ali during the 1960s. It is certainly true that this relationship—or, perhaps better described by the Yiddish term Dave Kindred uses for it, this shtick—was in large part responsible for Cosell's rise to fame. It is important, however, to place Cosell's relationship with Ali, as well as Cosell's other very public endorsements of civil rights, within a larger historical context. The origins of this political idealism are in the Jewish neighborhoods of Brooklyn, in the increasingly ethnic and working-class character of American culture that emerged from the popular culture of the 1930s, and in the ambitions of those who entered the cultural and entertainment fields during the 1950s. At the same time, the political stances taken by Cosell, which were carefully crafted around themes of civil liberties and individual rights, have roots that stretch back to the anticommunist witch-hunts and purges of the 1950s.

In 1951, when Carl Foreman, with whom Stanley Kramer produced the film *High Noon*—a picture generally seen as a critique of the bullying tactics employed by Joseph McCarthy and HUAC—was called to testify about his past political affiliations, Kramer severed their business partnership. He continued to make "message" movies, however, including *Judgment at Nuremberg* (about the trials of Nazi officers following World War II), and *Guess Who's Coming to Dinner* (a comedy of manners about an elite young white woman who brings home an African American fiancé to meet her parents). Like his fraternity buddy Kramer, Cosell would avoid the anticommunist blacklist—though he does use the term to describe the refusal of ABC to allow him on national television during the early 1950s. But Cosell's career would progress more slowly. It would take him more time to find a space in which he could comment on race and society within the world of sports. When he did, he would evoke the values of liberal pluralism and Americanism that emerged out of the 1930s, but in a way that found a responsive audience among young sports fans and television viewers in the 1960s.

3 On the Network "Blacklist"

For five years, beginning in 1959, I was locked out of
network television. Five years stolen from a career that
started late. Five years at the peak of one's ambition.
Blacklist is a harsh word. Put it this way: When the man who
runs the company thinks you can't perform, he has every
right not to put you on the air. That man's name was Tom
Moore. The company he ran was ABC.
—Howard Cosell, *Cosell*, 1973

In *Cosell,* the best-selling autobiography written by Howard
Cosell, with editorial assistance from Mickey Herskowitz,
during his rapid ascent to mega-fame in the early 1970s, Cosell refers to his failure to land a job on network television
as being "blacklisted." In his choice of that loaded term, he
indirectly recalls the fear and insecurity that characterized
work in broadcasting during the Red Scare of the 1950s. Yet
Cosell actually claims that he was kept off network television not because he was thought to have been a communist,
but because Tom Moore of ABC found him to be too abrasive, too much of a New Yorker, and implicitly too Jewish.
The force behind this "blacklist" was not a government
agency or congressional subcommittee putting pressure on
the network, but an advertising-savvy broadcasting executive trying to build up a struggling network, for whom Cosell provided the "wrong image."[1]

Although there is too little information to give a clear picture of Cosell's actual involvement with the Television Writers
of America, at the very least the episode detailed in the previous chapter illustrates the terrifying and stifling atmosphere
created by the Red Scare, at a time when Cosell was seeking
to gain a foothold in sports broadcasting. As Paul Buhle has
illustrated in his extensive scholarship on Hollywood during
the Red Scare, Jews in the entertainment industry had to be

especially concerned about being tagged as communists. Although the great entrepreneurs of the television networks—David Sarnoff of NBC, William Paley of CBS, and Leonard Goldenson of ABC—were all Jewish, many in the television industry worried that American audiences, and particularly southern audiences, saw Jews as perennial foreigners, "un-American" by definition. It should come as no surprise, then, that as Howard Cosell worked to gain acceptance as a sportscaster during the 1950s, he would invoke the language of the Red Scare, as his struggles were very much about overcoming his status as an "outsider," as a man whose obvious connection to an ethnic past simply could not be erased from his public persona. Yet ironically, it would be those same ethnic traits and personal qualities that kept him off the air in the late 1950s and early 1960s that would come to be seen as an asset by the network as sports broadcasters began to grapple with a new phenomenon: the political mobilization of African American athletes during the 1960s.

———

A 1958 press release from the ABC Radio Network contains a phrase that Cosell would often use to describe a cornerback who would make a key interception or a third baseman who would catch a sharply hit line drive: "In the Right Place, at the Right Time." The public relations document gushes about the network's new upstart radio commentator and boxing analyst: "Cosell can be seen in the dressing rooms of fighters, both before and after every major bout, at the ballparks and just about every other place sports news is likely to develop." It continues:

> The lawyer-turned-broadcaster never has been refused an interview—his log of guests reads like a sports who's who. You name them—Ted Williams, Stan Musial, Casey Stengel, Bud Wilkinson, Jackie Robinson, Bob Cousy, Otto Graham, Paul Brown, Cary Middlecoff, Sam Snead, Althea Gibson, Lew Hoad, Pancho Gonzales, Paul Hornung, Frank Gifford, Fred Haney, Floyd Patterson, Rocky Marciano, Ray Robinson, Bobby Bragan, Branch Rickey, Maurice Richard, Muzz Patrick, Bill Russell, Wilt Chamberlain—and chances are he or she has appeared on one or more of Cosell's programs.[2]

It had been over five years since Cosell began *All League Clubhouse,* nearly four since he had given up his law practice. He was continuing to work hard to keep his career as a sports broadcaster afloat. In July 1957 he began to appear regularly on the ABC television network with a nightly sports commentary program that aired from 6 to 6:15 called *Sports Focus*. It had begun as a summer replacement for the children's program *Kukla, Fran and Ollie*.[3] Newspaper previews touted *Sports Focus* as a new kind of interview show, one that diverted attention from the mechanics of sports and instead provided audiences with an intimate look at the human side of their sports heroes. Cosell explained his approach to one reporter: "'What kind of pitch did you hit? When did you know you had the fight won? What was your greatest thrill in sport?' You don't hear those kinds of questions on my show[,] . . . and you're not going to unless they're the most important ones at the moment of the interview."[4] In other words, said the novice broadcaster, described by another reporter earlier that same year as "a lanky young man," "I try to prove that sports figures have the same personal dimensions as other celebrities." Only three years after entering broadcasting, Cosell was being heard on over two hundred stations across the United States and was attracting the attention of the national sports beat writers. Although he positioned himself as an alternative to the play-by-play announcer—"frequently, I think you can get a hotter insight into a sports story from an interview than you can from play-by-play"—in June 1959 he began calling live sporting events himself, describing from ringside his first heavyweight championship boxing match for ABC Radio, in which a Swede, Ingemar Johansson, knocked out champion Floyd Patterson in the third round.[5]

Yet in 1959, looking ahead to the future that he faced as a broadcaster, Howard Cosell was anywhere but in the right place at the right time. A new director of programming, Tom Moore, did not take to Cosell and canceled *Sports Focus*. He was relegated back to radio and local television in New York.[6] It was a time, however, when Cosell grew and developed as a broadcaster and producer, and came to the attention of a young executive named Roone Arledge, who saw in the nasal-voiced New Yorker a sportscaster who could speak to the political and social issues that were increasingly becoming part of the world of sports. Fortunately for Cosell, he worked for a network that had made the decision, revolutionary in American broadcasting history, to bank its future on sports. By the mid-1960s Cosell would be lifted from the "blacklist" largely because the man chosen to captain the ABC Sports juggernaut was none other than Arledge, a maverick television executive, a pioneer in the marketing of sports on television, and, as chance would have it, Cosell's biggest champion.

———

During the 1950s sports programming on television had not yet developed into the complex system that it would become in the 1960s and 1970s. By the late 1950s CBS had begun televising regular National Football League games, and networks had been broadcasting boxing matches and baseball games since the medium had first been established. But the network that employed Cosell, ABC, did not even have a sports division during the 1950s. At the time ABC was considered the "third network," a minor league broadcasting entity. Unlike the other two television networks, which came into existence independently, ABC developed out of NBC's Blue Network, which coexisted alongside NBC's more substantial Red Network. In 1942 NBC was forced to divest itself of one of its two networks after losing an antitrust suit that was eventually affirmed by the Supreme Court. In 1943 Edward J. Noble (founder of Life Savers) purchased NBC Blue, and in 1945 he renamed the network the American Broadcasting Company. In 1953 ABC, gaining final approval from the Federal Communications Commission, merged with Paramount Pictures, which was headed by Leonard Goldenson.[7]

From its beginning as a network, ABC was at a financial disadvantage in comparison to its rivals. Without the capital and resources of CBS and NBC, it could not afford to produce programming or news of the same quality, and ABC also had trouble gaining access to local affiliate stations in many markets across the country. Arledge writes in his memoir that insiders called ABC the "Almost Broadcasting Company." Instead of creating its own sports department, ABC purchased its sports programming from an entity called Sports Programs, Inc., created and run by a crusty New Yorker named Ed Scherick. Arledge describes Sports Programs as having offered one-stop shopping for a network looking for sports programming. Scherick acquired rights, obtained advertising sponsors, and supplied all of the personnel and equipment necessary to put together a sports broadcast.[8]

Scherick had been putting together sports broadcasting packages since 1954 for coverage of baseball, pro football, and college basketball games. In 1958 he obtained rights to broadcast the Bluegrass

Bowl, a low-tier college bowl game played in Louisville, Kentucky, between Oklahoma State and Florida State. At the time, neither was considered a powerhouse program. The stadium held only 8,000, and because the game-time temperature was six degrees above zero, only 2,100 people showed up. Since the stadium had stands on only one side of the field, the broadcasters had to build a press box on a tower looking down into the stands or else face the prospect of airing a football game that would look as if it were being played on an isolated frozen tundra. The game was noteworthy, however, for two principal reasons. It was the first college football game broadcast by Scherick, who would later bring a comprehensive NCAA football package to ABC, and would become the first head of ABC's sports division. It was also the first live sports broadcast on television for Howard Cosell.[9]

Up until this time, with his short-lived *Sports Focus* show, Cosell was the closest thing that ABC had to a sports department. Cosell's nightly fifteen-minute program was in fact the only regularly scheduled sports programming on the network.[10] This would change, however, as Tom Moore, an energetic and aggressive new executive from Mississippi, became increasingly involved in ABC's operations as director of programming. Having made his mark in sales as a spokesperson for Forest Lawn Cemetery in Los Angeles, Moore became a sales executive for CBS radio and ABC television. He worked his way up the network hierarchy to the lead position in programming by 1958. He played a large role in shaping an image of ABC that would last for many years, for he was one of the first television executives to seek out a specific demographic niche with the aim of delivering a particular audience to advertisers (in his case, young viewers between the ages of eighteen and thirty-five).[11]

Sports became a key part of Moore's strategy. He developed a strong working relationship with Scherick, and agreed that if the network were to gain momentum and catch NBC and CBS, it would have to develop a stronger selection of sports. Eventually Moore would persuade ABC to purchase Sports Programs, Inc., and develop its coverage of sports in-house. In 1961 he hired Arledge to serve as vice president for sports. But while Moore worked to build a sports programming department at ABC, he also was determined to keep Howard Cosell off the air.[12]

In writing about his experiences at ABC, Cosell is respectful of Moore. He credits the executive with developing a focus on sports programming that helped to build ABC into a major network. According to Cosell, Moore wanted ABC to gain access to local affiliate stations in markets around the United States. By the end of the 1950s, the two other major networks, NBC and CBS, had already taken the stations with the strongest frequencies, and in many markets ABC did not even have an affiliate. Moore's idea was to gain entry to these markets by developing a monopoly on sports programming that could be packaged with other shows the network had to offer. According to Cosell, however, Moore's decisions also reflected an anti-urban, anti-Semitic prejudice which arose out of his concerns about creating a national audience.

Cosell recalls talking about his ambitions with Ed Scherick, founder of Sports Programs, Inc.: "He was dead honest with me. Tom Moore didn't want me on the air. I wasn't his kind of image."[13] Cosell remained on local television and radio, and worked to make an impact on the network as a producer of sports documentaries, something new to television at the time. He created his own company, Legend Productions, and was able to assemble teams to make a number of innovative documentaries about sports, past and present.

Yet Cosell remained on the fringes of the network hierarchy. He conveys his sense of exclusion from the network's plans when he describes his experience producing the first of these documentaries in 1963, a retrospective film titled *Babe Ruth: A Look behind the Legend.* The program was based on an article written by the baseball writer Roger Kahn, who agreed to write the screenplay for the show. Once completed, the film was screened for an audience of television reviewers, but before they could get a word out in print, it was almost canned. Ted Shaker, the ABC executive in charge of affiliate relations—and someone firmly within Moore's camp—tried to get the program dropped. Despite this opposition, Cosell was able to lobby successfully for the show to air. The reviews of *Babe Ruth* were glowing. John P. Shanley of the *New York Times* wrote, "Thanks to a combination of talents, the effort was an outstanding success," going on to call the program a "realistic and compelling study of the man."[14]

In his autobiography Cosell gleefully recounts how Shaker and Moore reversed themselves after the Babe Ruth program aired. His recollections emphasize how Cosell perceived his absence from network television as the result of blacklisting, reflective of a stifling corporate culture that dictated the tastes and choices of network programming executives: "You could understand Shaker. He was a CBS type. The proper dress, the button-down collar, the right residence (Darien), two yardsticks for sports announcers: either the mellifluous voice or the gentleman jock—neither of which I conformed to. A New York City boy, reared in Brooklyn; a New York City *Jewish* boy, if you will. The nasal twang. It all added up to the wrong image in the eyes of Ted Shaker and Tom Moore."[15]

Over the next year and a half Cosell would produce three more documentaries: *Requiem for an Arena,* a retrospective on the Polo Grounds produced during the ballpark's demolition; *Run to Daylight,* a profile of Green Bay Packers coach Vince Lombardi; and *One Hundred Yards to Glory,* one of the first in-depth television reports about Grambling College and the tradition of successful football that had developed there under the leadership of coach Eddie Robinson. Once more the films were well received. Arthur Daley of the *New York Times* wrote of *Requiem for an Arena* that it recaptured memories of the ballpark "with tender and loving care" and called it a "superb documentary."[16]

Yet Cosell still had trouble making it onto the network behind the microphone, and his success as a producer only caused executives like Moore to typecast him even more firmly as someone who could contribute exclusively "behind the scenes." Ironically, Cosell was being denied access to the network microphone for the same personality traits that had enabled him to get a foot in the door at ABC in the first place: his aggressiveness, his intelligence, and his honesty. Whereas earlier his tenacity and penchant for getting taped interviews with players had made him a valuable reporter, the new team of executives at ABC saw him as pushy and conniving. Cosell was clearly a very intelligent and insightful interviewer and sports commentator, but he also could annoy his listeners, frequently reminding his audience of his erudition by using polysyllabic words where simpler ones might have sufficed. These characteristics emerged early in Cosell's career as an interviewer and a sportscaster, and fans commented on them from a very early stage. In what must be one of the very first letters to a newspaper complaining about Cosell's verbosity, a viewer named J. Clyde Ferryfoot wrote to the *Washington Post* in September 1959: "I have now heard Chuck Thompson and Howard Cosell chew the microphone to death at enough football games to know I am being conned. Mr. Cosell, authoritatively prolix, astounds us with his command of minutiae whenever Mr. Thompson will let him, which is often enough for us to grow weary of both."[17]

Ferryfoot was not the only one who found Cosell "authoritatively prolix." *New York Times* media critic Jack Gould mocked Cosell's reporting of the second heavyweight title fight between Patterson and Johannson in January 1960, in which Patterson regained his crown with a knockout of the Swedish champion: "Mr. Cosell, in reporting the fight's afterglow, achieved the heights of inarticulate fervor. The nature of his questions, which Mr. Patterson turned aside with attractive dignity, was extraordinarily trying. Also the pandemonium following the fight did not turn out to be the most fruitful period in which to bring an announcer's autobiography up to date."[18]

––––––––

Cosell provoked reaction with more than his vocabulary. During the early 1960s his "tell it like it is" honesty created a stir when he took aim at one of the most revered sports icons of his time: Casey Stengel. In 1962 WABC radio, which broadcast the Mets' games, hired Cosell to join former Brooklyn Dodger pitcher Ralph Branca for pregame and postgame interviews with players and coaches.[19] The stint lasted only two years, but it was long enough for Cosell to develop an intense dislike for Stengel, the Mets' manager. While New Yorkers flocked to see the Mets play, and most often lose, under the leadership of a skipper who had taken the crosstown Yankees to five consecutive World Series titles only a few years earlier, Cosell would have none of it. To him, the old skipper was a fraud who was largely to blame for the expansion Mets' abysmal performance. In 1981, during an oral history interview, Cosell recalled that he "ripped the shit out of Stengel and the press ripped the shit out of me." He continued, "I was telling the truth about Casey Stengel, he was a terrible person, he hated young people, he tortured them."[20]

Early in his career with the Mets, Cosell's honesty was still something that at least some sports columnists understood as an asset. In a column in which he reviewed the performance of Cosell and Branca, Red Smith wrote in May 1962—the first season for the Mets—"One reason why Cosell commands respect as a sports commentator is his candor. On controversial topics, he speaks his mind in forthright terms and gives his work a flavor sadly lacking in the bland pabulum that is the staple diet of natives in radio's vast swampland."[21] When the cause Cosell was advocating was less than popular, however, reporters were less likely to celebrate his candor. By August 1963, toward the end of Cosell's second season with the Mets, Cosell began to call publicly for Stengel to be fired. Arthur Daley of the *New York Times,* who called Cosell "the electronic oracle," noted that the broadcaster had lost faith in the baseball icon: "The disillusioned Cosell has caromed a dornick off the corrugated brow of the hitherto unassailable Mr. Stengel. The sorry mess in which the Mets find themselves, it was inferred, is due mainly to the O'l Perfessor's mishandling of his heroes. A new broom would sweep cleaner."[22] Daley dismissed Cosell's critique as "arrant nonsense" and argued that Stengel was doing a better job managing the Mets than he had done managing the Yankees.

Cosell kept up his public criticism, however, even after leaving his job as Mets announcer. In August 1964 he told a local newspaper near his home in Pound Ridge, New York, of his distaste for the team's skipper. The Mount Vernon *Daily Argus* reported: "He speaks venomously of Casey Stengel, and abhors the fact that 'the Mets outdraw the Yankees two-to-one' even with their record of 'almost complete failure.' This record he blames largely on the manager. And he decries the idolizing of these failures by today's youngsters. 'Why should kids grow up worshiping total failure?'"[23]

Given his desire to get back on network television, Cosell probably did not do himself much of a favor by attacking a sacred cow like Casey Stengel. Nevertheless, many sports reporters and television critics, despite their misgivings about Cosell, did harbor a certain respect for what they often saw as his forthright character and directness. Although Cosell was no longer welcome to appear on the ABC network, he was still a regular on the local New York affiliate, WABC-TV, and this allowed people who were influential in network television to get to know him as a television performer. Even so prominent a television critic as Jack Gould of the *New York Times,* who had been very dismissive of Cosell's reporting of the second Patterson-Johannson fight, began to express a more charitable view by 1964. Writing about a "hard-hitting" local television panel interview that Cosell had hosted with Yankees general manager Ralph Houk, Gould begins by praising Cosell for the independence he displayed in his reporting, even though he "may have one of the more irritating manners of delivery on the home screen." He then goes on to describe the program:

Last night, on Station WABC-TV, Mr. Cosell presented what for TV was something of an extraordinary event; a nonservile interview with [a] sports celebrity. . . . Mr. Cosell's half-hour last night did point up that TV does have a function in covering the controversies in the business of sports, particularly at a time when so many TV interests have a direct or indirect stake in professional athletics. That so many other TV sportscasters sidestep realistic reporting of sports understandably invites only a raised eyebrow.[24]

While Moore still refused to put Cosell on network television, some at ABC felt that Cosell's ability to generate controversy could generate viewers as well. Among the suits at the network, there was one prominent executive who had begun to admire Cosell's new style of sports coverage: Roone Arledge. After coming to the network as a producer of college football games in 1960, Arledge had gone on to become something of a nonconformist within the company. He helped to redirect the orientation of network television sports so that it brought fans into an intimate relationship with the game being broadcast—introducing innovations such as slow-motion replays and multi-camera cuts. With Scherick, he worked to develop and produce *ABC's Wide World of Sports,* a taped sports highlight show that presented fans with a banquet of sporting events each week—from college sports to NASCAR. In 1964 ABC created ABC Sports, Inc., out of its sports department, and Arledge became its vice president.[25] With his penchant for drama and spectacle, it's not surprising that Arledge became an admirer of Cosell's from a very early stage. Almost as soon as he became vice president of ABC Sports, Arledge started looking for a way to slip Cosell onto the airwaves, despite the wishes of Tom Moore.[26]

Moore had told Arledge outright that Cosell was not to appear on national telecasts, so Arledge decided to employ "stealth and slipperiness." In his memoir Arledge remembers telling Cosell that he wanted him back on the air:

It wasn't under cover of night that I summoned Howard to my office, but for all the secrecy involved, it might as well have been.

"Roone," he said, when I told him what was up, "we are today witnessing an occurrence on the scale of Milo T. Farnsworth's invention of the cathode ray tube: the television rebirth of an acknowledged genius. You are to be congratulated, young man, on your sagacity."

"Howard," I said, "cut the crap."[27]

Arledge was a magnificent storyteller, and we have only his word that this conversation ever took place. What can be confirmed from Cosell's accounts is that Arledge was indeed the executive who brought him back to network television in 1965 to become a regular on *Wide World of Sports*.[28] In addition to Cosell's reputation as a forceful interviewer whom athletes liked, Arledge had become attracted to Cosell after he saw him do an interview in 1962 with a young boxer named Cassius Clay.[29] Clay, of course, soon changed his name to Muhammad Ali and revealed his allegiance to the Nation of Islam. He was among the first African American athletes to assume a militant and assertive stance in response not only to a sports infrastructure controlled almost exclusively by white men but also, more generally, to a society still guided by racial hierarchies and white supremacy. As the 1960s developed, African American athletes would increasingly move in this direction.

––––––––

At the time, almost no white journalists had yet won the trust of this new generation of African American athletes. Perhaps because of his reputation for candid interviewing and reporting, Cosell soon emerged as one of the few white reporters, working in a medium that employed, by and large, only white reporters, who seemed to be able to get interviews with African American athletes. A look at Cosell's career during the early 1960s reveals that he had already begun to develop a strong relationship with important black athletic stars. In fact, perhaps one of the earliest was Jackie Robinson, who had become the first African American to play in the major leagues during the modern era when he broke in with the Brooklyn Dodgers in 1947. After his retirement Robinson wrote a syndicated column that appeared in African American newspapers around the nation. He often took the opportunity to praise Cosell, even during the time when Cosell was banned from appearing on network television. For example, in stark contrast to Jack Gould's negative review of Cosell after the second Patterson-Johannson fight in 1960, Robinson praised his performance. While sharply criticizing the organizers of the fight for their inability to control the crowd, Robinson has only positive words for Cosell.

I think Howard Cosell did a fine job of reporting the fight's aftermath via radio. Howard and I fought our way through [to] Patterson's dressing room right after the fight. Inside the club-house with the victorious champ, who had just made ring history by regaining his heavyweight crown, it was amazing how anyone could have fashioned an accurate description of what was going on. But Cosell's colorful commentary prompted fellow sportscaster Lindsey Nelson to send Cosell congratulations for an excellent report. . . . I have long been an admirer of Howard's because, in my opinion, he is the best sports interviewer in the business and it was a pleasure to watch him work under very difficult conditions. I think it was Dick Groat of the Pirates who once said he likes to be interviewed by Cosell because Howard brings up questions that are thought provoking and, therefore, stimulate a very interesting interview. There was definitely a lot of confusion surrounding the ending of Monday's fight, but this certainly had nothing to do with ABC's Howard Cosell.[30]

The next day Robinson published another comment which sug-gested even more that Cosell had a strong rapport with African Amer-ican sports stars. Robinson's column of June 30, 1960, was a response to one by Stanley Woodward, who was at the time the sports editor of the *New York Herald Tribune*. Woodward had written a column titled "New Segregationist," in which he accused Floyd Patterson and his entourage of discriminating against beat reporters covering the event. Woodward noted that Jackie Robinson was allowed to follow Patter-son into his dressing room before any reporters were allowed to enter. He likened the sight of Robinson and Patterson smiling together to that of white politicians in Alabama smiling as the police beat black voters. Thus, by strong implication, Woodward had accused Patter-son of discriminating not just against boxing writers but against *white* reporters more generally.[31]

Robinson mocks Woodward's posture in his column and takes um-brage at "Stan's use of the fact that Patterson and I are both Negroes as an excuse for his own ineptitude in getting the Patterson story." He counters that he did not, in fact, enter the locker room arm in arm with Patterson, but instead, as he puts it, "fought my way through the crowds and special police later on, along with ABC's Howard Cosell—who happens not to be a Negro."[32]

Cosell may not have been a "Negro," but Robinson's story suggests that he may have been one of the first white reporters to enter the room. Indeed, Cosell worked well with African American athletes. In the early 1960s it was not uncommon to see Cosell's photograph in the pages of an African American newspaper, or to find him listed as the master of ceremonies for an event honoring an African American athlete. In May 1963, for example, the *Los Angeles Sentinel* published a photo of Cosell with Jackie Robinson and football star Jim Brown to publicize International Golf Week, for which Robinson was serving as chair.[33] The following February, the *Chicago Daily Defender* published a photo of Cosell with tennis champion Althea Gibson, in which Cosell is presenting her with an award for having been named "New York Athlete of the Century" at a benefit dinner.[34]

As much as Cosell seemed to support the efforts of African American sports stars, however, he was not yet an open champion of attempts by black athletes to address social issues such as racial discrimination. This can be seen clearly in Red Smith's coverage of a banquet for Floyd Patterson, for which Cosell served as toastmaster in January 1961. Patterson was now the heavyweight champion, and was making plans for a rematch with Johannson in Miami that March. Having experienced racial discrimination before while fighting in the South, Patterson requested that the fight promoter, Feature Sports, post a $10,000 bond ensuring unrestricted seating in the hall where the fight was to take place.[35] At the dinner, Cosell asked Patterson about this request in an interview that was projected over the public address system for all who were in attendance to hear. "You know," said Cosell, "there are some people who think this means you now have a cause on your mind when you should be giving all your attention to the main job, winning the fight." Patterson replied: "A cause? No, my mind's on winning the fight. But I believe it's up to any of us who get a chance, anybody [who] gets to be the heavyweight champion, for instance, to do whatever he can for the advancement of our people."[36]

It is important to recognize that all of these experiences with African American athletes—his friendship with Jackie Robinson, his participation in honoring African American stars—took place before Cosell ever developed his famous television interview relationship with Muhammad Ali. His questioning of Patterson, however, also suggests that Cosell's thinking about sports and civil rights would undergo a transformation during the 1960s. Cosell asks a cagily worded question about "some people" who think that the champ is more interested in a "cause" than in fighting. In doing so, he lends legitimacy to the idea that athletes have no business advocating for political ideas, even those surrounding basic issues of social justice and equality, while they are participating in the arena.

By the end of the 1960s, Cosell would change his attitude on this score, becoming one of the few sports journalists to defend African American athletes who proudly asserted their rights and unflinchingly addressed continuing racial injustice in the United States. In some ways this transformation in Cosell's thinking paralleled one in his relationship with Floyd Patterson. Cosell had an association with Patterson that was almost as intense and significant as the one he would develop later on with Ali. In his book *Cosell,* he credits Patterson, along with Patterson's trainer Cus D'Amato and boxing writer Bill Heinz, with developing his interest in boxing. He writes about how he had become close to Patterson early in the young fighter's career; how he sympathized with him as a young man who had grown up a troubled child but had turned his life around through boxing; and how, after Patterson had been knocked out by Johannson in their first bout, he had introduced the ex-champ to Jackie Robinson, who inspired Patterson to return to the ring and become the first defeated heavyweight champ to regain his title. Yet by the end of Patterson's career, the fighter had broken ranks with Cosell. While in 1961 Cosell could suggest that Patterson was putting a cause before his boxing career by demanding an integrated arena for his third fight against Johannson, by 1965 Cosell was angered by Patterson's insistence on calling Ali by his former name, Cassius Clay, thus refusing to respect Ali's religious and political wishes.[37]

In 1965 Roone Arledge was finally able to get Cosell back on network television at ABC, first on the network's baseball broadcasts, and then as a boxing analyst for *Wide World of Sports.* It was this second job that would introduce his public dyad with Ali, a road show that would carry the two of them along for over a decade and a half. It also marked the beginning of Cosell's new attention to the racial dynamics of sports, which were beginning to change rapidly as the integrated world of big-time athletics moved into its second generation, and as African American athletes felt a new urgency to address the inequalities and injustices being exposed by the civil rights movement.

4 Telling It Like It Was in the Civil Rights Era

The story I always tell is when I was in college, it was the late sixties, Ali's in exile now, okay. A Saturday afternoon. I want to say it was at an NIT basketball game or something like that in Madison Square Garden. And Ali walks through the arena. He's wearing a white T-shirt and a black leather jacket. And the black leather jacket wasn't Gucci, you know, it was really a badass outfit in that era. Ali was really getting hissed by the crowd. It wasn't this celebrated moment, "There goes the champ," okay? . . . Cosell was the prime voice for Ali's defense. . . . And I think that's why a lot of people, a lot of America, disliked Cosell as much as others revered him.
—Television producer Joseph Valerio, interview with the author

In his dual biography of Muhammad Ali and Howard Cosell, sportswriter Dave Kindred tells the story of a meeting that took place in 1967, the day that the New York State Athletic Commission took away the boxer's license to fight and stripped him of his heavyweight title. According to Kindred, the meeting included writer Norman Mailer, *New York Daily News* columnist Pete Hamill, journalist/*Paris Review* editor/gadfly George Plimpton, and *Village Voice* reporter Jack Newfield. At a table in Greenwich Village's fabled Lion's Head bar, this group of self-described "left-wingers, alcoholics, and other bohemians" decided to take action in defense of Ali, whom they saw as a victim of racism. His banishment from boxing, they felt, was a blatant violation of the United States Constitution's Fourteenth Amendment, guaranteeing due process of law against the power of any institution to deprive a person arbitrarily of life, liberty, or property. (The Supreme Court would later agree, in an 8–0 decision, with Justice Thurgood Marshall recusing himself.) This "committee" decided that their cause needed a voice, one prominent enough and credible enough to take Ali's cause to the nation. Their choice was Howard Cosell.[1]

Plimpton took their request to the broadcaster. According to Kindred, Cosell said no, expressing a fear that if he spoke out, he would be assassinated by "some crazed redneck sharpshooter" firing through his office window. Cosell reportedly told Plimpton: "My sympathies are obviously with Muhammad. He has no greater friend among the whites[,] . . . but the time, at this stage in this country's popular feeling, is not correct for such an act on my part."[2] This story suggests that Cosell was not the only, nor even the most courageous, white journalist to come to Ali's defense. Yet despite Cosell's reluctance to join forces with such an esteemed "committee" in support of Muhammad Ali, he was a logical candidate for these writers to pick as their public voice; in fact, his was probably the only voice on network television that might have been sympathetic.

Only two decades before, American sports institutions had been bastions of white privilege, stability, and exclusion. That they would become the site of political activism—not only among African Americans but also among a number of young, rebellious athletes more generally—turned sports such as football, baseball, boxing, and basketball into significant cultural battlegrounds over issues of race, masculinity, and the cultural norms and ideals of post–World War II American society. Few if any sports reporters were in the same position to take on these issues as Howard Cosell.

Jim Spence, as coordinating producer of *ABC's Wide World of Sports,* worked closely with Cosell on coverage of Ali, one of the biggest stories in sports during the 1960s. This was at a time, of course, when prizefights were major sporting events and boxing champions were superstars. Cosell was perhaps the only television reporter who could have brought Ali to audiences in such an intimate and critical way, says Spence, who credits Cosell's intelligence, his political courage, and of course his sympathy with Ali for the relationship that the broadcaster and the boxer would forge. "The two developed a great chemistry, so that Howard was able to ask the hard, direct questions and evoke answers no one else could have produced," writes Spence.[3]

Indeed, in the view of Roone Arledge, unlike many other white media figures, Cosell had no fear of militant black athletes, a fear that clearly would get in the way of an open, honest journalistic

NOVEMBER 1969
PRICE $1

Esquire

THE MAGAZINE FOR MEN

We believe this:
Muhammad Ali deserves the right to defend his title. See page 121

1 Richard Benjamin
2 Theodore Bikel
3 Truman Capote
4 Howard Cosell
5 Ernest Gruening
6 Michael Harrington
7 James Earl Jones
8 Roy Lichtenstein
9 Sidney Lumet
10 George Plimpton
11 Budd Schulberg
12 José Torres
And inside,
90 others.

Cover of *Esquire*, November 1969, featuring prominent cultural figures who supported Muhammad Ali. Pictured in the ring with Cosell are actor Richard Benjamin, singer and actor Theodore Bikel, writer Truman Capote, Alaska senator Ernest Gruening, activist Michael Harrington, actor James Earl Jones, pop artist Roy Lichtenstein, film director Sidney Lumet, writer George Plimpton, screenwriter and producer Budd Schulberg, and boxer Jose Torres. Photo courtesy New York Public Library.

conversation. Arledge recounts an incident that occurred when Cosell was first getting to know Ali. The two ABC broadcasters were summoned to the champion's hotel suite. Recalling the event, Arledge attempts to reconstruct the atmosphere surrounding the occasion: "This, I should say, was the heyday of Black Power and burning ghettos in American cities, and the idea of Black Muslims, of people like Elijah Muhammad and Malcolm X in their black suits and white shirts preaching against whitey, drove fear into the hearts of even the most liberal citizens." Clearly, Arledge was a little nervous. "My pulse began to pitter-pat," he recalls, as they stepped into a silent room full of the aforementioned "Black Muslims." Cosell, Arledge writes, broke the ice within a few seconds by yelling loudly, "All right, everybody who isn't white, get out!" To Arledge's astonishment, the room burst into laughter.[4]

Boxing writer Bert Sugar recalls a similar story of bravado when Cosell came to interview Sonny Liston. Like Ali, Liston was black, but unlike Ali he was not particularly committed to political principles. He was an angry, tough man who had been arrested more than twenty times and whose intimidating stare wilted many an interviewer. As Cosell walked in, Liston snapped at him, "You ain't my friend." Cosell shot back: "Sonny, you're a professional and I'm a professional. So cut it out!"[5]

————

Cosell's first national television interview with Ali was on May 22, 1965. It was not by far the first time the two had met. In fact, Ali greeted Cosell by saying: "Howard Cosell . . . the world's greatest newscaster. How ya feelin'?"[6] Ali had become champion when he defeated Liston in Miami on February 25, 1964, and he was now training for a rematch in Lewiston, Maine, set for May 25, 1965. Shortly before the first fight, while he was still known to the general public as Cassius Clay, reports had circulated around Miami that he had been seen with Malcolm X, at the time the most public spokesperson for the Nation of Islam. Malcolm X scared many white journalists, particularly those in the sportswriting fraternity. He preached a message emphasizing the alienation of black people from America and encouraging empowerment through separatism. His rhetoric was loud, direct, and angry. In fact it was so angry that at the time that Malcolm had met with Ali, he had been suspended from the Nation of Islam for commenting that the assassination of John F. Kennedy had been a case of the "chickens coming home to roost."

The promoter of the 1964 bout, Bill Faversham, had considered canceling the fight because of the potential for controversy. In the end it went on, and Ali defeated Liston, defying the expectations of most. After the bout, and after having been declared champion, Ali let it be known that he was a member of the Nation of Islam. To the minds of most white sports reporters, Ali had joined a "hate group," and consequently, few agreed to refer to him by his newly adopted name. Instead they insisted on calling the champ by his former name, Cassius Clay. During his first interview with Ali, Cosell attempted to skirt the issue. After bantering back and forth with the champ over training and mental preparation, Cosell wrapped up the interview saying, "We leave the heavyweight champion of the world, Muhammad Ali, or Cassius Clay, if you will."[7]

Even this halfhearted acknowledgment was more than any other television broadcaster, and the vast majority of print reporters, could stomach. Ironically, George Plimpton, one of the "committee" members who allegedly tried to persuade Cosell to become a spokesperson on behalf of Ali, mused: "I always thought Cassius Clay was such a wonderful name. Why does he give that marvelous name up, Cassius Clay for Muhammad Ali—foreign, mysterious, Arabic."[8] Cosell later wrote insightfully about the connotations of Ali's former name.

> I said that I was "amused" at the reaction of much of America and in particular some of the writers. I was—at first. Later I grew angry and finally furious. Didn't these idiots realize that Cassius Clay was the name of a slave owner? What intelligent proud black in the 1960's would wish to bear the name of a white Kentucky senator who, before the Civil War, bought and sold black flesh? Had I been black and my name Cassius Clay, I damned well would have changed it! The insinuations and objections of whites, in particular the ones that appeared in the press, can best be called racist snarls.[9]

Indeed the Civil War–era Clay was a slave owner, but, as Dave Kindred points out, he freed his slaves as a young man in the 1830s, became a crusader opposed to the injustices of slavery, and ran for president as an abolitionist.[10] Cosell may not have grasped some of the nuances of this history, but his general point was logically sound. He supported Ali's right to name himself, a right that had been held exclusively by slaveholders until abolition. The name of any African

American was by definition an extension of that history. In a some-what topsy-turvy analogy, Cosell compared his own name change from Cohen to Cosell to Ali's, writing that this provided a connection between the two.

> Coincidentally, I wonder how many people would know Howard Cosell as Howard William Cohen? And for the record, Cosell—once spelled with a K—*is* the family name. It was changed back not for show-biz reasons but by the family, to comply with the wishes of our late father. As a Polish refugee, my grandfather had been unable to make his name clear to a harried immigration inspector. The official simply compromised on Cohen and waved him through. So I understood, better than most, that names are not necessarily engraved on marble tablets, never to be disturbed.[11]

This admission reveals two important things. First, it reestablishes the terms of Cosell's name change. Sportswriter Jimmy Cannon had famously stated that Cosell was the first person to "tell it like it is" after changing his name and putting on a toupee. Of course Cannon's implication was that while Cosell claimed unflinching honesty, he had tried to hide his Jewish identity by changing his name, just as he hid his baldness under a hairpiece. Cosell answers this criticism by throwing a dart at Cannon's widely shared sentiment: that a name change from Cohen to Cosell was a pathetic attempt to assimilate, to conceal his Jewish self behind a gentile veil, as so many other celebrities tried to do. Rather than its being a move to assimilate, Cosell asserts that it was actually a reversion to an even more authentic Jewish past—that it was instead the name Cohen that was fraudulent, and that by changing his name, he fulfilled the wishes of his ancestors. In this sense the name Cosell was as much an assertion of Jewishness as the name Muhammad Ali was an assertion of blackness. (As I explore in the next chapter, the timing of this statement, coming soon after the 1972 Olympics, was critical to the development of Cosell's more assertive self-identification as a Jew.)

Of course, for most professional writers, Ali's name change was inseparable from the boxer's association with the Nation of Islam. The fury created by the controversy almost immediately alienated him from the boxing establishment, as can be seen in his first title defense. Originally Ali had scheduled a rematch with Liston for November

1964 in Boston, but this had to be canceled when Ali needed hernia surgery. Ultimately the fight had to be rescheduled entirely, but no big city was willing to host it. The Ali-Liston rematch ended up being set for May 1965 in Lewiston, Maine. It ended quickly in the first round with Ali delivering a knockout with a short, almost imperceptible right hand to Liston's forehead. The quick, anticlimactic ending of the match left boxing fans skeptical of a fix. Cosell remarked after the bout, "If boxing can survive this, it can survive anything."[12]

Dave Kindred argues that, in the wake of the Lewiston fight, Cosell changed his public approach to Ali. Whereas before he had been a "professional broadcaster," Kindred argues that Cosell became "a new kind of media creature. He became a journalist/carnival barker reporting the news even as he invited rubes inside the tent to see a new kind of heavyweight champion."[13] Certainly Cosell's bantering interviews with Muhammad Ali established themselves in the 1960s as a regular feature on *ABC's Wide World of Sports,* and ultimately as an iconic fixture of American broadcasting. Their interview and review of Ali's title defense against Cleveland Williams in 1966 certainly illustrates Kindred's point. More than a sports journalist, Cosell appears to be a playful buddy of Ali's, cajoling him into demonstrating the secrets of his success in the ring. After coming back from a commercial break, Cosell, seated next to Ali with a small table between them, turned to his guest.

> COSELL: I'd like another showdown first [jabbing his index finger at the floor with mock seriousness]. I'd like you to stand up with me, and I'd like you to demonstrate, right here in the *Wide World* New York studio, the Ali Shuffle.
>
> ALI: Right now?
>
> COSELL: Right now. All right?
>
> [The two begin to stand up.]
>
> ALI: You're serious?
>
> COSELL: I'm serious . . . if you'll get off my mike.
>
> ALI: Well, I'll tell you what, Howard, this is unexpected. I didn't know you would invite me to do this. [Cosell starts to jab Ali with his left hand in the champ's stomach, and Ali puts his hand out to stop him.] Now, hold it. The Ali Shuffle is a dance that will make you scuffle. Now, you must be in a boxing pose. [He directs Cosell's hands.]

COSELL: Uh-huh.

ALI: This only takes about one and a half seconds to do. And immediately after a second goes by, it takes about half a second to follow up a combination. During the time that I'm doing this shuffle, for a minute, you're going to be confused.

COSELL: All right.

ALI: Throw you off track. And this shuffle can be used for a defense retreat or an offensive attack. You must get in a boxing position [Ali redirects Cosell's hands again], and have a little dance like we're boxing, and just one second, I have to time it, one second. [Ali shuffles his feat quickly. Then he slowly comes across with his right and Cosell laughs.] See?

COSELL: That can bewilder a novice like me. . . .

ALI: That's right.

COSELL: But it shouldn't bewilder a professional.

ALI: Well it will bewilder a professional, you just saw it [referring to the tape of his fight against Cleveland Williams]. . . .

[After sitting down, Cosell turns to the camera.]

COSELL: What we've just seen, perhaps, is the heavyweight champion of the world in what should be his true profession, that of a professional dancer.[14]

This brand of media exhibitionism clearly did not bother Roone Arledge one bit. In fact it was precisely what he was looking for—coverage that emphasized the entertaining, storytelling elements of sports. Soon after Ali became champion, ABC began broadcasting some of his heavyweight bouts live on *Wide World of Sports*. The first was held in London against British star Henry Cooper in Arsenal Stadium on May 21, 1966. After four hours of preliminary bouts, ABC had the main attraction on the fight card delayed for a half hour so the network could show audiences in America a film of Ali dancing with top hat and cane through the streets of London. By the time the fight began, the impatient crowd was infuriated, and when Ali won by a technical knockout in the sixth round after opening a gash over one of Cooper's eyes, British gang members ran down between the seats and over the heads of spectators, storming the ring.

Cosell had been calling the event with veteran Chris Shenkel and former champion Rocky Marciano. Shenkel's hand was broken by a rampaging fan, and even Marciano refused to enter the ring. Cosell, however, was undeterred, following behind production assistant Joe Aceti through the ropes into the ring to get to Ali. A bobby, not recognizing the American sportscaster, almost clubbed Cosell and had to be restrained by Aceti. When Cosell finally got to Ali, the champ threw off an attacking fan and said, "I thought it was just someone offering me congratulations."[15] As Cosell recalls, Ali "started off by thanking everybody in the world, and he began to go through his litany about the Muslims and the Grand Prophet. . . . I cut him off. 'We've been through all that before, Muhammad,' I said. 'How about thanking the president of the United States?' And he said, 'Oh, yes, yes. Him too.'"[16]

Cosell continued to provide ringside analysis of Ali's fights for *Wide World of Sports.* By this time Ali had begun to have trouble arranging fights in the United States, so his next bouts were in Europe—once again in London against Brian London, and in Germany against Karl Mildenberger. By the end of 1966, when Ali did his shuffle routine in the studio, Cosell had become the face of boxing on ABC, and his interplay with Ali had become a central component of the program. As Cosell's interview with Ali in the ring after the Cooper fight suggests, the two did not always enjoy a uniformly harmonious on-air relationship. As much as Cosell defended Ali's right to speak out about his religious and political beliefs, the way that Ali acted on them could make Cosell angry.

In 1967, for example, Ali returned to fight in the United States, and went up against World Boxing Association heavyweight champion Ernie Terrell in the Houston Astrodome to determine the single, unified heavyweight champion of the world. At the weigh-in before the fight, Terrell refused to call his opponent by any name other than Cassius Clay. Ali pledged to make Terrell say his new name after humiliating him in the ring. During the fight, Ali could be seen shouting between jabs, "What's my name!" Despite his defense of Ali's right to choose his own name, Cosell thought this was unnecessarily cruel—charging that Ali had intentionally held back from knocking out Terrell just so he could keep on hitting him and humiliating him a little longer. Cosell later wrote, "Ali, in my opinion, had behaved very badly in that fight and had, indeed, turned on me in the ring interview afterward."[17]

On *Wide World of Sports* after the fight, Cosell had Ali analyze the bout in the studio, and the tension between the two surfaced early.

Ali began narrating the first round by saying, "I'm glad the people in the American television audience who have been distorted by the press in their view of the fight . . . they can actually watch this now." He continued: "I understand that [Terrell's] intentions were to corner me. As you see, he's missing his jabs by a long range. And I understand from reading the press write-ups that blindness caused him to miss in the later rounds. And I'm sure that if he was blind, which I don't believe he was . . . uh, he can't hit me now." After a pause, Cosell spoke:

> COSELL: I'd appreciate it if you'd stop editorializing unless I ask you a question as we go. I don't want to distract the viewers from the fight. And I want to make it very clear to the viewers around this country that when you say the press is distorted, this is you speaking, your opinion, not the views . . .
>
> ALI: [interrupting] not only . . .
>
> COSELL: [continuing through the interruption] necessarily of ABC, or Howard Cosell.
>
> ALI: Right, and this is not only me speaking, the movie that you're watching now is speaking also.
>
> COSELL: Let's let the film speak for itself.
>
> [pause]
>
> ALI: And I'll speak along with it.[18]

Writing about this interview in *Cosell,* Cosell reports fan reaction that reflected the larger, precarious relationship between African Americans and Jews in the United States during this era. The interview, according Cosell, brought in a flood of mail: "I was no longer a nigger-loving Jew bastard as I usually was in any adverse mail that reaches my office. I was the black-hater. I actually got, for the first time in my life, a letter signed by a whole dormitory in Michigan State telling me that I was antiblack." Cosell reveals that the interview even created a strain in his friendship with Jackie Robinson.[19]

Similar tensions can also be seen in Cosell's coverage of Ali during the winter of 1967, when Ali refused to be inducted into the United States military to fight in Vietnam. For many white Americans, the fear and animosity they had felt toward Ali after his conversion to Islam returned. At the same time, Ali also spoke eloquently to African Americans throughout the country who saw in him a role model of pride and confidence. He openly addressed the oppression faced by African Americans in the United States, stating often, "I've said it once and I'll say it again, the real enemies of my people are right here, not in Vietnam."

Objecting to the war on religious grounds, Ali arrived at the army induction center in Houston on April 28, 1967. Cosell was there to cover the event. As most remember it, he provided Ali with sympathetic treatment. In fact Cosell was personally opposed to the war in Vietnam and sympathized with Ali's position in many respects. Cosell's recollection, however, also displays some of the ambivalence that many Jews felt at the time. While supporting Ali's right to protest, Cosell was uncomfortable supporting draft resistance.

Standing outside the federal courthouse wearing a khaki raincoat and a hat, he spoke into a handheld microphone. "This is the federal induction center," Cosell intoned, leaning against a recruiting placard for the U.S. Marines, "a place where in a matter of moments the heavyweight champion of the world, Muhammad Ali, born Cassius Clay, will arrive, presumably not to take the step forward and not to take the oath that would induct him into the United States military service." Writing about the incident afterward, Cosell reported his dialogue with Ali.

> "Are you . . . going to take the step, Muhammad? Are you going—to take—the step?"
>
> In spite of all his orders, and all his intentions, and all his denials, just as we were about to enter the building he flashed me a quick grin and said, "Howard Cosell—why don't *you* take the step?"
>
> "I did," I snapped back. "In Nineteen forty-two."[20]

Cosell may have personally opposed the war, and may have respected Ali's right to object to it. Yet his rejoinder to the boxer certainly was not a ringing endorsement of the decision to resist induction. The very fact that Cosell repeats this conversation in his memoir—that he recollects his response as a sharp comeback—even suggests that he found Ali's action offensive. Cosell was effectively drawing a distinction between the right to protest and the obligation to serve one's country. As much as Cosell believed in and defended dissent, he also believed, as many of his generation did, in the fundamentally exceptional character of the United States, that despite any differences, there lay a foundational agreement among Americans about the democratic promise of their country. The idealism of the popular front opened the door of this American promise to Jews in the United States in the 1930s and during World War II. This idea was further nurtured with the erosion of anti-Semitic barriers in American life after the war.

Yet the actions, speeches, and perspectives articulated by Ali, the Nation of Islam, and the Black Power movement directly contradicted this idealism. Militant African Americans questioned, or even abandoned, the very notion that they were a legitimate part of an American national plurality. Their nation was a Black Diaspora, and their history in America was one of oppression and exploitation. Encapsulated in Cosell's brief exchange with Ali are all of these tensions: Cosell's commitment to dialogue and dissent; Ali's radical refusal to join the military and rejection of the American nation-state; and Cosell's frustration as Ali turns his back on the ideals of American nationhood.

By refusing induction, Ali quickly drew criticism from throughout the country, even from Jackie Robinson. In measured tones Robinson expressed concern that white Americans would see Ali's action as a mark of disloyalty that would stain all black people. He said: "I'm sorry that he's done it. I respect Cassius as one of the greatest fighters of all time. I hope that the American people will understand that this is an act of one man, not an act of all the Negroes in this country." The boxing establishment reacted swiftly, stripping Ali of his heavyweight title almost immediately. Although Cosell allegedly refused to serve as a spokesperson for the Newfield-Mailer-Hamill-Plimpton committee to save Ali, he did continue to appear on the air with the ex-champ. Dave Kindred makes clear that Cosell never actually stated that he agreed with Ali, only that he thought that the boxer's constitutional rights had been violated.

Nevertheless, the support that Cosell did extend to Ali was enough to incite a tremendous amount of anger among fans. Later, when Cosell was subjected to insults and even death threats as a member of the *Monday Night Football* broadcasting team, he would trace the scorn of fans back to his defense of Ali. Late into his career Cosell would speak of the stripping of Ali's title as one of the greatest injustices to have occurred in the history of American sports. While Ali struggled to regain his title, Cosell asserts, viewers would send hate mail demanding that ABC drop that "Nigger-loving Jew."[21] This is a story repeated by others who have written about Cosell. Bert Sugar writes that when Cosell supported Ali, "letters poured into Cosell's office that started with endearing salutations such as 'You nigger-loving Jew bastard' and went downhill from there."[22] Roone Arledge writes in his memoir, "Howard Cosell was the only media person who addressed the champ [as Ali], which brought him sacks of mail calling him 'nigger-loving Jew.'"[23] Kindred, writing about Cosell's commitment to defending Ali's constitutional rights, states: "He did it at the risk of his reputation and his livelihood in a business—television—not famous for principled stands that might offend advertisers. He did it, too, Cosell often said, despite thousands of letters he received in which the correspondents referred to him as 'a nigger-loving Jew bastard.'"[24]

Unfortunately, any such letters that might have been sent to Cosell no longer exist; ABC doesn't have them, according to librarians who guard the network's collections of papers; nor does Cosell's family; nor are there any in the largest public repository of materials related to Cosell's career, the Roone Arledge collection at Columbia University. This, of course, does not mean that viewers did not send such hateful mail. Cosell's family members who were interviewed for this book remember the threatening letters that arrived in the 1960s. What is more, death threats against Cosell during his time on *Monday Night Football* are a matter of public record, contained in the files of the National Archives. Yet it is always noteworthy when a story has a credibility that extends beyond firsthand evidence. Perhaps that credibility stems in part from the way the phrase "Nigger-loving Jew" creates a logical link between Cosell's concern for African Americans' civil rights, on the one hand, and his Jewishness, on the other.

When asked about Howard Cosell, sportswriter Frank Deford noted that Cosell's Jewish identity was an important part of his public persona. Even though Cosell rarely if ever noted on air that he was Jewish (he did do so in his writings), Deford understands that Cosell's persona was indeed Jewish. And he feels that, in general, much of the criticism that was directed toward Cosell throughout his career grew out of anti-Semitism.

He was sensitive about being a Jew and [about] how Jews had been discriminated against. I mean, I suppose any Jew,

particularly at that time, had to face a certain amount of anti-
Semitism, and certainly he did as he became famous. . . . [S]ome
people [said,] "Oh, that's not true," you know. "We just can't stand
Howard Cosell. . . ." I don't have any doubt that there was a
considerable amount of anti-Semitism devoted to him in the same
way that the black athletes would be singled out as arrogant, or
an instigator—all that sort of thing—because they were black. . . .
There's no question in my mind that there was an undercurrent of
anti-Semitism that marked a great deal of his existence; that it
wasn't just "We don't like Howard Cosell"; it's "We don't like him
because he's a Jew-boy."[25]

Like others, Deford never saw any actual evidence of hate mail directed at Cosell, but he also notes that the kind of prejudice and ste-
reotyping someone like Cosell might face is not always expressed in a
direct fashion. "I think that most people are more polite about that. If
you're racist or anti-Semitic or something, . . . you keep it to yourself.
I think that's the undercurrent. . . . I would hear it. . . . I would hear
it because I'm not Jewish. So people would say it in front of me."[26]

Not all of Cosell's enemies, of course, were necessarily anti-Semites.
Many were print journalists. Cosell's most vocal public critic was actually Jewish himself, a sports columnist named Dick Young, who wrote
for the *New York Daily News,* the *Sporting News,* and the *New York Post.*
Kindred describes a scene outside Fenway Park during the 1967 World
Series between the Boston Red Sox and the St. Louis Cardinals that
sums up their relationship. Young, along with a gaggle of other print
journalists, had been shut out of the Red Sox clubhouse after the game.
Impatience turned to outright anger, which was transformed into full-
throttle rage when Cosell blew past the crowd of reporters, bombasti-
cally shouting the word "Tel-e-vision!" The doors to the clubhouse
opened for Cosell, then closed quickly behind him, leaving the newspaper reporters still waiting.[27]

To Young, Cosell was a threat, someone who represented a medium
that was in and of itself arrogant and destructive. Television, and even
radio, cut in on the territory of print sports journalists. Young did not
like this one bit, and he let it be known in his columns on Cosell. As
Deford puts it:

Young is a very fascinating guy himself. Very tormented. I
mean Dick, very much like Howard, he got very bitter in his later

years and became sort of a sad case. . . . He, like Cosell, was a very outspoken guy, and like Cosell was a very important figure. Dick Young was one of the first guys, if not the first guy, to go into the locker room after a game and get quotes. He was a terrific journalist. Just fabulous. He wasn't that good of a writer, but he was just the epitome of what a good tabloid writer-reporter was. So, Cosell comes along and, no question, [Young] was threatened by him.[28]

In fact Young himself remembered this rivalry in a 1983 column that he wrote for the *New York Post* in response to a *Sports Illustrated* profile of Cosell that Deford had written. In the column he paraphrases Deford, who asked Young if it was true that he would shout obscenities in the background during locker room interviews to spoil the recordings that Cosell was trying to produce for radio. Young provides less a denial than an excuse for his behavior.

In the first place, it was nothing aimed at Cosell, individually, I told Deford. We, the newspapermen, were becoming increasingly annoyed with all the radio station guys who would hold out their microphones in the middle of a clubhouse crowd and pick up the questions asked by sportswriters, and the answers. We viewed the radio-tapers as parasites, I told Deford. They would contribute nothing. They would pirate our material, then, because of the nature of the two media, beat us to the public with our own stuff. To combat this, the reporters hit upon using profanity for fouling up the tapes.[29]

Although he was like Cosell in the way he reported the off-field lives of athletes, Young did not share Cosell's admiration for African American athletes of the most recent generation. While Cosell praised Jackie Robinson as both an athlete and a social pioneer, Young was more, in the words of sports historian Ron Briley, "distanced"; while Cosell leveled criticism against the managers of sports—from team owners to boxing regulators—Young reserved his fire for the athletes themselves, whom he regarded as overpaid and spoiled. When Young began his career in the 1950s, his approach was actually a new one, and it brought a level of journalistic integrity to sports coverage that had been lacking in the era of reporters like Grantland Rice—writers who tended to act as personal publicists for America's sports heroes.

Unlike Cosell, however, he did not embrace the young athletes who had begun to speak out on political topics during the 1960s. Briley writes: "By 1968, Young was reminiscent of an establishment figure such as Lyndon Johnson, who could not understand the forces of change at large in the land. Once voices of reform, Johnson and Young were now defenders of the status quo."[30]

This was particularly true in their treatment of Ali. Whereas Cosell sympathized with Ali, Young denounced him as a "Black Muslim," a religion that Young described as a "sad little sect." In total contrast to Cosell, Young refused to call Ali by his new name, and referred to him only as Cassius Clay.[31] While Cosell used his coverage of sports during the 1960s to probe issues of race and racial discrimination in American society, Young ignored these issues entirely, or was openly hostile to African American athletes who used their status as a platform for protest. Young had difficulty understanding athletes who became involved with the Black Power movement. As Briley comments, "Young seemed to assume that black athletes who complained of mistreatment were using race as a crutch"[32] Not surprisingly, Cosell labeled Young a "right-wing cultural illiterate."[33] Young was not, however, anti-Semitic. But as Young remarked in his column, "Cosell needn't be Jewish to be disliked."[34]

For critics like Young, Cosell's defense of Ali was only a ploy to advance the sportscaster's career.[35] It is actually true that although Cosell's defense of Ali provoked the ire of fans around the United States, it was also probably the single most important step that launched Cosell to fame. For Ali's part, Cosell's continued coverage throughout the late 1960s, past the point when most other sports reporters had given up on the ex-champ, was instrumental in keeping the dethroned heavyweight's name before the public until he finally did return to the ring in 1970. Bert Sugar writes that whether it was planned or not, Cosell's defense of Ali "was a masterful public relations coup for ABC and 'Wide World.' As Ali was consigned by public opinion and the press to the musty old archives former heavyweight champs are supposed to occupy, his name was kept alive in an almost total absence of exposure by Cosell and 'Wide World.'"[36] Referring to the network's willingness to keep Cosell on the air, Sugar stated in an interview: "ABC had no choice. . . . I mean, when you're last—although, charitably speaking, they were number four in a three-network race—you'd do anything, and to that end, Cosell was good for them because he brought them rating points—Nielsen rating points—and advertising."[37]

In his first book, Cosell reports an incident in which he jokingly chided Ali about their co-dependence, of course emphasizing how much Ali owed to the public relations opportunities created by a shrewd television sports reporter. Remembering a meeting between the two at Ali's hotel room before a fight in Germany, Cosell writes:

> I studied Ali's face for a moment. "You know," I said, "[football star Jim] Brown became famous on his own. When you stop to think of it, I did, too. But you, Muhammad, without me you're a nothing. Nobody would know your name."
>
> He wasn't sure if I was kidding. "What you talking about?" he said, frowning. "I'm the one that made *you*. I made you an international traveler."
>
> I leaned closer. "I'll tell you the honest-to-God's truth. Not even Brown made it entirely on his own. He'd be the first to tell you. I *helped* make him. But I *made* you. Nobody would know your name."
>
> His personal photographer, Howard Bingham, was with him. "That's ridiculous," he broke in. "Everybody knows Muhammad Ali."
>
> I shrugged. "Ask Jimmy Brown. He knows something about publicity. Where would you be without all the shows, without 'Wide World of Sports,' without me doing your fights, without the interviews in the ring? Yes, I made you, and everybody knows it."
>
> Ali got to his feet and dismissed the conversation with a wave of his hand. "Ahh, I'm going downstairs." And he left.[38]

Ali had a strong argument that it was *he* who made Cosell. As we have seen, Cosell's national broadcasting career was floundering until Ali emerged. Certainly, as Sugar confirms, Cosell played an important role by keeping Ali's name before the public during the fighter's court appearances over his refusal to submit to the draft (although Cosell's conversation with Ali in Germany took place before this turn of events). Cosell, however, needed Ali to actually fight—and to win—in order to have something to cover in the first place.

Moreover, the sport of boxing played to Cosell's strengths—not necessarily because Cosell was especially knowledgeable about the sport (although few would go as far as Bert Sugar, who has asserted,

"He didn't know boxing at all").[39] Boxing is a sport that involves long periods of downtime. The actual fight is only a small blip on a larger timeline that includes weeks, and more often months, of hype, buildup, controversy, and endless battles over arrangements, promotions, and of course money. Cosell's strength was his ability to place a sporting event within the context of a storyline, a narrative. He recognized that sports were interesting to most audiences only to the extent that they became meaningful on a larger social and cultural level. In a real way, Ali, as a successful and charismatic boxing champion, allowed audiences to see what Cosell could do.

It would be a mistake to look at Cosell's relationship with Ali in isolation from his larger development as a critical commentator on sports during the 1960s. Of course, as Cosell's career advanced during the decade, he continued to address race in work that extended far beyond his coverage of Ali. He did not give up working on the sports documentaries that he had helped to produce during the period of his absence from network television. In 1967 Cosell produced with sportswriter Jerry Izenberg the documentary *One Hundred Yards to Glory,* which brought to national attention the success of the Grambling College football team, an athletic program at one of the nation's oldest historically black institutions.

In addition, Cosell continued to explore topical issues related to sports on his weekly program *Speaking of Sports* on the ABC Radio Network, and in 1967 he became the sports editor for ABC's nightly news program *Peter Jennings with the News.* Although he did not appear every night, he was assigned to comment on what the network referred to as "page one" sports stories. Calling Cosell "one of the most astute, knowledgeable, and entertaining sports commentators in the nation today," William Sheehan, ABC vice president and director of television news, announced that as sports editor, Cosell would be available to offer commentary on a program that aimed to provide a "well-rounded news report of interest to all members of the family."[40]

Cosell's ABC News sports commentaries covered a variety of topics. A profile of Boston Red Sox slugger Tony Conigliaro highlights the player's resolve in his attempt to come back after being hit in the eye by a pitch the year before. Cosell provides narration for a piece that is almost a short documentary, following Conigliaro as he takes swings at batting practice during the day and sings at a hotel lounge where he moonlights at night.[41]

In January 1969 Cosell did a preview piece on Super Bowl III. Standing before the camera in the grandstands at the Orange Bowl and holding a football, Cosell boldly predicts that there is no way that Joe Namath and the New York Jets of the American Football League can upset the Baltimore Colts, champions of the National Football League. The Colts will win, he pronounces, "by a score of 30–10."[42] A week later, after the Jets did in fact pull off a 16–7 upset victory over the Colts, Cosell contritely admitted his mistake, and with solemn intonation compared the feat to the victory of David over Goliath. "What I really saw," he says, "was the end of an era, the death of the establishment." He describes sitting next to Art Modell, owner of the NFL Cleveland Browns and president of the National Football League. "At the start of the game," Cosell says, "the smile was there, almost open contempt [for the Jets and the AFL]; a little later, a growing disbelief; after that I couldn't tell whether or not it was hysteria; in the end, it seemed to be apoplexy."[43]

Among Cosell's most memorable commentaries, however, are those he did during the 1968 Olympics in Mexico City, where once again he rose to the defense of African American athletes who took a strong political position. In particular, Cosell expressed support for Tommie Smith and John Carlos, who, after winning medals in the 400-meter dash, raised their fists on the ceremonial stand during the medal presentation in a Black Power salute. On October 18, 1968, two days after their protest on the medal stand, Smith and Carlos were sent home, banished from the Olympic village and censured by the U.S. Olympic Committee. Cosell provided the following commentary for that evening's news:

> Doubtless, the preponderant weight of the American public opinion will support the committee, but nothing is solved really. The U.S. Olympic Committee, in the manner of the fabled village of Brigadoon, appears on the scene once every four years. It is, in the main, a group of pompous, arrogant, medieval-minded men who regard the [Olympic] Games as a private social preserve for their tiny clique. They view participation in the Games as a privilege, not as a right earned by competition. They say the Games are sports, not politics, something separate and apart from

the realities of life. But the black athlete says he is a part of a revolution in America, a revolution designed to produce dignity for the black man, and that he is a human being before he is an athlete. He says his life in America is filled with injustice, that he wants equality everywhere, not just within the arena. He says that he will not be used once every four years on behalf of a group that ignores what happens to him every day of all the years. He says he earns participation, wins fairly, and that he will use his prominence earned within the arena to better his plight outside of it. He says, Don't tell me about the rules. The U.S. doesn't dip its flag in front of the reviewing stand, and that's a rule all other nations follow. He's aware of backlash but says he's had it for four hundred years. And so the Olympic Games for the United States have become a kind of America in microcosm, a country torn apart. Where will it all end? Don't ask the U.S. Olympic Committee. They've been too busy preparing for a VIP cocktail party next Monday night in the lush new Camino Real. Howard Cosell reporting from Mexico City.[44]

This commentary illustrates what Cosell could do when he was really determined to make a statement. It pits the logic and rationale of the Olympic protest against the flimsy pretenses of the U.S. Olympic Committee. Like a boxer landing a flurry of blows on a defenseless opponent, Cosell ends with his final uppercut, the jab about the cocktail party, sending the USOC to the mat. Yet he does not explicitly endorse the use of the Olympics as a political platform. He only notes the hypocrisy of the USOC for punishing black athletes on this account.

In a similar light, on October 25 Cosell summarized the 1968 Olympics for ABC News, this time taking a direct shot at the president of the International Olympic Committee:

I should bring to you as the Nineteenth Olympiad comes to its close what I take out of this as a fundamental premise: that it is false any longer to pretend that the Olympic Games anymore are sports and not politics, because they have become exactly the latter—politics. And I think that it is time for the International Olympic Committee, with its archaic curmudgeon of a president, Avery Brundage, and the various national Olympic committees, including our own, to take a look at themselves, and to seek to bring the Olympic Games back to the dream of Pierre de Coubertin [founder of the modern Olympics], if indeed it is at all possible.[45]

Cosell did not always hold the strong opinions that he expressed in these editorials. Months before the Olympics began, a group of African American athletes who called themselves the Olympic Project for Human Rights (OPHR) proposed a boycott of the 1968 Games in Mexico City. Cosell opposed it. The boycott idea later faded, but many African American athletes still planned to protest to raise awareness of the struggles facing African Americans and the African Diaspora more generally. As we can see from his commentary, however, Cosell had at least come to support strongly the right of African American athletes to use the Olympics as a forum for political protest.

The most prominent leader of the OPHR was Harry Edwards, a sociologist who had once been a collegiate track and field athlete. Edwards was angered by the degree to which educational institutions and the U.S. Olympic Committee exploited African American athletes. He argued that athletes at high-profile universities were provided scholarships to play and promote their schools, but they received minimal educational benefit for their efforts.[46] Likewise, he argued that African American Olympians won medals for their country but received unequal, discriminatory treatment at home. He remembers that Cosell initially spoke out sharply against the boycott idea but later changed his mind at the urging of Jackie Robinson. In fact Robinson was central to introducing Edwards to Cosell, which marked a turning point in the sportscaster's thinking. As Edwards recalls:

My connection with Howard Cosell became much more direct after we declared an intention to stage a boycott of the 1968 Olympics. Howard, when he heard the news, called Jackie Robinson in the middle of the night. . . . According to Howard, Jackie said: "Jeez, this is the most outlandish thing I've ever heard of. Why would they do something like that?" Then Jackie called back that morning around 7:30—after he listened to Howard's radio show—and said: "Howard, I mean, you call me in the middle of the night and ask me my opinion on something. And now [I don't] find out what the deal is until I get up this morning and start reading the papers and everything and see what these guys are about." And Howard's response was, "Hey, you wouldn't have done it like that." And Jackie's response was: "Hey, you know, if I were a young athlete today, I wouldn't do it the way that I did it back in 1946 and through the early fifties. This is a new age and a new time, and I understand where these young guys are coming from." And then Howard was magnanimous enough to say, "Well, let me invite Dr. Edwards back to New York to be on my radio show." And he actually flew me back to New York from California, and I sat on his radio show.

Afterwards we talked, before the show we talked—and we talked about a broad range of things, not just the '68 Olympics, but the game that had been canceled at San Jose State as a result of the protest that we waged there over issues of race and sport on campus, and general discrimination in the campus community. And for the first time I think he really began to understand what we were concerned about. . . . He said, "Maybe it's time. These are not trivial issues that are being raised," and [he] actually began to raise those issues during the course of one program after another.[47]

In the end, most prominent African American athletes chose not to boycott the Olympics. But Edwards accomplished perhaps an even more daunting feat: he changed the mind of Howard Cosell. This did not happen often, but there are many reasons why Cosell might have changed his thinking. One was his tremendous respect for Jackie Robinson. As important as his affection for Robinson, however, was Cosell's utter disdain for Avery Brundage, the president of the International Olympic Committee, whom Cosell considered to be a sinister anti-Semite. Edwards remembers conversations in which Cosell expressed this sentiment.

We discussed things that I'm quite certain still stuck in his craw. We discussed the Olympic Games and United States Olympic Committee in terms of Avery Brundage and the 1936 Games [held in Nazi Germany], when [Brundage] took these Jewish athletes off the team rather than send x-number of Jews on the American team to Berlin for what came to be known as the Nazi Olympics.

[Cosell] was very much aware of the politics of the Olympics going back to that time and the fact that the United States Olympic Committee and the International Olympic Committee were complicit in those politics—not just the up-front stuff, like the counting of medals between the East and the West, the United States and the Soviet Union, being in the forefront of that titanic ideological struggle camouflaged under international athletic competition. He was aware of the politics behind the scenes and the kinds of deals that were cut and decisions that were made. So when we began to discuss the politics of the Olympics with him, when I first discussed that on his program, he was never one of those people who said, "Yeah, but you're introducing politics into sports." . . . I never once got that from Howard Cosell, because he understood—going back to the Nazi Olympics, not just in terms of what Hitler did, but in terms of what happened on the American Olympic team, and those Jewish athletes who were taken off the team, even though they should have been on the team—he understood what that meant. He understood what Brundage was implying when Brundage made the statement, "I don't understand why these Negroes are talking about boycotting the Olympic Games when the Olympics are the only forum that they can stand on where they have equal standing with other human beings."[48]

Edwards refers to the decision by Brundage, then the chair of the USOC, to replace two Jewish sprinters, Marty Glickman and Sam Stoller, the day before they were scheduled to run as part of the 4×100 relay team. Brundage had been a supporter of the Nazi regime, arguing that it had been unfairly branded as anti-Semitic. Glickman understood his removal from the team as an act of blatant anti-Semitism, however, and Cosell and Edwards agreed.[49]

In fact, the organizers of the Olympic protest had a keen understanding of how exclusive and ultimately divisive the U.S. Olympic Committee had been in its dealings not only with blacks but also with Jews. When the OPHR announced its proposal to boycott the Olympics in December 1967, its leaders called a press conference in New York City in which Edwards, Louis Lomax, and Martin Luther King Jr. issued a set of six demands to be met if African American athletes were to perform. The second item on the list was "Removal of the anti-Semitic and anti-black personality Avery Brundage from his post as Chairman of the International Olympic Committee."[50] According to Edwards, this demand was included not only to gain sympathy for the movement from Jewish sportswriters and broadcasters like Cosell, but also out of a genuine understanding of how central anti-Semitism had been to the operations of the USOC.

————

Once again, Cosell's critical perspective became an important aspect of his work at the 1968 Olympics, allowing him unique access to the Smith and Carlos protest, one of the most significant events of the Games. ABC had bid a record $4.8 million—more than twice the amount bid by rival NBC—to become the first American network to broadcast the Summer Olympics live.[51] At the time, this bid was considered an extravagantly large one, and some inside the network accused Arledge of unnecessarily inflating the company's offer, giving away more than the network could recoup in advertising revenue. Yet Arledge was a rebel within the world of network television executives. ABC chairman Leonard Goldenson, a former Hollywood film executive, had decided to give him a long leash, hoping that his record for innovation would help ABC catch up to the more established NBC and CBS.

Goldenson's gamble on Arledge may not have recouped all that the network spent, but Arledge's gamble on Cosell was certainly redeemed after Tommie Smith's protest on the medal stand. As Smith and Carlos ascended the dais with gloved hands and in stocking feet, Arledge anticipated the kind of sensational moment that he had paid so much of his network's money to cover in bidding for the Mexico City Games. "Get in there!" he recalls shouting to his cameramen from the control room in the ABC broadcast center. "This is Black Power! Get in on them!"[52]

When the ceremony ended, Arledge sent Cosell in search of Smith and Carlos for an interview. Despite having trouble tracking Smith down after the sprinter had been expelled from the Olympic village, Cosell finally caught up with him and persuaded him to do an interview. After Cosell asked Smith to explain the meaning of his protest, Jim Spence, who was producing the interview, prompted Cosell through his earpiece to ask, "Are you proud to be an American?" Cosell famously did so, and Smith answered, "I'm proud to be a black American." Brundage would later complain to Arledge that it was bad enough to have broadcast the protest, but it only made matters worse that it was Cosell who covered the story.[53]

Arledge's comments echo Cosell's own account in his 1973 memoir. He recalls that "there was a threat that the blacks might boycott the Games," and Arledge advised him to cover any attempt at a protest with depth and honesty. Arledge, according to Cosell, was "aware of the long-standing criticism of sports broadcasting that the announcers were shills, and that in their desire not to offend anybody they could never hit an issue head on. Once and for all, especially in what would be the biggest sports coverage in the history of television, Arledge wanted to put that notion to rest."[54]

For Arledge, the Tommie Smith–John Carlos incident affirmed his belief in Cosell's value to the network. The commentaries Cosell delivered were certainly controversial, and not necessarily popular with the viewing audience, but they created a buzz, and ABC needed buzz. Howard Cosell had given viewers another reason to pay attention to him. A letter from a California viewer published in the *Van Nuys News* expressed an opinion of Cosell that many would come to share over the next decade and a half. Responding to a positive review of Cosell's performance from the paper's television critic, Ernie Kreiling, the writer states: "I can't agree with you on Howard Cosell and his idea of sports reporting. Reporting is supposed to be neutral and objective, not loaded with personal opinions and prejudices. I want it straight and I'll make up my own mind." Kreiling responds: "Cosell refers to sports as the toy department of life. It's only fun and games for grown-ups, so hardly worthy of the reverence you suggest. On a more basic level, his kind of colorful reporting makes for better listening I find."[55] Cosell had become a polarizing television persona, but he captured the attention of viewers, and that is exactly what Arledge wanted.

For Cosell's part, he recalled the 1968 Olympics as a joyous adventure. In *Cosell* he writes, "Unlike the 1972 Games in Munich, the 1968 Games in Mexico City are one of my life's more pleasant memories."[56] As we will see, the International Olympic Committee's refusal to shut down the 1972 Games after Palestinian terrorists murdered eleven Israeli athletes left Cosell feeling especially angry and bitter toward Brundage. Yet it is curious that Cosell would remember Mexico City so fondly. Mexican political leaders had hoped to use the Olympics to show the world that their country had achieved the rank of a fully modern nation. They hoped to defy their country's "mañana" stereotype by competently putting on a spectacle worthy of international admiration. Instead, students and workers protested, asking how a country afflicted by such grinding poverty that it was unable to provide basic social services for its population could afford the luxury of spending enormous sums to produce an Olympic Games. The protests led to the greatest bloodshed ever to impact an Olympics when Mexican riot police, known as *granaderos,* sprayed gunfire through a crowd of over ten thousand protesters on October 2, 1968, just a few days before the Olympics were to begin.[57] Although the Mexican government acknowledged that thirty-five people died as a result, estimates compiled from eyewitnesses have established that roughly 350 people lost their lives in what became known as the Tlatelolco massacre.[58] Such a tragedy would have merited the cancellation of the Games just as much as the terrorist killings in Munich.

Cosell never discussed this event in any of his recollections of the 1968 Olympics. In his memoir he does address the concerns of the protesters. "Mexico is a poverty-stricken country," he writes. "Mexico City itself is filled with hunger, dirt and decay. . . . [I]t is hard to escape the poverty, and so it was hard for me, intellectually, to justify a nation's expenditure of multimillions of dollars for two weeks of international fun and games. It still is." Yet in the end, Cosell does justify it by pointing out the national pride that the Olympics evoked. Recalling the nationwide celebrations that took place when Mexican athletes won medals in swimming and race-walking, he writes: "The Mexico City Olympics were an Olympics with a heart. In Munich they had a computer."[59]

In fact it is ironic that Cosell would ignore the massacre in Mexico City, for there was a widespread perception that the two protests— the African American protest exemplified by the actions of Smith and Carlos on the one hand, and the Mexican protest on the other—were connected. Both Mexican officials and U.S. intelligence agencies saw any potential displays of Black Power sentiment as potentially incendiary acts of political dissidence and sought to shut them down as rapidly as possible. For their part, in the wake of the Tlatelolco massacre, African American activists and athletes at the Olympics feared that the secretive violence of the Mexican regime against its own people—later to be called the "dirty war"—might be turned against them as it had been against the student protesters just before the Olympics began. According to Harry Edwards, the members of the OPHR were so concerned that civil rights leader Louis Lomax, one of those who had helped the organization draft its central protest document, persuaded him not to attend the Games out of fear for the safety of all involved. Edwards recalls, "We were constantly aware of how violent and dirty that situation was in Mexico."[60]

While Cosell may have missed an important story here, his Olympics commentaries and coverage effectively mocked the notion that the Games represented a pure expression of American harmony on the fair playing field provided by sports. Cosell would not always defend Smith and Carlos so staunchly. Amy Bass, analyzing a 1976 documentary on the Olympic Games, observes that Cosell criticizes them in that film, accusing them of interjecting political protest into the Olympics, and introducing a sequential chain that he would ultimately connect to the terrorist murder of the eleven Israeli team members during the 1972 Games in Munich.[61]

Yet Cosell was a very different sports reporter by 1976, embittered by his experience in Munich and jaded by his years as the ringmaster of the circus that had come to be known as *Monday Night Football*. His commentary at the 1968 Olympics represents a different point in his career, when his critical perspective on sports and society, and his keen sensitivity to racial injustice, would not allow him to regurgitate banalities about sports as isolated from American society. Cosell shared something important with the African American sports stars whom he championed. Like Muhammad Ali, or Grambling football coach Eddie Robinson, or Jackie Robinson, or Smith and Carlos, Cosell was to his own mind an outsider. The protest of African American athletes at the 1968 Olympics was about more than civil rights to Cosell; it was about thumbing one's nose at the self-righteous snobbery of the same WASP elite that had "blacklisted" him from network television for five years because of his ethnic accent and appearance. It was precisely the edge created by Cosell's anger that made him unique, that fired his intense ambition, and that would ultimately win him unparalleled fame and creative license on network television.

5 Bigger than the Game

Cosell did not creep onto the scene; rather he burst
onto it—and to some people, not as a journalist but as
"that obnoxious Jew from New York."
—Jim Spence with Dave Diles, *Up Close and Personal*, 1988

In June 1966 Roone Arledge wrote to congratulate National
Football League commissioner Pete Rozelle for negotiating a
merger with his league's rival, the American Football League.
Part of that merger was an agreement to hold an interleague
championship game, an event that would someday come to
be known as the Super Bowl. Ever adept at recognizing a programming opportunity, Arledge wrote Rozelle, "I assume it is
too early for you to know what your plans are concerning
television rights to the inter-league Championship game, but
I would like you to know that we are very interested in being considered as the carrying network for this game and we
would appreciate the opportunity of discussing this matter
with you prior to its resolution.'" In 1966 the idea of ABC winning the rights to cover such an important game was laugh-
able. In just a few years, however, Rozelle would come up
with a new idea for the NFL schedule, and ABC would be chosen as the network to broadcast it: *Monday Night Football*.
Cosell would not merely be a part of the "package" of announcers relaying the game to viewers each week; he would
be the first one hired, and the key ingredient to establishing
the show's brand.

If there were any viewers left in the United States who
did not know who Howard Cosell was before the fall of 1970,
they would learn more than enough about him in the decade that followed. In five years he had risen from relative
obscurity to become one of the most recognized sports personalities in the country. Over the next decade his fame and
fortune would rocket to almost unprecedented heights. He

would become not just a famous sportscaster but a celebrity. His professional credits would range from the sublime (his somber field reports from the 1972 hostage crisis at the Munich Olympics) to the ridiculous (*Battle of the Network Stars*). No program was more important to Cosell's newfound status as an icon of American popular culture, however, than *Monday Night Football*. Huge audiences tuned in every week—more than ABC had ever experienced before—often simply to watch football, but just as often to hear the back-and-forth banter in the broadcast booth between a New York Jew, Howard Cosell, and a good-ol'-boy Texan, a veteran football quarterback named "Dandy Don" Meredith.

Paradoxes seem to be a defining feature of Howard Cosell's life, and *Monday Night Football* would contain paradoxes of its own. During the first season, the team chosen to work together included Keith Jackson doing play-by-play alongside the Cosell–"Dandy Don" show. Arledge had long wanted former football star Frank Gifford to be the third man in the booth, but in 1970, when *Monday Night Football* was inaugurated, Gifford could not get out of his contract with CBS. The following year, however, Gifford became free. Arledge signed him, and Jackson was reassigned to broadcast college football games. Most saw this at the time as a slap in the face, but Jackson ended up becoming the iconic voice of college football, and one of the most revered play-by-play sportscasters in television history.

While Cosell's fame also grew, many of those who knew him saw a change in his personality as the 1970s progressed. They saw how the success of *Monday Night Football,* and Cosell's celebrity along with it, increased in almost inverse proportion to Cosell's happiness. By the end of the decade, Cosell was not just one of the most recognized sports personalities in America; he was one of the five most recognized people in the nation. Yet he also became increasingly tormented personally, and according to many of his oldest colleagues, he grew defensive, paranoid, and angry.

The reasons for this personality change are probably too complex to grasp completely. Cosell, however, writes about a number of developments during the 1970s that affected his perspective. One, of course, was *Monday Night Football*. As much as the program provided Cosell with a regular national audience, it also cast him in a role with which he was not always comfortable, and in ways that he felt played to the prejudices of the viewing public. Another was the 1972 Olympics in

Munich, an event disrupted by a bloody terrorist attack against the Israeli Olympic team by Black September, an organization that promoted Palestinian rights. The tragedy raised Cosell's consciousness about being a Jew as no event had since World War II.

By the late 1960s Howard Cosell could look in the mirror and see a star. He even counted Hollywood movie stars among his buddies. In *Cosell* he devotes a chapter to one of his celebrity friends in particular: Woody Allen. He writes in the opening sentence, "The first time I ever saw Allen Konigsberg of Midwood High School in Brooklyn, was in the Spring of 1965."[2] Here Cosell does not extend to Allen the same courtesy of respecting a name change that he had extended to Ali, but then, these were very different name changes. Allen's was like Cosell's, whose opening sentence is meant to show how the two had risen from the same place and from the same ethnic background. If a name change is about leaving behind the baggage of one's family history, Cosell seems to feel free to run back and fetch those bags for Allen.

Maybe this was because Cosell finally felt that he was important— that he could show off to the public his intimacy with a genuine rising star. After all, Allen was not just a casual friend. He had actually used Cosell in his most recent movie, the 1971 hit *Bananas.* Cosell admits that his relationship with Allen was not always so positive. In 1965 Cosell and Emmy had gone to see Allen perform standup comedy in Fort Lauderdale. "I didn't like any of it," he writes. The next year, while he was in London, Cosell was invited by movie star pal Telly Savalas— who was in England shooting a film—to join a poker party. Allen, sitting at the end of the table, shooed Cosell away, saying that there were already too many people playing.

In 1968, however, the two met again, this time in San Francisco. Allen was filming his first feature, *Take the Money and Run,* while Cosell was in town to cover the Jerry Quarry–Jimmy Ellis fight. This time it was Allen who approached Cosell in a Dixieland jazz nightclub. Now it was the big comedy star who wanted to sit at Cosell's table. After ribbing him a little about the poker game, Cosell invited Allen to sit with him at ringside for the Quarry–Ellis fight.

In *Bananas,* Cosell opens the film playing himself. The movie is a farce about a product tester from New York who, while vacationing in the fictional Latin American country of San Marcos, accidentally

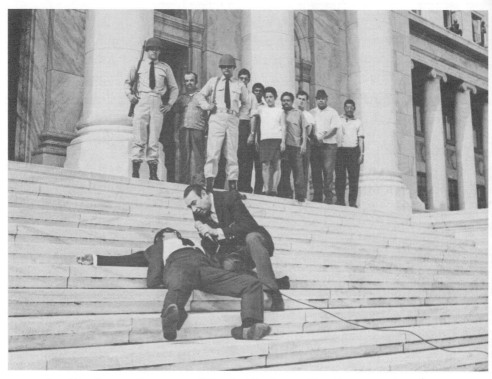

Cosell in the opening scene of Woody Allen's 1971 film, *Bananas*. Harry Ransom Humanities Research Center, University of Texas at Austin. Photo courtesy MGM Media Licensing and Woody Allen.

becomes a rebel leader and, later, the country's president. In the opening scene, the previous president of San Marcos is assassinated. Cosell, wearing a blazer with the *Wide World of Sports* crest, announces the event as if it were a prizefight. The movie begins with another famed prize fight announcer, Don Dunphy. After opening the fictional segment, he introduces Cosell, who, surrounded by bystanders, begins to deliver a play-by-play of the assassination:

This is tremendous, Don. Just tremendous. The atmosphere heavy, uncertain, overtones of ugliness. A reminder in a way of how it was in March of 1964 at Miami Beach, when Clay met Liston for the first time and nobody was certain how it would turn out. The crowd is tense. They've been here since ten this morning. And . . . and I think I see . . . the door beginning to open. El Presidente may be coming out. The door opens. It's he. It's El Presidente.

A man wearing a dark suit and sunglasses walks out onto the marble steps of a palace and waves to the crowd; a hand holding a gun emerges from the left side of the screen and fires two shots. The man retreats into the palace, but the door is locked as the crowd becomes unruly. Cosell is barely audible; the gun keeps firing.

And down! It's over, it's over for El Presidente![3]

The film ends with a parallel scene in which Dunphy once again introduces Howard Cosell, this time in a hotel suite where Allen's character, Fielding Mellish, and his fiancée, Nancy (played by Louise Lasser), consummate their marriage. Covering the scene again as a prizefight (including doctors who have to take a look at a cut over Mellish's right eye), Cosell leans into the bed to interview the newlyweds.

Each scene draws its humor from Cosell's public image, and in each, Cosell plays up for the camera the qualities that marked him as a public figure. In fact, Cosell performed these scenes without a script. Blessed with a photographic memory, he could smoothly and confidently provide narration looking straight into the camera, and he could do so while making much more comprehensive use of the English language than just about anybody else on television. This was something that Cosell would do throughout his career. In the days when he broadcast radio commentaries, he could talk to his producers and staff for an hour before going on the air, and then provide a crisp, coherent commentary that fit the ninety-second slot for his program almost to the second. When he gave his famous narrations of NFL highlights during halftime on *Monday Night Football,* he needed to watch the reel of highlight footage only once before providing his commentary. According to Cosell, all Allen did to prepare him for his scenes in *Bananas* was to say, "Do your thing."[4]

Cosell recalls that shooting the assassination scene was an all-day affair. According to Cosell, during their lunch break Allen expressed his heartfelt admiration for the way Cosell would "fight the establishment" with his sports coverage. He remembers how happy he was to hear such praise, but his euphoria would be short-lived. "A few months later," Cosell writes, "after 'Monday Night Football' had begun and the adverse mail was streaming in, I thought to myself, 'How could Woody have been so wrong?'"[5] Fame, as Cosell would soon discover, could be a double-edged sword. As employed by Allen, Cosell was enough of a popular culture icon to be the subject of parody even before *Monday Night Football*. Working in the booth each week broadcasting football games, however, would test Cosell in new ways, and would introduce him to the less appealing aspects of fame.

In the press release announcing the "package" of broadcasters who would be in the booth each Monday night, ABC stated that Cosell would "provide fair, accurate commentary on the NFL games, pointing out the bad plays as well as the good ones." It went on, "Cosell has been closely associated with football on television for many years and the production company he heads has produced some of the most outstanding football shows ever seen on network television."[6]

It is not hard to read between the lines of this document. First, despite pronouncements to the contrary, Cosell was not being included because of his football expertise. Second, he would be on a very long leash. Of Meredith the announcement states simply that his role would be that of a onetime star quarterback who would provide "expert analysis of plays." A more accurate understanding of his role would emerge only later. Cosell, however, was hired to be controversial. After the *Monday Night Football* broadcasts had just begun, a reporter asked Arledge if he was worried about the controversy that Cosell would generate. He remembers answering: "Worried? That's exactly what I'm looking for!"[7]

Arledge, in fact, had been able to persuade ABC to go out on a limb and make a $25.5 million bid for *Monday Night Football*. He felt that securing the program was essential for the network to maintain its local affiliates. Virtually from the beginning he had Cosell in mind as a commentator in the booth. Frank Gifford recalls an early conversation in which Arledge explained his intentions.

I remember the first time he mentioned *Monday Night* to me. . . . [W]e were playing golf . . . and he said something to the effect of, "What do you think about the game on prime time?" And I said it would be fantastic. We talked some more, and he said, "What do you think about Howard Cosell?" . . . [I said] not much. At the time[,] because I could not get out of my contract, he got Keith Jackson from college football to do the play-by-play. And then I suggested Don Meredith. So I thought he was going to go with Don and Keith. But then he said: "We need a reporter type like Howard. He won't get involved too much in the game." Roone really admired his reportorial skills, and in all honesty, Howard wasn't afraid to ask the questions that were never asked in sports at that time.[8]

The idea was to attract attention—to draw on the very contentiousness and abrasiveness of Cosell's personality to bring in audiences. As Arledge put it: "You hate him, at times want to strangle him, but he wouldn't let you ignore him. He forced you to watch."[9] At the same time, he did not feel comfortable pairing Cosell alone with a play-by-play commentator. Traditionally, football broadcasts had always included an ex-player to provide expert commentary, or "color." Arledge's solution was to expand the number of people in the booth from two to three. He settled on Keith Jackson for the play-by-play but had trouble finding a suitable former player. Following Gifford's suggestion, Arledge hired recently retired Dallas Cowboys quarterback Don Meredith, an easygoing Texan with a charming demeanor and a down-home sense of humor. Arledge was intrigued by this contrast of personalities. He encouraged Cosell and Meredith in particular to loosen up the typical commentary for professional football games—to treat the game as entertainment.

Keith Jackson remembers having a conversation with Cosell on a bench in Central Park after having been brought aboard to do play-by-play for the first *Monday Night Football* season: "Everything seemed to indicate that it would be one of two things. Either it would be extremely successful, or it would be an extreme failure. And it had a better-than-average chance of being successful because it was going to introduce the persona of not only Howard Cosell but of Don Meredith." Jackson remembers that the addition of Meredith and Cosell brought the personalities of the broadcast crew into the game in a way that had not been done before. In particular, Jackson, Meredith, and Cosell offered an intriguing mix of backgrounds.

> It was kind of funny. Here we have a New York Jew, a Georgia cracker, and a Texas cowboy. Now, how the hell can you put that together and expect it to work? But it did. I mean, Don practiced at being completely off the wall, and completely confusing Cosell on occasion—not often, but [on] occasion. And Don handled it. . . . [I]f he didn't understand something that Howard was saying, he'd just simply say, "I don't understand a dang thing you said." Well, that took all of the bite out of whatever it was that Howard said, and so while the viewer was laughing . . . they loved to see Howard get put down. That's what he incited [in] the television audience. There was a certain segment of the television audience that loved to see him get put down. But at the same time there was a very large segment of the television audience that watched professional football that understood what he was saying. . . . I would say that [not] every viewer ever liked him, but there was a large segment of the American public who eventually started listening to him and said, "By George, the guy knows what he's talking about."[10]

Jackson, Meredith, and Cosell had their trial run on August 28, 1970, in a preseason game between the New York Giants and the Pittsburgh Steelers. At least one complimentary letter came into the mailbox of Roone Arledge. Dan Jenkins of *Sports Illustrated,* one of the top football writers in the country, who would later write a satirical novel about life in the NFL titled *Semi-Tough,* sent a note praising the broadcast team. A proud Texan, Jenkins was undoubtedly happy to see Meredith in the booth, but he had positive things to say about everyone who put the broadcast together. "Dear Roon," he wrote:

> Just wanted to tell you personally that I thought more stars than Terry Bradshaw were born last night with your telecast of the Giants and Steelers. High on your list of accomplishments must go to the hiring of our pal, Dandy Don Meredith—and the use of our other pal, Howard Cosell, on pro football. I knew Dandy and Howard would be great, and they were. And you were right again. Keith Jackson is a fine, sobering anchorman for the

two. What you've got, of course [here he writes in reference to the team of three astronauts who went to the moon in 1969], Collins (Keith) flying the space ship while Armstrong (Dandy) and Aldrin (Howard) roam the moon. Listening to Dandy, as natural and funny as if he were sitting in the back room at Clarke's, was a real pleasure—especially when measured against cliché-type competition. Here's hoping you keep 'em turned on, and let 'em go. They're guaranteed to become the Huntley-Brinkley of pro football, but far more lively, and a welcome breakthrough in the business of telecasting the pro game. Congratulations to all my friends at ABC-TV Sports, of which I am continually proud.[11]

Arledge's response to Jenkins was appreciative, if somewhat more cautious. He agreed that Meredith had turned in a good performance, but he also wrote, "Howard Cosell was not as effective as he normally would be because of some logistical problems we had, but I expect to be hearing some incisive and hopefully, intelligent commentaries from him in the future."[12]

Indeed, both Cosell and Arledge hoped that *Monday Night Football* would bring in new audiences. Not surprisingly, ABC's own market research showed that professional football viewership was overwhelmingly male. Arledge immediately set out to determine audience numbers for football games shown in traditionally male locations such as taverns.[13] But he aimed to broaden the audience for football on Monday nights, in part by using the entertainment value Cosell brought to maintain the interest of people who were not necessarily football fans. Before the first broadcast Cosell tried to debunk the notion that *Monday Night Football* would make "football widows" out of women in their homes for two days of the week instead of just one. "We're going to make certain that our telecasts appeal to women," he said. Contrasting the coverage that ABC would provide to that of previous network football broadcasts, Cosell told a reporter:

First, we're adding something new. It is called humor. No football game is going to stop the war in Vietnam, curb inflation or clean up one ghetto. We'll treat the game as a game. Second, we're going to have journalism instead of shill-ism. Most sportscasters work for a team[,] and this shows. I have talked with [NFL] commissioner Pete Rozelle, with Vince Lombardi [former coach of the Green Bay Packers and coach at the time of the Washington Redskins], and with Al Davis [owner of the Oakland Raiders]. They all agree with me. If a game is dull, I'll call it a dull game.

He continued: "No more of those marching bands at halftime. Instead, we'll have a ten-minute film feature, the highlights of the best Sunday pro games. And finally, we'll bring some literacy and erudition to football."[14]

The first regular-season broadcast of *Monday Night Football* was on September 21, 1970. The Cleveland Browns were hosting the New York Jets in Cleveland's Municipal Stadium. Cosell lived up to the promise of the ABC press release and honestly stated that he thought the Browns' star running back Leroy Kelly, who gained only forty-four yards on twenty-six carries, was "not a factor" in the game. Such criticism seems relatively tame by current standards, but at the time many viewers saw Cosell as editorializing far too much.

According to Cosell, his first broadcast brought in, once more, a "flood of mail," and other reports confirm this.[15] The *Chicago Daily News* wire service reported after the game, "ABC is being bombarded with complaints that sportscaster Howard Cosell, a member of the Monday Night telecasting team, 'talked too much' and 'obviously favored New York in his commentary.'"[16] Arledge reports that "sacks and sacks" of mail were delivered to ABC—not the kind that begin "'In my opinion,' but [letters that] stated 'We the undersigned,' and ended with three hundred names."[17] The perception that Cosell supported the New York team may have been due to his accent (something frequently noted by television critics), yet a New York bias was also noticed by one of the most prominent television critics in New York. Jack Gould of the *New York Times* wrote: "If the New York Jets lost, so did Howard Cosell, the ABC sports reporter. His parochial partisanship for the Jets was grating enough[,] but his miscalls of what happened on the field, particularly with respect to penalties, suggested boxing is really more his bag."[18]

Such criticisms may have had some merit, but if so, it would be unfair to level such a charge of bias entirely against Cosell. In the week after the game Arledge wrote a letter to the Jets' star quarterback Joe Namath expressing appreciation for allowing Cosell to interview him before the game. Namath had felt nervous before the opening contest of the season and did not want to distract himself by talking to Cosell. In the letter Arledge thanks Namath and writes, "It is a tragedy that the JETS didn't win a game that you so clearly dominated, but it is a long season and I'm sure that you'll come out on top in the end."[19]

In papers around the United States, comments about Cosell were even less polite than Gould's criticism. Loel Schrader of the Long Beach, California, *Independent* wrote: "Monday night pro football telecasts *seemed* like a good idea. But then the network blew it by hiring Howard Cosell as 'second' man. Cosell wouldn't permit himself to be upstaged at the Second Coming."[20] About the nicest comments came from syndicated columnist Cynthia Lowry, who wrote in a column that appeared in papers throughout the United States that the Monday night game "was even interesting for viewers who couldn't care less about sports. The big colorful cast had a star, Joe Namath, and even a comedian, a commentator named Howard Cosell with a Brooklyn accent and a penchant for using jaw-breaking words."[21] Previewing the next week's Monday night matchup, Paul Ernst of the *Columbus (Nebraska) Telegram* wrote, "I hope Howard Cosell does a better job of announcing."[22] Chuck Dell of the *Lima (Ohio) News* wrote positively about Keith Jackson, but considered Don Meredith "barely tolerable" as a color commentator, and stated outright, "Howard Cosell has gotta go." He went on to elaborate: "About Cosell, what can you say? [Baseball announcer] Ken Coleman summed it up best at a meeting in Boston Tuesday when he facetiously remarked: 'Howard Cosell should make a good pro coach someday.'"[23] Perhaps the harshest criticism came from Jim Murray, the acerbic sports columnist for the *Los Angeles Times*. Known for making a point and then piling it on, Murray found in Cosell an easy target to unleash his biting wit.

> First you get Howard Cosell, the man of a thousand syllables, who comes on as if he were reading the tablets of Sinai to a group of retarded children who are hard of hearing and unfamiliar with the language. Howard is the master of the innocent insult. A lawyer by profession, a broadcaster by accident, he is capable of some of the most impersonal slaps in the face in the history of television. "Johnny Unitas, they say you can't throw the long ball anymore, that you're through as a long threat." . . . He doesn't interview people, he prosecutes them. He implies he wants a

definite yes or no, and no volunteering from the witness. . . . The unwary might think they had tuned in on a third degree of a known child molester. He's beautiful. He speaks with all the deliberation of a guy who has an arrow in his chest. He treats the game as if it were a pointless interruption of an otherwise brilliant monologue. "Bot (the way he pronounces 'Bart') Stah (the way he pronounces 'Starr'), they're booing you," he may say accusingly. You expect, in the next breath, to hear, "How do you plead?"[24]

Cosell expected the negative criticism, yet even early on there were signs that he had trouble accepting it. *Cosell* contains more than a slight note of resentment directed toward Meredith, who soon became very popular for his Monday night role. "A new hero had been born" with *Monday Night Football,* Cosell writes. "Dandy Don Meredith. And a new goat: Howard Cosell." Despite his expectations of being "ripped" by the fans and the press, Cosell remarks, "The damn thing got to me."[25]

Ironically, it was Cosell himself who first envisioned the roles that he and Meredith would play on *Monday Night Football.* According to Cosell, before the debut of the program Meredith had deep reservations about becoming a broadcaster. Just before beginning at ABC he had institutionalized his daughter, who suffered from blindness and mental retardation. Meredith was emotionally sensitive and had trouble adjusting to the demands of his new profession while also handling the crisis taking place within his family. He was ready to back out of his commitment to *Monday Night Football,* but Cosell writes that he was able to persuade him to stay—in part by outlining the roles that each would play. "Middle America will love you," Cosell remembers telling Meredith. "Southern America will love you. And there are at least forty sportswriters in this country who can't wait to get at me, . . . You'll wear the white hat, I'll wear the black hat[,] and you'll have no problems from the beginning."[26]

Meredith told a very similar story in an Associated Press piece about him that appeared in November 1970.

> Meredith said he is the guy in the white hat on Monday night games with sometimes abrasive Cosell in the black hat. Meredith has nothing but praise for Cosell. "I remember we were in New York after a game and I was feeling depressed. He took me to a

bar and said—you know how he talks—"don't worry about a thing, kid. Just be like the champ. Be yourself. You be Don Meredith and I'll be Howard Cosell!" Meredith said later he got to thinking that Cosell makes $300,000 a year just being Cosell. "That's when I decided I was going to start being myself," Meredith said. "That Cosell is a real pro."[27]

This routine would, of course, prove to be very popular in the long run, but early on the negative sentiments toward Cosell in the broadcast booth were not just insulting; they threatened to bring a quick end to his job. Leonard Goldenson, ABC's founder and president, recalled that after the first *Monday Night Football* broadcast, the head of the Ford Motor Company, Henry Ford II, phoned him. "Take that guy Cosell off," Ford told him. "He's hogging all the time. He and Don Meredith talk so much I can't enjoy the football game." Cosell had always considered Goldenson to be one of his strongest allies at the network. Nevertheless, Goldenson agreed to look into taking Cosell off the air. Only after Arledge persuaded the network boss to give Cosell a few more weeks was the controversial "second man" allowed to stay in the booth.[28]

Eventually advertisers like Ford came around and continued to support *Monday Night Football*—with Cosell. Perhaps the reason for keeping him had less to do with the flood of mail ABC received than with the flood of viewers ABC attracted. The first broadcast drew 33 percent of the available audience, according to the A. C. Nielsen rating service.[29] This was a far better share than either of the rival networks managed to achieve, despite the fact that *Monday Night Football* was going up against programs considered to be very tough competition: Bob Hope or *Movie of the Week* on NBC, and popular comedies such as *Mayberry R.F.D.* and stars like Doris Day and Carol Burnett on CBS.[30] Cosell, however, continued to feel the sting of criticism from viewers who spoke out against him. Of the reaction to his first appearance on *Monday Night Football,* he writes: "Was football that important to this country? Was it a moral crime to introduce objective commentary to the transmission of a sport event? If so, how did we as a people get this way? Remember, this was 1970—an endless war was raging in Vietnam. The economy was in trouble. Unemployment was high. Racial problems were still in the news. The fact that there could be such outrage against a sports commentator, after one football telecast, had to be a reflection of the values of many Americans."[31]

Cosell may have been asking his questions rhetorically, but indeed football was proving to be very important to television audiences throughout the United States. *Monday Night Football* very quickly became more than just a highly rated television program. It was a television phenomenon. In many ways it was the springboard from which ABC was able to launch itself as a network that could compete with NBC and CBS. Goldenson writes that only three weeks after his call to take Cosell off the air, Henry Ford II called again and said: "Leonard, I apologize, I really enjoy the patter that's going on between these two guys. I withdraw my objection."[32] About Cosell, Goldenson makes the very common observation that "half the audience likes him; the other half hates him. But they talk about him. I don't know how 'Monday Night Football' would have succeeded without him."[33] The success of *Monday Night Football* meant that ABC now had a platform for promoting its program schedule, the major role played by sports programming. This meant more revenue for the network as audiences multiplied for ABC's other shows.

As much as *Monday Night Football* was changing the profile of ABC, many saw it changing the habits of Americans in general. As a sign of the social dimensions of the program, the Club Cal-Neva in downtown Reno, Nevada, called out in a newspaper advertisement, "Attention! Football Widows: Fix him a TV dinner and come join the other ignored wives EVERY MONDAY NIGHT." Guests got a free glass of champagne with a ninety-eight-cent chef's special. In an editorial the *Courier-News* of Blythville, Arkansas, took note of the impact that *Monday Night Football* was having on traditional cultural practices and community events.

> Monday night, a Blytheville man was the scheduled speaker at a civic club. He arrived at 7:25 for the 7:30 meeting to find club members who had finished dinner and were awaiting his appearance. Meeting time for the club has been changed to 6:45. It's a time change dictated by the National Football League, which this year scheduled a television game for each Monday evening at 8. Monday night football is as American as carbon monoxide. And the American Broadcasting Company, either through

Machiavellian genius or the sort of blessed fortuity which accounts for a spilled laboratory test tube leading to a cure for cancer, has two top bananas and a straight man wedged firmly in the middle.[34]

The editorial goes on to describe the banter between Cosell and Meredith as central to the program's entertainment value.

> The press-box action is divided between Don Meredith and Howard Cosell. Meredith, the retired Dallas Cowboy (out of SMU) quarterback, plays Judge Julius Hoffman to the counterpoint of Cosell's Jerry Rubin. Cosell, who someday might be arrested for crossing state lines with the intent of inciting a riot, has all the charm of an asp . . . and, come to think of it, he has the profile of one, too. Cosell, you feel, never will achieve happiness until either Meredith or one of those NFL linebackers re-distributes the Cosell nose with a fist, on camera and in color. Cosell, who never learned that a little dab'l do you, abrades the down-home gentility of Meredith. The Cosell Agnewism is a fingernail run down the blackboard of Don Meredith's soul, thus the drama, from Monday night to Monday night, is not only on the football field, as new tests of the Meredith patience unfold.[35]

In addition to likening Cosell to a venomous Egyptian snake, this editorial suggests how completely, by the end of the 1970 football season, *Monday Night Football* had become integrated into a cultural fabric that increasingly blurred the lines between entertainment and current events. The editorial's reference to Judge Julius Hoffman and Jerry Rubin concerns the trial of anti–Vietnam War protesters who had been charged with inciting a riot at the 1968 Democratic National Convention in Chicago. The comparison is notable as it parallels a celebrated trial in which several of the defendants routinely mocked courtroom decorum in a manner reminiscent of the Marx Brothers in *Duck Soup*. The term "Agnewism" refers to Vice President Spiro Agnew, who, like Cosell, often peppered his speech with inflated polysyllabic vocabulary.

Similarly, *Time* magazine ran an editorial on *Monday Night Football* in December 1970 titled "The Don and Howard Show," which once again highlights the cultural and personality contrasts between Meredith and Cosell as central to the program's success.

Meredith's Texas drawl and bucolic quips sound as if they belong on one of ABC Monday Night Football's competitors, Mayberry R.F.D. Which makes them a highly effective counterpoint to Cosell's rasping New York pedantry. As Meredith told TIME's Mark Goodman last week, "If Cosell says, 'They have a paucity of plays,' I say something like, 'If you mean they ain't got a whole bunch, you're right.'" As a result, the Don and Howard Show has become so entertaining that at times it comes close to upstaging the action on the field below. There have been rumors that Cosell might bow out next season, which would be unfortunate. Still, Meredith has amply demonstrated that he can carry the ball by himself.[36]

Later in his career, when he would write bitterly about his experiences on *Monday Night Football* in his book *I Never Played the Game,* Cosell would claim to have been the reason for the show's success and would dismiss the contributions of Meredith almost entirely. Yet the first season of *Monday Night Football* was also an emotionally tormenting one for Cosell. Before the sixth game of the season, a matchup between two top teams—the Los Angeles Rams and the Minnesota Vikings—he admits, "I behaved badly, boyishly, monosyllabically all day, with [producer Chuck] Forte, with Dandy, with Keith, with all of them."[37] Cosell acknowledges that he had become a "pain in the ass" to the *Monday Night Football* staff, and to himself. Meredith also continued to struggle with his emotions, feeling uncomfortable behind the mike, and sensitive to criticism. According to Cosell, he and Meredith calmed each other down during the season, alternately threatening to quit and then talking the other back into staying. Yet Cosell's perceptions of Meredith also reveal a tension between the two.

A late-season game between the Cowboys and the St. Louis Cardinals serves as an illustration. This was the first game that Meredith broadcast back in Dallas, and it promised to be a happy affair as his old team was favored. It was the Cardinals' night, though, as they jumped out to a 21–0 lead at halftime and finished with a 38–0 slaughter. Cosell remembers that his partner was an embarrassment: "Meredith went wild in the booth over the performance of his old team. He couldn't understand their absolute futility and he all but exploded with personal emotion." Afterward, Cosell notes, he saw Meredith in the hotel lobby with a "sheepish" grin on his face. "He knew he had gone berserk over the ineptness of the Cowboys."[38]

By contrast, Arledge remembers this as the broadcast that cemented *Monday Night Football*'s status as the entertaining program he had hoped it would become. "The worse it got for the Cowboys, the more Howard needled [Meredith], and the more Don moaned. 'Roger Staubach is now four for four in the passing department,' he said after an interception. 'He's completed two to his team, and two to the other.'"[39] To Arledge's mind, Meredith provided a signature performance with his famous halftime statement, "You don't know what trouble is till you're down 21–0 in the Cotton Bowl." As the crowd below the booth chanted, "We want Meredith!" Dandy Don responded, "I'm not going down there on a night like this." Arledge writes: "The final score was 38 to 0, a blowout that should have had TV sets turned off coast to coast. Instead, we kept our biggest audience of the year, and beat a Johnny Carson special. Howard, the smart-aleck New Yorker, and Dandy, the aw-shucks cowboy who puts him down, were enshrined, and a principle was proved: The show was bigger than the game."[40]

Another difference in perception arises in the accounts of the game that took place the following week in Philadelphia. At the University of Pennsylvania's Franklin Field, the Eagles hosted the New York Giants on a frigid November evening. Cosell remembers that he had a fever and was barely able to make it through a pregame party thrown by the Eagles for the press. He then did further damage to his system when he ran wind sprints on the track with his old friend from the 1968 Olympics, John Carlos. After that, he returned to the party, then climbed the rickety steps that led to the overhanging press box, open to the air. Cosell remembers that as the game developed, he grew increasingly lightheaded; he was unable to pronounce "Philadelphia" and eventually felt so sick that he threw up all over Meredith's new cowboy boots. "If anyone ever looked like an on-camera drunk, I did," he writes.[41] According to Arledge, Cosell was in fact drunk. Not only had he ingested "a martini or two or three at the hospitality suite" before the game, but also he was further fortified by a "bandolier" for his "silver bullets" (what Arledge reports Cosell to have called his martinis) in an ice bucket next to his station in the broadcast booth provided by Eagles owner Leonard Tose.[42] As Cosell continued to work national telecasts of football and baseball games, others would allege that he drank on air, and that his increasingly bitter deportment may have been related to the effects of excessive drinking.[43]

At the conclusion of the 1970 football season, ABC had some very good news for advertisers who sponsored *Monday Night Football*. The program was the second-highest-rated television program on ABC, just after the Sunday night movie. While there may have been "Monday night widows," Cosell proved to be correct about the program's ability to attract female viewers. An average of 5.34 million women watched the show during its first season. This contrasted with CBS and NBC football telecasts, which drew only 3.78 million and 3.61 million women, respectively. Similarly, *Monday Night Football* had an audience of 2 million teenagers, while CBS and NBC telecasts drew 1.65 million and 1.46 million. Most important to the network, however, were what industry insiders call "key demographics." Television advertisers want not just large audiences but affluent ones. Among viewers earning $15,000 or more a year (considered by the network in 1970 to be "upper income"), *Monday Night Football* drew almost double the audience for NBC football games, and about one third more than for CBS. The ratings were virtually the same or better for viewers with a year or more of college education, for viewers who were professional or white-collar workers, and for households with five or more family members.[44]

Yet for all its success, Cosell finished the first year of *Monday Night Football* beset by the same insecurities that had plagued him at the beginning of the season. In fact they would continue to haunt him throughout the remainder of his career on the program. In a way, the personality traits that had once served him as a probing journalist exploring the connections between sports and society were now being exploited to cast him as an object of ridicule. Cosell became increasingly resentful of ex-athletes who made their way to the broadcast booth—the "jocks" who constituted a new elite in what Cosell liked to call the "jockocracy." He found this perception validated in 1971, when Meredith won an Emmy Award for sports broadcasting. As much as Cosell had worked to mentor Meredith, and had grown to like him, he felt that the former quarterback was a lazy commentator, that he would come to the broadcast booth every Monday night underprepared and would rescue himself only through his hip cowboy wit.

Cosell consistently decried those who took sports too seriously, yet ironically, the more insecure he grew, the more seriously he took himself. As *Monday Night Football* increasingly focused on the spectacle surrounding the game, Cosell's self-seriousness became something to laugh at more than something to revere. Since he first entered broadcasting, Cosell had been pompous, arrogant, and verbose, but at least during the 1960s, when he defended Ali and Smith and Carlos, his opinions commanded respect. Now he was being paid a lot of money because of the entertainment value involved in ridiculing the class geek. For someone who had such faith in an American consensus, he was now one of the most divisive public figures in American society. Later, in his exceedingly bitter memoir *I Never Played the Game,* Cosell would say as much: "Intellectually, looking back on it, my work on *Monday Night Football* is a matter of monumental indifference to me. I'm a man of causes, and I never had a cause. My real fulfillment in broadcasting has always come from crusading journalism, fighting for the rights of people such as Jackie Robinson, Muhammad Ali, and Curt Flood, and obviously there was none of that on *Monday Night Football*."[45] In general, the intersections between sports and political protest that defined the 1960s would decline during the 1970s, leaving Cosell with less opportunity for the crusading that drove him in his career. One event in particular proved to be a dramatic watershed for Cosell, once again bringing a political issue to the forefront of a major sporting event.

The year 1972 was for Cosell a time of paradigmatic changes. In April, New York Mets manager and former Brooklyn Dodger Gil Hodges died. Returning from his funeral, Cosell and his camera crew ran into an old friend, Jackie Robinson. Cosell asked if he could shoot an interview in his limousine on his way home, and Robinson consented. By this time, Robinson—who had been such a key influence in Cosell's life and career, who had advised him, criticized him, defended him, and whom Cosell had championed and respected probably more than any other person in public life—was himself clinging to life. He had suffered for years from diabetes. He was blind in one eye and had a severe cataract in the other. He had suffered two heart attacks. More than this, tragedy had befallen his family. His son, who had returned from Vietnam only to struggle with bouts of drug addiction and crime, and who had recovered and been working with other youths at a drug rehabilitation center, had recently been killed in a car accident.

When Cosell thought about Jackie Robinson, he thought about someone who had sacrificed on the ball field and endured vicious racist taunts from fans and prejudice from teammates and opponents alike, all to make the game of baseball seem as if it were a genuinely democratic and inclusive pastime. Cosell asked Robinson if he felt he had been particularly burdened with suffering. While he acknowledged having been dealt a great many difficulties, Robinson insisted, "Oh, we've had a great life, we've accomplished so much."[46]

Robinson was more than just a friend and ally of Cosell's. He was in many respects a representative of an earlier era when the cause of civil rights for African Americans, as understood by white liberals like Cosell, was a relatively simple and straightforward matter. In the late 1960s, as the federal government attempted to redress the deep-seated consequences wrought by three centuries of racial oppression, the sentiments of many whites turned against civil rights. Even as the majority of Jews remained loyal to the principles of the Democratic Party and liberal political reform, many began to question the extent to which the injustices of the past might be corrected, especially with regard to affirmative action. As much as Jews supported Lyndon Johnson's Great Society, the vast majority opposed quotas based on race when used as criteria in hiring and school admissions. In particular, Jews confronted a new kind of double consciousness in post–World War II America. On the one hand, they had been treated almost strictly as outsiders before the New Deal and the Second World War. Yet in the decades since, the benefits they had enjoyed from the New Deal and postwar reforms sometimes put them in conflict with African Americans over a number of volatile issues. Policies of the Great Society that treated Jews as no different from other whites struck many Jews as unfair, especially those of Cosell's generation, who had strong memories of their earlier treatment in American society.[47]

In some ways these developments among Jews in the United States paralleled even larger ones internationally. Since World War II, Jews had won a major victory as Theodor Herzl's dream of a Zionist state was finally realized with the declaration of an independent state of Israel in 1948. In the years that followed, Israel successfully fought wars—immediately following its independence and again in 1967—each time gaining territory. The success of Israel stood in stark contrast to the images of victimization that had characterized the history of European Jewry before and during World War II. Most in the Arab world and the Middle East, however, saw Israel in a very different light. For years, Jews had fought the British colonizers who managed Palestine, but to Palestinians, Jews had become the new colonizers. Jews felt justified in declaring Israel theirs because they were the oppressed, but to Palestinians and Arabs, Jews were the oppressors. All of the complications that accompany this history were about to confront Cosell as he left New York for Munich and the Olympics in August 1972.

In September 1970 King Hussein of Jordan had declared martial law in response to a threat of insurrection from a Palestinian rebel group. His government killed or banished thousands of Palestinians living in Jordan. In response, a group of Palestinian men formed a terrorist organization named in memory of this incident, "Black September." Over the next two years they planned and carried out only a few actions, but those that they did execute were dramatic in scope. On November 28, 1971, a coalition of as many as four different terrorist groups opened fire on Jordan's conservative prime minister, Wasfi al-Tel, during a visit to Egypt. Wasfi was killed instantly. In May 1972, two men and two women hijacked a plane from Vienna and forced it to land in Tel Aviv. Israeli authorities shot out the tires of the plane and began negotiations. These ended when Israeli commandos, disguised as mechanics, stormed the plane, killing two hijackers and one passenger. The two female hijackers were arrested.[48]

Despite the group's connection to the cause of Palestinian rights and liberation, not all agree as to whether Black September was under the direct control of or even an arm of the Palestinian Liberation Organization (PLO). It was an extremely fluid terrorist "cell." Nevertheless, the PLO refused to condemn the terrorist actions of Black September, thus implicitly linking the two organizations. This small group operated under the rule of different leaders responsible for each of its actions, and each loyal to different branches of Palestinian leadership.[49] One of the leaders was Abu Daoud, who in 1972 planned the most spectacular and deadly of all Black September actions that year, one that would make the organization's name recognized around the world and would bring the fight between Israelis and Palestinians to the forefront of world events.

Before coming to Munich for the 1972 Olympics, Howard Cosell had probably not heard of Black September, but he knew plenty about the history of Jews in Germany, or at least about the history of Jews in Nazi Germany. He also knew about the 1936 Olympics, and about Avery Brundage and the history of anti-Semitism in the U.S. Olympic Committee. Four years earlier Cosell had sat behind the Olympic broadcasters' desk in Mexico City and boldly denounced the treatment of John Carlos and Tommie Smith after their Black Power protest. At the time, he could easily parallel the bigotry that had denied Jewish athletes the opportunity to compete in 1936 to the banning of Smith and Carlos.

At the time of the Mexico City Olympics, he was a rising star in television sports journalism. Now, however, despite having achieved unparalleled heights of fame and fortune, despite having by all accounts a blissfully happy marriage and family life, Howard Cosell was uneasy. In part that uneasiness came from his being in Germany, watching the opening ceremonies of the Olympic Games, where he felt very close to the history of Jewish oppression. Seeing the teams from nations around the world enter the Olympic stadium in Munich, he writes, "I got a sense of World War II and the days that preceded it—it was almost like seeing Warsaw and Prague again. I couldn't shake it. Right then my whole background surfaced in me. I felt intensely Jewish." He'd had similar feelings during trips to Germany to cover some of Ali's fights in the mid-1960s, but the spectacle of the Olympics in Munich seems to have affected him even more deeply. Up until this time, the story of his life had been one of separating himself from his Jewish background. Now, he reflected, "Dachau was only 22 miles away."[50]

Cosell acknowledges that he felt no overt anti-Semitism in Munich—in fact, quite the opposite. Germans seemed to go out of their way to show that, thirty-six years after Hitler's Olympics, the country had changed. The most warmly greeted Olympic team to enter the stadium on the day of the opening ceremonies was Israel's, and the Israeli athletes were routinely cheered more than any others, even though none had a chance of winning a medal. Indeed, in an effort to counter the perception of Germany as a militaristic society, security was lax at the event. The West German Olympic Organizing Committee wanted to project a new image of Germany, one that was casual and open.

Understanding this, leaders of Black September planned a spectacular action, one that would assuredly catch the attention of the global media. During the second week of the Olympics, early on the morning on September 5, eight people dressed like athletes and carrying sports duffels climbed a fence around the Olympic village. Not knowing who they were—athletes had been routinely scaling fences to get into the village all week—some members of the U.S. Olympic team helped them throw their bags over the fence. These were of course not athletes but members of Black September, some of whom had worked on maintenance and construction at the village. Inside their bags were automatic rifles.

By 4:30 am they had arrived at the Israeli Olympic team's pavilion, had broken in, and had killed Moshe Weinberg, a weightlifter, and shot Joseph Romano, a wrestling coach, leaving him bleeding to death. During the struggles in which Weinberg and Romano were killed, some residents were able to escape. The captors, however, took the remaining nine people in the building hostage, demanding the release of over two hundred prisoners held in Israel, as well as the leaders of a radical German terrorist group, the Baader-Meinhof Gang, who were in prison in Germany.

Cosell had been sent to the Olympics mostly to cover boxing and conduct interviews with notable athletes. On the morning of September 5, however, he received a phone call informing him that terrorists had broken into the Israeli pavilion and taken athletes hostage. He was sent to cover the events inside the village with television news reporter Peter Jennings, with whom he was to share a camera crew. By the time Cosell arrived at the village, security had clamped down. Jennings was already inside, but Cosell was unable to get in. Finally, along with newspaper sportswriters Jim Murray and Shirley Povich (whom Cosell had long despised), he was able to sneak into the Olympic village by disguising himself as a representative for Puma, the athletic shoe company.

Eventually Cosell found Jennings and the camera crew and settled beneath an overpass just outside Building 31, where the Black September terrorists were holding the Israeli hostages. He found a close friend of Moshe Weinberg and interviewed him. But when he found out that the day's Olympic events were being allowed to continue, Cosell became enraged. He resisted being removed from the area by police, using his trademark putdowns against the German authorities. He hugged the ground when warned that there might be a shoot-out. "In a weird way," he recalled, "totally disconnected from reality, I felt I was back doing the opening scene" in Woody Allen's *Bananas*.[51]

Over the next twelve hours, people covering the hostage crisis understood as little about what was actually going on as they did about the politics that were at its roots. Israeli government officials, led by Prime Minister Golda Meir, refused to negotiate with terrorists as a matter of policy, and held to that position throughout the day. Television viewers saw a haunting black and white image of a masked gunman on the balcony of Building 31 as ABC's Jim McKay reported the bits of information that were coming out of the Olympic village. By evening a resolution seemed to be near. German authorities had apparently offered some sort of promise of safe transport out of the country. In the middle of the night, the hostages were taken to a nearby airport via helicopter. Following a report that came over the wire from the Reuters news service, McKay announced that the hostages had been freed.

In fact, the Germans were attempting to lure the terrorists into a trap. The plan backfired, leading to a standoff on the tarmac. A German marksman shot and killed one of the gunmen as he walked on the tarmac outside one of the two helicopters that held the hostages. There was a short firefight, and one of the German marksmen was killed, as was one of the helicopter pilots, who was trying to escape. After an hour of silence, German commandos in armored vehicles attempted to storm the two helicopters. The hostage takers lobbed a grenade into one helicopter and sprayed it with bullets. They then shot and killed all of the hostages who were bound together aboard the other helicopter.

By this time McKay had retracted his announcement that the crisis was over. "The word we get from the airport is that, quote, 'All hell has broken loose out there,' that there is still shooting going on. There was a report of a burning helicopter. But it all seems to be confusion. Nothing is nailed down." After sixteen hours in the studio, McKay was told by Arledge over his earpiece that official word had come down. All of the hostages were dead; three of the hostage takers had survived and been taken into custody. McKay looked into the camera and told his viewers: "They've now said there were eleven hostages. Two were killed in their room this—ah, yesterday morning. Nine were killed at the airport tonight. . . . [T]hey're all gone."[52]

For Cosell, the events of September 5 and 6 brought back memories of Jewish oppression that had been all but suppressed over the past twenty-five years, as he had climbed the ladder of success. He had thought of himself as a "hybrid character"—married to a Protestant, the father-in-law of a Catholic, a man with no formal religious training himself. "But I did grow up in Brooklyn, of Jewish parents, in the age of the Depression and the threat of Hitler," he wrote. "Again, I had never felt so intensely Jewish as when I watched this scene: two Israelis already dead; more to die here in Germany, where Hitler inflicted his scars; the Arabs, incredibly, this tiny coterie of desperadoes, holding forth."[53]

———

As important as the hostage crisis was personally for Cosell, most viewers remembered the event for Jim McKay's dramatic coverage. Cosell became better known for his reporting of a blunder by the United States track team which once again turned him into a lightning rod for criticism. Ironically, it was Stan Wright—one of the first African American track coaches ever hired by the U.S. team, and the man who had four years earlier guided Tommie Smith and John Carlos—who was at the center of the controversy. On August 31, 1972 (about a week before the hostage crisis), Wright had been charged with getting three athletes—Eddie Hart, Rey Robinson, and Robert Taylor—to their preliminary heats. In the morning, the three easily won their first-round races, and were to run in the quarterfinals later in the day. Wright, relying on an eighteen-month-old schedule, thought that this race was at 7 pm, but as he was relaxing with the sprinters in the Olympic village late in the afternoon, he saw on television that one of the heats for his sprinters was already beginning. Taylor was able to get to his semifinal race on time and eventually won the silver medal in the finals, but Hart and Robinson were too late and were disqualified.[54]

In an interview with Cosell, Robinson bitterly blamed Wright. Cosell, feeling that the complaint should not be aired without allowing Wright to respond, arranged for an interview. During a key exchange, Cosell pressed Wright.

COSELL: But as a matter of accepted routine, with all that's at stake, all the years, really, of work and preparation and so on, don't you check on a given day with the appropriate Olympic authorities?

WRIGHT: Yes, I did.

COSELL: As to the schedule? What happened?

WRIGHT: I checked as to our heats and I checked the stadium before I left, checked the assembly area, asked them about the schedule I had. They said that's the way it was going to run—be run—and I left on the assumption that that was correct.

COSELL: I feel deeply sorry for you, but we all have to answer to the American public. Why in the world was America the only country to have the wrong information?

WRIGHT: Well, I can't answer that because those a little higher up on the echelon, as far as I'm concerned—

COSELL: What do you mean by that?

WRIGHT: Well . . . I think you know what I mean.

COSELL: No, I don't. I'd like you to tell me.

WRIGHT: Well, I'm not in a position to tell you because I really don't know myself, but I don't feel I have to answer to America; I feel I have to answer to these two youngsters, and this is why I feel so deeply about it. I'm concerned about them. They were the ones that did not make the heat, they were the ones that are suffering the grief of, as you say, long preparation. Great sprinters, outstanding sprinters, representing their country, and they didn't get a chance because there was a misunderstanding on my part on the schedule.[55]

Cosell finished his broadcast of this incident with a special commentary which he delivered, as he almost always did, without a script. It concluded:

Now, what about the coach, who has just openly admitted his mistake, who has made a terrible mistake quite clearly, but who has been a very decent man all his life and a very fine track coach? . . . Without attacking or unnecessarily pillorying Stan Wright, the plain fact is for you people in America that only the United States of America had the wrong information. It is clear that the *Paris Tribune* as published today in Munich had the right time information for those one-hundred-meter heats. It's clear that every responsible reporter in Munich, West Germany, had the right time information. The American Broadcasting Company had the right time information. So, no matter how they try to pass the buck, no matter how they try to whitewash, our people are to blame. And the ones who suffer are the ones who are supposed to flourish: the two decent young men who've had such dedication and such purpose, and now such terrible, terrible despair and disappointment. That's what happened here in Munich, West Germany, today, even as others exulted in the Mark Spitz victory.[56]

In later years Wright would defend himself and complain that Cosell's criticisms were unfair, pointing out that the outdated schedules had been given to him a month before the races, not eighteen months before. What is more, three other national teams during these Olympics had missed races under similar circumstances.[57]

Perhaps Wright should have thanked Cosell, though, because his harsh words ended up deflecting the nation's anger away from the beleaguered coach and back toward Cosell. Letters and newspaper columns overwhelmingly attacked Cosell for rubbing Wright's nose in a mistake that he already regretted. Readers of the *Chicago Tribune,* for example, had harsh words for Cosell. David Edington and Doug Carey, thirteen-year-olds from Northbrook, wrote: "Howard Cosell 'cut up' Stan Wright, the U.S. Olympic team sprint coach, far more than was necessary. Mr. Wright made a mistake, which he admitted, and he felt bad enough without Cosell's rude and uncalled for comments." Donna Essling from Aurora said: "I was infuriated by the tactless treatment given Coach Stan Wright by the high and mighty Cosell. I do hope that sometime Howard Cosell might descend to the lowly level of a human being, so he too would be capable of making a mistake." Wendy Pankrac from Berwyn asked: "How much longer do U.S. sports fans have to put up with Howard Cosell? Brash, unfair, insensitive—the poorest excuse for the commentator imaginable."[58] Thomas McCann from West Lafayette, Indiana, told the paper, "Right after I saw Howard Cosell recently take apart the U.S. track coach on TV, I realized I had seen the cheapest piece of sensationalism of my life."[59]

John Henry Auran, a senior editor at *Skiing Magazine* recounting his experiences as a coach at that year's Winter Games in Sapporo, Japan, also defended Wright in a letter to the *New York Times,* saying: "Cosell and most of the press covering this affair missed the real story. It's the United States Olympic Committee which should be put on the griddle."[60] Dave Wimbish, sports editor of the *Arizona Daily Sun,* wrote, "For Cosell, I thought his Thursday night performance was the most disgusting since he threw up on Don Meredith at halftime one Monday night last year."[61] Norm Unis of the *Eureka (California) Times-Standard* accused Cosell of goading Robinson and Hart into condemning Wright by asking them leading questions, before "turn[ing] to the suffocation of Stan Wright, coach of the U.S. speedsters, who unknowingly chose to go with outdated schedules of elimination heats, causing tardiness and [the] ouster of Robinson and Hart."[62]

None of these people accused Cosell of unfairly attacking an African American coach out of racial prejudice. Yet the change in perceptions since 1968 certainly is dramatic. Four years earlier in Mexico City, Cosell had drawn criticism for defending the medal stand protest of Smith and Carlos. He had, in the eyes of his critics, been too quick to endorse an expression of Black Power. Now he was criticized for being too harsh in his questioning of a black coach. For Jim Spence, who worked with Cosell on the Stan Wright interview, the criticism of Cosell was not justified. "Cosell properly chastised the coach for not having fulfilled his responsibility properly," he said. "While he was always sensitive to the plight of the black man, he also was a journalist, so he didn't let his sensitivity overcome his journalistic sensibility."[63]

As true as this may have been, the circumstances had changed a great deal since 1968. This can be seen dramatically in the case of a protest on the medal stand in Munich that paralleled the one in Mexico City but had a very different outcome. In 1972, Americans Vincent Matthews and Wayne Collett had won the gold and silver in the 400-meter dash. In contrast to the orchestrated protest of Smith and Carlos, however, Matthews and Collett merely refused to recognize the ceremony. Atop the medal stand they chatted casually as the national anthem played, at one point twirling their medals around their fingers and scratching their beards. Like Smith and Carlos, both were angry over the treatment of African American athletes by the U.S. Olympic Committee and the slow pace of change both in sports and in American society more generally. Matthews, who had competed previously in the Olympics, was also upset that he had been required to pay his own way to get to the Olympic trials. After the incident, the two were sent home from the Olympic Games even more quickly than Smith and Carlos had been. Cosell caught up with Collett and asked him about the protest.[64]

COSELL: If you were in the same situation again, would you stand at attention?

COLLETT: Probably not.

COSELL: Why not?

COLLETT: As I said before, I couldn't with a clear conscience. I feel that, you know, looking back on it now, my actions on the victory stand, probably mirror the attitude of white America toward blacks—totally casual, ignoring them, as long as we're not embarrassing you we're okay. That's how I feel.[65]

What was perhaps most striking was not Collett's explanation for his actions but Cosell's lack of response. Unlike with Smith and Carlos, there was no courageous defense, no outraged editorial on the television news, no stern chastisement of the U.S. Olympic Committee for ejecting these two young men from the Olympics. In fact Cosell's indifference to the protest of Matthews and Collett mirrored not only the indifferent style of the sprinters' protest but also the reaction of the international media. Apart from some editorials in African American newspapers such as the *Chicago Defender,* the *Pittsburgh Courier,* and the *Amsterdam Press,* few took the time to comment on this event, either positively or negatively. As Douglas Hartmann has pointed out, "Unlike the reception Smith and Carlos received, Matthews and Collett were mostly ignored, almost immediately and conveniently forgotten."[66]

About two weeks after the end of the Olympics, Cosell was eating dinner with four players for the Washington Redskins in Bloomington, Minnesota, before a Monday night game against the Vikings. A newspaper reporter asked him for his reaction to the criticism that he had received for his questioning of Stan Wright. Cosell asked, "What criticism?" The reporter noted that *Sports Illustrated, Newsweek,* and a host of others had complained about Cosell's questioning of the track coach and his commentary. "Where did you get your facts?" Cosell demanded. "Who gives you the right to perpetrate such garbage? I don't like your attitude. Grow up! Get out and meet the people of this country, like I do each weekend." The Redskins players—John Wilbur, Charley Taylor, and Chris Hanburger—quietly wiped their mouths with their napkins and left the table as Cosell continued his rant: "I pity American sportswriters. In fact, I'll call your editor right now and tell him you've quit."[67]

The next morning Cosell saw the same reporter at breakfast and decided to bestow some kindness upon him, offering to answer any question. "I did the finest work of my life in Munich," he proclaimed. "Since the conclusion of the Olympics, I, more than anyone else, have been in constant demand by the public. Johnny Carson called me three times in Munich. It's no surprise. I was brilliant. I produced for ABC television the most-wanted figures in the Olympics on a moment's notice. I asked questions, like in the Wright interview, that were no different from those questions asked by sportswriters during press conferences." As a sports announcer, Cosell claimed, he was entitled to ask the same questions a sportswriter would ask. "Yet a segment of the nation's sportswriters chose to make a martyr of a man who ruined 18 years of preparation by two athletes. They made a martyr of Wright and attacked me personally in a vicious manner."[68]

Cosell's openly narcissistic point of view was nothing new. Nor were his hot temper and sharp tongue. But he had rarely displayed these unappealing aspects of his personality so brazenly before in a public setting. Despite his pronouncements about having done the "finest work" of his life, his experience at Munich had left a terribly bitter taste in his mouth. He was astonished that even International Olympic Committee (IOC) president Avery Brundage would have the Games continue during the hostage crisis, not suspending the events until 4 pm on September 5, when the hostage crisis had been under way for hours. Adding to Cosell's outrage, Brundage resumed the schedule after only one day of mourning, counting that twenty-four-hour period as having begun retroactively the day before, with the 4 pm suspension of competition. In a speech at the Olympic stadium in Munich, Brundage compared his decision to carry on despite the murder of eleven Israeli athletes to the IOC's decision to exclude the openly racist country of Rhodesia from the Olympics, stating: "We lost the Rhodesian battle against naked political blackmail. We have only the strength of a great ideal. I am sure that the public will agree that we cannot allow a handful of terrorists to destroy this nucleus of international cooperation and goodwill we have in the Olympic movement. The Games must go on."[69]

Brundage's elitism, his anti-Semitism, his insensitivity to the Israeli victims, and his willingness to put the ritual and ceremony of the Olympics before everything else all reminded Cosell of the same attitudes that he had chafed against four years earlier. "He has many admirable qualities," Cosell wrote of the IOC president. "The only trouble with Avery Brundage is that he believes in all the wrong things."[70] Less diplomatically, Cosell once called Brundage "a hypocrite and a parasite." Reflecting in an interview on the 1972 Munich hostage crisis, Cosell said it revealed that "there's always going to be prejudice and hatred in the world toward Jews, and because I was born of Jewish parents[,] I would always in the long run be Jewish." He added that Brundage's decision to continue the Games was "endorsed by millions of people in this country" and that this reflected a general indifference in the United States and the world toward the plight of Jews.[71]

The 1972 Olympics were a vivid reminder for Cosell of Jewish victimization. He often pointed out the nearby presence of the Dachau concentration camp. Yet the connection between this history and the causes Cosell lived to champion were becoming increasingly difficult to see clearly. This was particularly the case with African American civil rights. A movement among African Americans had come to identify strongly with the cause of Palestinian rights and become highly critical of Israel. To confuse matters even more, among those who were most forceful in their support of the Palestinian cause was the Nation of Islam, the African nationalist organization to which Muhammad Ali belonged.[72]

In other words, just as Cosell was reawakened to the oppression leveled against the Jews, some of those whose rights he had defended were coming to understand Jews in the Middle East as the oppressors. Cosell clearly had difficulty assimilating these two contrasting perceptions. In a 1981 interview he flatly stated, "I don't think the Palestinians deserve a state." Asked to elaborate, he answered: "I think that when the British Mandate ended and the independent State of Palestine was created, there were terms then that provided for appropriate land for them within the Arab states[,] and I don't think there's any need to parcel off that which is Israel's and that which became Israel's after the Six-Day war. I consider the Palestinians outlaws." Asked how he would answer those Palestinians who were displaced by the creation of the Israeli national boundaries, he said, "I answer that by being Jewish, two thousand years and more."[73] This was one of the few instances one can find of Cosell's actually identifying himself as Jewish, and not "born of Jewish parents." In any event, Cosell's thinking did not easily absorb the complexities of the conflicts between Palestinians and Israel. Instead, Cosell divided his universe starkly into good and evil, and over the years ahead he would come to believe that the world of network television sports was filled with a lot more evil than good.

6 Essential Contradictions

When he walked in a room, you'd know it. It rattled the
windows. He craved attention and loved it, good or bad.
Attention was attention. But once he had the stage he made
the most of it.

—Keith Jackson, interview with author

Most of Howard Cosell's associates describe him as someone who, in person, was much like he was on television. A 1972 *Washington Post* profile called him a "most vulnerable man" who can "quote, endlessly, the shafts and needles hurled at him in print." The article's author, Lawrence Laurent, concludes, "Each must hurt, or Cosell wouldn't recall each incident so vividly."[1]

Indeed, Jim Spence remembers that throughout his career, and especially as the 1970s progressed, Cosell was a constant presence in the offices of ABC network executives, angrily waving an unflattering press clipping. In 1972 he vowed to Laurent that he was going to get even. He had a contract to write a book titled *I Never Played the Game*. "He is aware that the title has at least two meanings: First, he was never a professional athlete and, second, he has refused to abide by the conventions that are dear to many sportscasters and to even more of the public."[2] Cosell, of course, did write a book that was published in 1973, but its title was simply *Cosell*. In it, he tells his story of the 1968 and 1972 Olympics; levels harsh criticisms at the International Olympic Committee; praises Jackie Robinson and Vince Lombardi; gives readers a glimpse into his own biography; writes about Muhammad Ali, Floyd Patterson, and Sonny Liston; and provides overall an entertaining picture of the self-absorbed, pompous, verbose, and pretentious character that television viewers had come to know over the course of less than ten years. At the end of his career he eventually did use the title *I Never Played the Game,* and while many of the points made in that book are similar to those made in *Cosell,* it would have a much more bitter, even vindictive tone. In his first book, however, as in his next one, titled *Like It Is,* Cosell conveys a sense of his love for sports and his love of fame.

Increasingly during the 1970s, Cosell's life began to take on a kind of surreal quality. He had struggled for a long time to make it as a sportscaster, not getting his break on network television until he was in his mid-forties. Yet the pace and trajectory of his celebrity since then had been dizzyingly fast and steep, causing Cosell to question his ambition deeply . . . and quite publicly. Old questions about the worth of his work, questions that might very well have been raised by Isadore Cohen thirty years earlier, seemed to erupt within him, and he became a fierce critic of the sports institutions that had paved his way to notoriety and fortune.

————

Memoirs and interviews that mention Cosell often repeat stories that highlight certain characteristics of his personality. One, for example, is his remarkable intellect. As mentioned earlier, Cosell had a prodigious memory. His brain was like an enormous portable hard drive, and he could recall facts and sports trivia at a moment's notice. His radio commentaries and halftime highlight presentations were delivered with few if any notes; former producers, associates, and even his grandson Justin witnessed these feats at first hand. Yet he always wrapped up in the time allotted, almost to the second.

Another character trait was his loyalty to and love for his family. Cosell was married to Emmy until her death in 1991, and from all accounts was not only faithful to her but entirely devoted to her as well. Emmy and Howard often traveled together on *Monday Night Football* trips, to Olympic venues, and to boxing matches around the globe. When Cosell's daughter Jill's marriage to Peter Cohane ended in divorce, the Cosells helped their daughter raise her children. In fact her son Justin remembers his grandfather as a constant presence in his life from an early age, not as a famous celebrity who happened to be a relative, but as an ever-present patriarch who he later realized was an internationally recognized television personality.

It was Emmy, however, who held the family together. When the two met during World War II, she was attracted to Cosell's "bright, self-assured, brash" personality, but found that he had gentle, de-monstrative qualities as well. She characterized herself as much less emotive and much more stable. Those who knew the two recognized their contrasting personalities but also noted how each managed to complement the other. As Emmy put it, they capitalized "on each other's strengths."[3] Despite Howard's fame, Emmy loved her private life and kept her husband grounded. "At parties some women treat me with such contempt," she told a reporter in 1973. "They expect me to be glamorous." She claimed that she was able to handle the pressures of her marriage because of her own strong sense of self. "I came to marriage with a fairly undamaged ego," she said. "I was always rather happy."[4] Jill describes her mother as someone "who wore blue jeans, and read five books a week. My mother was an avid, avid reader."[5] Even those who did not like Howard were fond of Emmy. Ferdie Pacheco, Muhammad Ali's doctor, who had a stormy and ultimately contentious relationship with Cosell, remembers the influence Emmy had over her husband. "She followed the abrasive Cosell, mending fences. She almost succeeded in making him a nice man," he writes.[6]

As devoted and loyal to his wife as he was, Cosell also had a pen-chant for behavior at work that only can be described as sexual harass-ment. Those who knew Cosell and saw his treatment of women al-ways remark that it never went beyond verbal wordplay. Yet it is hard to imagine that the kind of conduct he sometimes displayed toward female co-workers would be tolerated in a contemporary work set-ting. Roone Arledge remembers that when they were traveling, Co-sell would flirt with flight attendants.

> "Watch this," he said to me once, as a most attractive crewmember approached with drinks on a flight to a *Wide World* shoot. "My dear," he then said, kissing her hand, "you must forgive the little boy in me, but I am overwhelmed imagining the caresses you bestow with these feathery fingers." He drew her closer, the better to ogle her cleavage. "Is it possible for a woman to have more succulent lips? A more sensuous neck?" I was ready to crawl under my seat, but the flight attendant was smitten, as Howard, in tones befitting a smutty Elizabeth Barrett Browning, described the pleasures of her swelling breasts and dewy thighs. By the time he was finished, she was telling him—I kid you

not—of the dampness she'd experienced while riding a horse nude in Oregon.[7]

Jim Spence also remembers that "it was a common practice whenever Howard came to the main floor of ABC Sports for him to make some remark about one of the secretaries." Cosell might comment about the size of her breasts or the shape of her legs, and might say something about how he could impress her with his prowess in bed. "To be sure, it was tasteless, but I'm certain it never went beyond that. The secretaries were shocked at first, but eventually they all came to understand that it was merely Howard doing his thing," says Spence.[8]

Such incidents strongly suggest that Cosell was far less sensitive to the movement for women's rights and equality that was taking place during the 1970s than he had been to issues of racial equality throughout his career. Even more to the point, his actions speak to an era in which those who worked in television found themselves in an extremely male-dominated world. In fact there were very few women who worked in executive or creative positions at ABC Sports. For those who did, it was a struggle to advance and prove themselves. Eleanor Sanger Riger was one. Spence describes her as having been "the most prominent off-camera woman in television sports." In his words, she worked "a notch or two below the major" sporting events, but remained loyal throughout her career. Nevertheless, records from her years at ABC show that she did not especially relish her subordinate position. By the late 1970s she repeatedly sent memos to Roone Arledge and other executives asking for more challenging and important production work. Often her requests met with no response. Decisions to pass her over for a male producer were relayed through a third party.[9] For Howard Cosell, however, there were few consequences for the way he behaved toward female employees at ABC, and despite his disenchantment with the world of sports in the United States, his work as a sports broadcaster would continue to be rewarded throughout the decade.

Although Spence and Arledge show a certain level of tolerance for Cosell's treatment of women, Spence notes that Cosell's conduct became increasingly inappropriate during the 1970s, even by the standards of the time.[10] He recalls one incident when Cosell made advances to a secretary on an elevator in the presence of a sports personality he was trying to impress. The secretary warily called Cosell's bluff. Cosell escalated his actions, unbuttoning the top two buttons of her blouse. She continued to stare him down, saying, "Well, go on Howard." Spence relates that Cosell "tittered like a nervous teenager on his first sexual exploration, chewed more vigorously on his omnipresent cigar, salivated on his chin, but uttered not another word. He was really out of control. He had created a situation to try to embarrass someone and wound up being himself humiliated."[11]

Such a story suggests that Cosell was having difficulty distinguishing the boundaries between acceptable and unacceptable behavior. Yet it also suggests something about Cosell's relationship with fame. To Spence, this anecdote illustrates how Cosell would increasingly try to show off his power as a public figure. Indeed, as loudly as Cosell proclaimed his commitment to high ideals, he also clearly loved notoriety. The gap between Cosell's ambitions and his ideals widened during the 1970s, and Cosell in turn became increasingly hostile as the decade progressed.

———

A few weeks after the end of the inaugural season of *Monday Night Football,* Arledge approached Cosell about the possibility of hiring Frank Gifford for the telecasts. Cosell immediately surmised that the experienced play-by-play analyst Keith Jackson would be dropped from the program, and he was outraged. It was a prime example of what he saw as networks hiring unqualified "jocks" to do work on network television that should have been done by seasoned broadcast professionals. Arledge went ahead with the decision—angering Jackson, who read about it in the newspapers rather than hearing it firsthand from Arledge. After the first broadcast in which the new threesome worked together, at the preseason Hall of Fame game in Canton, Ohio, Cosell seized on Gifford's gaffes in the broadcast booth, sarcastically anointing him "Faultless Frank." Indeed, Gifford did make a lot of mistakes. *Monday Night Football* was his first stab at doing play-by-play, and predictably he had a lot to learn. Yet Arledge surmised that Cosell was bothered not so much by Gifford's mistakes as he was by other things. "It wasn't Frank's stumbles, it was Frank himself: his ease and self-assurance, his status and connections, his appearance and grace," wrote Arledge. "Everything Howard was not."[12]

For his part, Keith Jackson did not believe that being replaced on *Monday Night Football* was unjust. He did feel, however, that Arledge mishandled the matter, and he respected Cosell for honestly speaking his mind. He recalled: "It was just pathetic that the network would handle it like they did, but they botched it up completely. . . . But in the course of that Howard became a primary defender of mine in that he thought that I got a raw deal. Well, I didn't feel that way, but I appreciated Howard taking a stand on what he thought was right.[13]

With Gifford's hiring, Cosell was for the first time the only non-ex-athlete in the broadcast booth. He felt alone—exposed to the jibes of viewers who he knew would identify with the good-looking, smooth-talking men who had played the game. Shortly into the 1971 season Cosell began to worry that Gifford and Meredith were teaming up against him, ganging up on him. What sounded to viewers like good-natured barbs on television were in fact getting beneath Cosell's skin, while he in turn saw his booth-mates forming an unholy anti-Howard alliance. "When push came to shove," he later wrote, "Gifford and Meredith were thick as thieves. They would never take sides against each other, and somehow I always was cast as the bad guy. I could never really trust either one of them."[14]

Cosell may also have been responding to the continued outpouring of negative sentiment from sports fans across the country. As he acknowledged himself, *Monday Night Football* provided him with a unique amount of exposure to the public. Before, when he was a *Wide World of Sports* boxing announcer and a news commentator, his on-air presence was spotty. *Monday Night Football,* however, put him in front of viewers for several hours every week. "I think it was too much chocolate," says Frank Deford in reference to Cosell's exposure to the public on Monday nights. "After a while, the act soured because he was just overexposed."[15]

Increasingly Cosell began to repeat a theme—an odd one for a sportscaster: sports have an inflated importance in American life. This theme was nothing new for Cosell. He had often opened up his repertoire to include topics beyond sports. As early as the 1960s he hosted a Sunday night radio program in New York from ten to eleven called *Speaking of Everything,* in which he grilled politicians and schmoozed with celebrities. He delighted in calling William F. Buckley "Billy" and in besting him on knowledge of trade union law.[16] In virtually every interview he gave in his life, he seems to have reminded the journalist writing the article that he had been trained as a lawyer, not as a sports journalist or broadcaster. Even when discussing sports, he had a penchant for probing the subject with a depth of seriousness

Never Before Revealed . . .
The Incredible Childhood of Howard Cosell

By GEORGE HUNTER, JAMES McCANDLISH, DICK SAXTY and DAVID WRIGHT

"He was the most obnoxious person I ever met in my life . . . even when he was 6 years old . . ."

"He was very fast and very shifty and his mouth was working all the time, just like it is today . . ."

"He was nasty. He was unattractive. And none of the other kids liked him. He was as abrasive then as he is today. He hasn't changed one iota . . ."

The other kids called him "Pinhead" — and little Howard Cohen was far from popular. They described him as pompous and insulting, and a tall, skinny show-off with a pointed head.

But he grew up to be the world-famous Howard Cosell — the fast-talking, controversial sportscaster — a man millions find just as abrasive today as his childhood chums say he was 50 years ago.

Boyhood pal Maurice Umans, now a Long Island advertising executive, told The ENQUIRER that he recently met another childhood friend from the Brooklyn neighborhood where he and Cosell grew up.

"The guy said 'Did you see what happened to Cosell, that S.O.B.?'" said Umans, 60. "Everybody in our neighborhood never liked him — now the whole world doesn't like him!'

"I'll tell you very honestly," said Umans, "I don't have much good to say about him."

Here's what The ENQUIRER learned when we delved into the childhood of Howard Cosell.

Cosell officially lists his birthdate as March 25, 1920, but he was actually born two years earlier in Winston-Salem, N.C. In 1921, his father, Isidore Cohen, immigrant Polish immigrant moved the family to Brooklyn where he found work as a traveling accountant for a chain of clothing stores.

Little Howard was not a good-looking boy, say old friends.

"King Kong was a beauty compared to Howard!" recalls Muriel Vegel, who attended school one year behind Cosell at Brooklyn's P.S. 9.

"The ugliest thing about him was his little head, which looked tiny compared with his body," said Vegel, now living in Indianapolis. "That's why we called him 'Pinhead' Cohen."

Young Cosell's personality was the same then as it is now, Vegel added. "He had exactly the same arrogance then that he has now. He was the most obnoxious person I ever met —

CLASS CLOWN: Howard was about 7 when he played a clown in 1927 school play in Brooklyn, N.Y.

Silver-haired Frances Slotnick now owns a bakery just a few yards from the Cohens' old residence. "I don't think he was a happy child," she said. "He was constantly thinking, brooding . . . how you can get on, get ahead. He was ambitious."

A child whose parents were less wealthy than his playmates' parents, Cosell grew up with an inferiority complex, say his friends.

"He came from the wrong side of the tracks," said a boyhood friend.

"Our area was the Jewish society of Brooklyn. Fathers were wealthy. And he'd come up from four blocks down — which was not society."

To get to see his pals, little Howard had to cross the Irish

'PINHEAD' & PAL: Nicknamed "Pinhead" because of his small, pointed head, Howard smiles with boyhood buddy, Ira Feldblum (left) when they were 17.

FRATERNITY BROTHERS: There's no mistaking Howard Cosell (top center) who was known as Howard Cohen when he posed with his fraternity brothers for the 1936 issue of the "Violet" — New York University's yearbook.

He Was an Obnoxious, Skinny Show-Off—Disliked by Everyone

neighborhood, and gangs of Irish boys would tear after him.

"They'd try to beat him up," remembered the friend. "He ran so fast he never got caught."

Cosell worshiped athletes and was crazy about sports, said Ira Topping, today president of a Long Island paper company.

"We were crazy Brooklyn Dodger fans," said Topping, who often met with Cosell to sneak into baseball games.

"The cops would chase us," he said. "Howard's fast running came in handy, because he never got caught.

"He was a good athlete. We played ball every single day.

"But he'd never play a sport where you could get rapped. The worst he'd play was touch football. We wanted to get him to play tackle — 'cause we all wanted a whack at him.

"He was very fast and very shifty and his mouth was working all the time, just as it is today. He'd win most of the games by arguing. We'd spend half the time playing and half arguing and Howard was the biggest mouth of all."

Cosell and childhood pal Ira Feldblum shared a wild enthusiasm for baseball. "We could quote batting averages," said Feldblum, now a Manhattan businessman. "In his pompous way as a kid, because he talked so much and was positive about things, you never knew whether he was right or wrong. He would never admit that he didn't know an answer."

Topping agreed: "He'd argue that a certain statistic was right whether it was or not. For instance, he'd say 'Don't you know so-and-so is hitting .327 against left-handed pitchers?' And he'd say it so authoritatively you'd believe him.

"He was nasty. He was unattractive and none of the other kids liked him. He was as abrasive then as he is today."

The boys started a neighbor-

hood fraternity, recalled Topping. "The bylaws said that Howard Cohen could never become a member."

Umans recalled, "He was disliked. He was obnoxious. He would try to impress everybody with his vocabulary. I always said that he would never use a two-syllable word if he knew a four-syllable word."

Cosell deliberately set out to learn difficult words, Feldblum said. "When he was about 16, he took a dictionary and memorized (difficult) words as synonyms for simple words.

"He developed a tremendous vocabulary and when he was 17 he started talking the same way he talks today. He became a big

TODAY: Howard Cosell.

pain in the ass. He'd start putting on this lingo act of his and it was unbearable.

"We'd say, 'Howie, speak English! We don't understand you! He was obnoxious."

Whenever the boys' interest turned from sports to girls, Cosell struck out. "In essence, I would say he was a pimply wallflower," said Feldblum.

"He had a small pointed head and was very skinny. None of the girls liked him. If we dated or had a party, it was a case of 'Don't bring Howard.'

"He never had a girlfriend. None of the girls wanted anything to do with him. He had an inferiority complex because of his looks. He compensated with his brains — but who the hell was interested in brains?"

Cosell had dreams of a career connected with sports — but he didn't like his name. "It was too Jewish for him," said Feldblum. So when he started writing for the Alexander Hamilton High School paper, it was under the name "Howard Cosell."

From that modest start, he worked his way up to what he is today — a radio and television sports broadcaster known by almost every American.

"Everybody thought that Howie would be successful because he was smart," Feldblum mused. "But how he got where he is today is beyond me."

SPECIAL INTRODUCTORY OFFER

20 weeks for $3.95

You save $3.05 over the newsstand price when you order your NATIONAL ENQUIRER subscription at this Special Introductory Rate. So mail this coupon today with $3.95 (cash, check or money order) to:

NATIONAL ENQUIRER   N-11-28
Lantana, Fla. 33464

PLEASE PRINT

NAME

STREET

CITY_____ STATE_____ ZIP____

This offer is NOT good for subscription renewals

A 1978 biographical profile of Cosell in the *National Enquirer.*
Page image courtesy of American Media, Inc.

most other television sportscasters avoided. In 1967 Larry Merchant of the *New York Post* said that Cosell made "the world of fun and games sound like the Nuremberg trials." He loved to denounce play-by-play announcers as "shills" who shamelessly promoted athletes and boyishly gushed over the sports stars they treated like heroes.[17] As early as 1967 Cosell had publicly called sports the "toy department" of broadcasting.[18] Yet in the earlier years of his career Cosell had his own sports heroes, particularly Jackie Robinson and Vince Lombardi. By the early 1970s these two were gone, Lombardi in September 1970 and Robinson in October 1971. By the middle of the decade Cosell could openly state that sports were beneath him, that they were a waste of time and a bore.

In March 1973 Cosell got a taste of a world that was bigger than sports and perhaps an even more colorful spectacle: politics. In the wake of various issues that had arisen during the previous year's Olympics— from a controversial ending to the gold medal basketball game which the United States lost to the Soviet Union, to the debacle of the missed starting time for the sprinters—Congress was considering legislation that would protect the country's amateur athletes in international competition. Specifically, the bill aimed to help individuals caught in a turf war between the two major amateur athletic organizing institutions in the United States—the Amateur Athletic Union and the National Collegiate Athletic Association. Claiming that the dispute between these two agencies had "gone on longer than the Vietnam War," Cosell endorsed federal intervention. He urged Congress not to leave the AAU and NCAA "where you found them, because where you found them is in the gutter."[19]

Later that year Playboy Press released Cosell's memoir *Cosell*. Christopher Lehman-Haupt of the *New York Times* mocked the book, calling it a "tacky self-congratulatory celebrity story."[20] Nevertheless, the book became a best-seller. Perhaps buoyed by its popularity, Cosell looked to step into the political ring himself. At a speech before the United States Naval Academy in Annapolis in April 1974, Cosell announced that he was considering a run for the Senate, challenging incumbent Republican James L. Buckley (brother of William F. Buckley) of New York. Richard Nixon, who would resign the presidency in August of that year, was already severely damaged from the Watergate scandal and the congressional impeachment hearings that were taking place. Given the consequent crisis of faith in American politics, Cosell saw himself as someone who could bring integrity to leadership. He remarked, "There are not 10 people in the United States better qualified to run for the Senate than Howard Cosell."[21]

Political columnist George Will commented on Cosell's prospective Senate bid in October 1974. In a column about NBC reporter Edwin Newman's book *Strictly Speaking: Will America Be the Death of English?*—a diatribe against the debasement of the English language on television—Will remarked on Cosell's use of exotic vocabulary on *Monday Night Football* telecasts, going on to note, "When Newman gets done examining the gaseous language of politics, it seems oddly reasonable that Cosell is thinking of running for the Senate." In many respects, Cosell's hinting at a run for the Senate was like his use of polysyllabic vocabulary in the booth on *Monday Night Football*. Surrounded by glamorous athletes to whom he felt physically inferior, Cosell played the intelligence card, highlighting his knowledge and his education as a counterpoint. His interest in a political career, in turn, was consistent with his growing belief that sports were beneath him. By the end of the decade, Cosell's condemnation of sports became increasingly blunt and decreasingly subtle. Sports, according to Cosell, had become "the single most corrupting influence in American society."[22]

In later years Cosell reported that Hugh Carey, who was governor of New York at the time, came to visit him at the Olympic Games in Montreal in 1976 and asked him to run against Buckley. Daniel Patrick Moynihan, who was the eventual Democratic nominee, defeated Buckley that year. Cosell would recall that he had turned down the opportunity mostly out of concern for his family: "Although I think I would have won, my family was dead set against it. My wife and my daughters and even now my growing grandchildren are entitled to some privacy and some peace, and the kind of print vilification, in their minds, that I would have received had I run [was] something they didn't want to undergo." Cosell also reflected on the influence he might have had as a senator, concluding, "As a freshman Senator, I couldn't in a million years have the impact, the power of persuasion, that I enjoy with my present forums."[23]

Cosell's grandson Justin remembers his grandfather discussing his possible Senate run, and recalls that he had real ambitions of winning— "You were actually thinking you were going to knock off Pat Moynihan?" Justin later asked him, to which Cosell answered, "I probably could have won"—but doubts that he would have been fulfilled by a career as a politician: "He would have probably hated the Senate. He would have had the same problems he did with the law. It's not immediate, it's research, it's all that stuff. As much as he enjoyed a part of that, he really liked the immediacy of television."[24]

Indeed, it may also be true that Cosell chose not to run out of a desire to protect his family. For all of his public bluster and arrogance, he was, according to both observers and family members, a very different person at home. Sportswriter Myron Cope noted this in his 1967 piece on Cosell for *Sports Illustrated*. After shadowing the sportscaster at work during the day, he went home with him to Pound Ridge, New York. "Away from the radio-TV jungle," writes Cope, "a curious change comes over Cosell. He speaks softly, with an occasional dash of humor that is missing in his broadcasts." Producer Chet Forte especially noted Cosell's strong relationship with his wife. "'It's always Emmy, Emmy, Emmy—I gotta phone Emmy. I ought be home. I gotta see what Emmy thinks of the way we're gonna do this show. I don't know if she builds him up or what,' he told Cope, "but after he phones her, he seems to snap out of it."[25]

The person Cosell's family knew was very different from the sportscaster so many people despised. His grandson Justin remembers that Cosell was there for him "constantly. I spoke to him almost every day of my life. . . . My parents divorced when I was ten going on eleven. My grandfather was at my father-son dinners. . . . He was a very paternal figure"—a patriarch, Justin adds, only because "he was Howard Cosell." In reality, the family had a matriarch—Emmy.

> My grandmother was . . . really the support system that gave him the strength to do everything he did. I don't think without her he would have done any of it, frankly. . . . He couldn't live without her. My grandfather used to tell me that the greatest love story he every saw was Rachel and Jackie Robinson. You know, I think that the most dynamic relationship I've ever seen between a man and a woman was between my grandfather and my grandmother. You know, for all his crap, for all his yipping, yapping, yelling, pomposity, arrogance, you know, multi-syllabicisms, all she would have to do is give him a look and he would slink into a corner. She was like a circus trainer.[26]

Frank Deford also remembers that Cosell was "putty in her hands. God, he loved her."[27] Frank Gifford has similar recollections of Emmy's influence on her husband when she traveled with him on *Monday Night Football* trips. "It could be the most exciting game you could imagine," says Gifford, "and I'd look over my shoulder and she'd be sitting there knitting. She just went through the whole night that way, just to be with him. And it wasn't that she needed him either. Emmy was his rock. She was everything. I don't know what kind of conversations they'd have, but I also heard her many, many times: "HOWARD!" And he was like a dog rolling over for a bone."[28]

In the 1970s Cosell bought a retreat for his family—a house on the beach in the Hamptons on Long Island. It was a kind of refuge for all of the Cosells. In Justin's words, it was "our own little Kennebunkport." Boaters would sail by and shout out to Cosell, and he would bask in both the sunshine and their adoration, smiling and waving back. During the summer months he would leave on assignments from there and then return for a few days with the family. The community of vacationers also welcomed him in, and he returned the favor by sometimes providing play-by-play for a local dog show or emceeing a charity event.[29]

Throughout this time, the lack of fulfillment Cosell derived from being a sports announcer continued to trouble him. Justin remembers that while his grandfather enjoyed sports as a hobby, his interests were far more wide-ranging. "In many ways the man was a genius," he remembers.[30] Cosell wanted his grandchildren to attend liberal arts colleges and, in an echo of his own father, attend law school—not necessarily to become lawyers, but to learn how to think and reason, and to sharpen their analytical and critical capabilities. Cosell had a love of learning. He read widely, and on his desk at ABC one might just as easily find a recent book about the Vietnam War or Watergate as *The Baseball Encyclopedia* or *Ring* magazine.

In the spring of 1976 Cosell was given the opportunity to teach a course as a guest fellow of Silliman College at Yale University. For his efforts he was paid the princely sum of $600, but the experience was one that he would relish for the rest of his life. He often brought up his teaching at Yale University in the broadcast booth. When the *Monday Night* crew covered Chicago Bears games, he rarely failed to mention that their star free safety Gary Fencik had been a student of his.

The course was titled "Big Time Sports in Contemporary America," a seminar for twenty-two students, mostly history, psychology, and American studies majors. They were treated to guest visits from some of the biggest names in sports at the time: National Football League commissioner Pete Rozelle; Roone Arledge; New York Knicks star Bill Bradley (who shortly thereafter was elected to the United States Senate from New Jersey, and ran for the Democratic nomination for president in 2000); Gabe Paul, the general manager of the New York Yankees; and CBS president Bob Wood. Cosell was so impressed by his students that he threw a party for them at the pricey 21 Club in New York City. "Some are near-geniuses," he told a reporter. "I will never, never forget teaching them." Despite the students' falling a little short of genius level, he was very impressed by the work they turned in. "Some of the term papers were over 30 pages and I read many of them to my wife," he said. "The subjects ranged from 'Do Sociological Realities Confirm Jean Paul Sartre's Views of Sport?' to the Louisiana Superdome and municipal funding of stadia. I gave out four A's. I came away with the feeling that those kids truly worked hard and cared deeply about what they were doing. . . . It was a very uplifting experience."[31]

As one might expect, Cosell's course did not go untouched by controversy. In this case, however, Cosell was more the foil for an argument over the hiring of another adjunct faculty member to teach a similar seminar. Herbert Aptheker was a radical historian who had been close to W. E. B. Du Bois, the revered African American activist and scholar. A Marxist and openly a member of the National Committee of the Communist Party of the United States, Aptheker was blacklisted from teaching during the 1950s. In 1976 members of the Yale faculty offered to bring Aptheker in to teach a seminar on Du Bois. In order to do so, he needed to have a department on campus sponsor him. The most logical choice would have been the history department, since Aptheker's most famous work had been on slave resistance and the intellectual life of Du Bois. The department, however, led by C. Vann Woodward, refused to act as Aptheker's sponsor. In fact, it actively lobbied to prevent the university from honoring the political science department's offer of sponsorship. The history department's actions prompted a vocal protest from students who saw the refusal to hire Aptheker as a revival of the 1950s blacklist, and it brought the department itself under new scrutiny. Aptheker's defenders noted in particular the seeming incongruity of allowing sportscaster Howard Cosell to teach a seminar but rejecting Aptheker for his supposed lack of qualifications.[32]

On April 9 the Organization of American Historians decided to consider investigating the Yale history department, urged to do so by a petition signed by about one hundred historians in support of Aptheker. The Howard Cosell argument seemed to catch on. Students circulated a leaflet that asked, "If Howard Cosell can teach at Yale, why can't Herbert Aptheker?" A young scholar-activist named Jesse Lemisch published an article in the *Newsletter of the Radical Historians Caucus* that posed the same question. Even the conservative political columnist George Will jumped into the fray—obviously defending the Yale history department on this issue—counterarguing that the "Cosell Criterion" constituted nothing more than a "strange attempt to portray Aptheker as a victim of persecution." Ultimately, Yale reversed itself by the end of April and agreed to let Aptheker teach his seminar the following fall.[33]

Rhetorically, Aptheker's allies found in Cosell's teaching at Yale an effective illustration of a university that chose to honor celebrity and publicity over academic standards and principles. Yet their choice of Cosell as a foil may not have been an appropriate one. First, Cosell and Aptheker had more in common than might initially be apparent. Both were Jewish and from Brooklyn, both were of the same generation, and both had developed a strong interest in defending African Americans. Those who supported Aptheker's right to teach were guided by principles that were as strongly articulated as those Cosell spoke of when he defended Muhammad Ali. True, Cosell had taken a less righteous stand against the blacklist in the 1950s, but he had also generated controversy within his own profession. Rozelle joked about this, saying that after the seminar was over, he gave Gary Fencik a football with the inscription, "Welcome to the violent slavery of the National Football League."[34] While the syllabus for his Yale course is no longer available, a later course syllabus includes books that are early examples of serious, and even radical, critiques of sports: Paul Hoch's *Rip Off the Big Game: The Exploitation of Sports by the Power Elite,* Robert Lipsyte's *SportsWorld: An American Dreamland,* and Harry Edwards's *Revolt of the Black Athlete.*[35]

Two years after teaching the Yale course, Cosell was back in the classroom, this time at his alma mater, New York University. Once more the class he taught offered a critical view of the role of sports in the United States. The brief catalogue description reads: "The seminar will focus on professional and collegiate athletics in contemporary America. Emphasis will be placed on the role and function of 'big-time' sports in modern society and the organization and promotion of sports for mass consumption. A consideration of the performers, managers, promoters, owners and consumers of sports, the infrastructure of big-time sports, and the role and obligations of the broadcasting industry vis-à-vis sports producers and consumers."[36] His fuller description of the class in his syllabus provides a sharper indication of how disillusioned Cosell had become with his life as a sports broadcaster. In the early 1960s Cosell had written a series of columns for *Sport* magazine about various athletes and the thrills they had provided for fans throughout their careers.[37] These writings are standard sports journalism, embellished with Cosell's flair for storyline and narrative. Those columns stand in stark contrast to his course description, which reads:

> Big-time professional and amateur athletics in contemporary America is a phenomenon of broad social and institutional implications. In this seminar we shall examine the economic, legal, political and social implications of and for sports—and ourselves as consumers of sports entertainment—of some of the social and institutional realities of our society. We shall focus specifically on the components of the big-time sports infrastructure which have developed in response to these realities: financing, ownership, management, legislation, regulation, promotion, packaging and brokerage. In doing so we shall take a hard look at the essential contradiction at the heart of all this: that which exists between sports as an American ideal— that whole cluster of positive and wholesome values with which we have traditionally colored athletics and athletes—and the more concrete and tarnished reality of big-time sports as they actually exist—the exploitation and manipulation of this ideal by vested interests, including Mr. Cosell's own, the broadcasting industry.[38]

Each week Cosell guided his students with questions such as: "Why is there an apparent disproportion of interest and energy devoted to sports?"; "Have Americans forsaken traditional values in their quest for the vicarious 'win?'"; "Is televised sports news or entertainment?"; "What is the impact of unfair college admissions to scholastically un-qualified athletes at the expense of others?"; "How do university coaching staffs abuse athletic recruits?"; "Is a non-chauvinistic Olym-pics possible?" He takes a few special shots at one of his favorite tar-gets, sportswriters: "How independent are sportswriters?"; "What are the ethics of such practises [sic] as per-diems and other forms of payment made by professional teams to sports reporters who regu-larly cover them?" His unit titled "The Sports Fan" provides some in-sight into his particular critique of sports and society: "This session will focus on the behavior patterns of the 'masses' as sports consum-ers and the values (winning and losing) which color their feelings and reactions."[39]

These questions and commentaries about sports reveal a distinct intellectual position with regard to the critical understanding of sports and society. As Cosell taught, sports were controlled from the top—by major institutions such as the government, professional leagues, and broadcasting networks and their advertisers. Audiences—the "masses"—were prey to these institutions. One gets little sense that American sports could be anything more than "bread and circuses," a contempo-rary answer to the Roman spectacles that pacified the plebeian masses. His argument, which is either strongly implied or openly stated through-out the syllabus, is that sports institutions are too powerful, too corrupt, and too wealthy to be effectively opposed by the rank and file, and what is more, ordinary people seem to eat up the trash that is fed to them on television anyway.[40]

Unlike the Yale course, the one at NYU was not a seminar but a large lecture class. Over two hundred students attended the first session in the university's Schimmel Auditorium. They applauded as Cosell en-tered the room that first evening. But these were not boaters outside his beach house in the Hamptons, and Cosell was not in the mood for such adulation. In fact he clearly hoped that by the end of the course, the stu-dents would no longer have such reverence for either sports or celebrity more generally. He told his class as he entered: "The first thing I want you to do is stop clapping. I did not come here as a national celebrity to

Cosell lecturing at New York University in the winter of 1978. Photo courtesy Mitchell Seidel.

tell you sports anecdotes." Instead, he told his students, he would spend the semester peeling away "myths" and dealing "with the reality of sports in America today." He would teach the students about the "almost grotesque over-emphasis on the importance of sports which pervades throughout American society today."[41]

The pleasure he had derived from his Yale seminar was not apparent on that first night at NYU two years later. He told students that viewers had complained to ABC when the network preempted college football to show news footage of Egyptian president Anwar Sadat visiting Israel. When they laughed in response, he shot back: "Do you really think that's funny? Well I don't. I think it's pretty goddamn sick." Later in the same session he called former New York Yankee Mickey Mantle a "drunk and a whoremonger" and said of current New York Yankee Reggie Jackson, "Sometimes Jackson can be the biggest pain in the ass in the world." He decried the inherent racism of sports that he had seen and reported on over his career and stated a new position: that women should be entitled to the same sports facilities as men. He ended by saying that he welcomed "reasonably penetrating" questions but did not want to hear any students ask, "Do you think Walter Payton will break O. J. Simpson's NFL rushing record? Because frankly, as Rhett told Scarlet, I don't give a damn!" Finally, he warned students that the class would not be easy.[42]

Shortly after the course began, the New York University newspaper, the *Washington Square News,* reported that Cosell was dissatisfied with it. Whether this was true or not, at least one student was not impressed. Mitchell Seidel was a photographer for the paper who was assigned to take pictures of Cosell in the classroom. He remembers expecting a high-minded treatment of American sports, but being sorely disappointed. "I actually sat in on that course for a day, just out of curiosity because I'd heard that Cosell steadfastly refused to go the 'Rocks for Jocks' route and shied away from just sports talk," Seidel recalled of the class. "Unfortunately, my attendance came in February, immediately after Leon Spinks defeated Muhammad Ali, and Cosell opened his session with the following words: 'Well, I suppose you want to know about the fight. . . .' So much for keeping away from jock talk."[43]

Cosell denied reports of his own dissatisfaction, saying only that he would have to miss a few classes because of his broadcast schedule, but that he would have guest lecturers fill in on the dates when he would be absent. Nevertheless, a class of two hundred students presented Cosell with issues of classroom management that he had not faced in his Yale seminar. On March 30 a student not enrolled in the course entered the lecture hall and began aggressively talking to and harassing Cosell. A security guard removed the student, who was later taken to Bellevue Hospital's psychiatric ward, where he was held for observation. A week later Cosell resigned, citing "conflicts in his schedule."[44]

This would not be Cosell's last foray into the academic world. In 1986 he taught a similar course at Brown University. In the early 1980s the Hebrew University of Jerusalem would establish the Howard Cosell Center for Physical Education. NYU even approached Cosell in the 1980s with a proposal to create the Howard Cosell Center for Sports and Entertainment Law and Policy. Yet more than Cosell's skills as a college professor, one can sense in the reports of these two different courses a change in attitude and perspective. From the first day of class at NYU, Cosell seemed to be annoyed with his students, assuming the worst of them. His tone was bitter and cynical as he warned students not to be enamored with his celebrity and not to expect anecdotes and player statistics. In many respects this change in attitude paralleled his declining interest in and valuation of sports. At the same time, another fading career paralleled Cosell's souring emotional perspective: that of the athlete with whom he was most closely associated, Muhammad Ali.

_____

Between March 1967, when he knocked out Zora Folley in the seventh round, and October 1970, when he knocked Jerry Quarry out in the third, Muhammad Ali had not been in a professional fight. His conviction for draft evasion, and his ban from professional boxing had prevented him from defending his title for three and a half years. When he did return to the ring, he was twenty-eight years old, still in his prime, but not in the shape he had been in four years earlier. Boxing fans no longer saw the lean, quick, graceful fighter they had once watched. The new Ali looked heavier, moved more slowly. He still had the confidence of old but not the training regimen.

In 1970 the obstructions that kept Ali from fighting began to tumble. He was no longer champion, but boxing commissions around the country were at least granting him the right to fight. First was Georgia, which did not even have a boxing commission, and then the most important venue of all, New York. After winning his first two fights after his suspension, first against Quarry, then a technical knockout of Oscar Bonavena in fifteen rounds, Ali was ready to take on the champion, Joe Frazier. Their fight was set for Madison Square Garden in March 1971. This gave Ali only three months to prepare, but he was, as usual, confident.

Both before the fight and in the ring, Ali mocked Frazier, calling him an "Uncle Tom." Nevertheless, it was Frazier's night. In front of twenty thousand, including some of the most glamorous celebrities of the time, Frazier knocked Ali down in the eleventh round and went on to win by a unanimous decision. This may not have been the end of Ali's career, but for the first time his skills as a boxer were successfully challenged. Nevertheless, Cosell saw this as Ali's finest moment. "He did go the distance," Cosell wrote after the fight, "and in the process he inflicted untold physical damage upon Frazier, who ever since that day has shown no sign of being the very good fighter that he had been. In my view the Frazier fight was an authentication of Ali's greatness as a fighter."[45]

In May 1971 Ali received perhaps the most important unanimous decision of his life. The United States Supreme Court overthrew his conviction, making him now truly free to fight. Cosell remembered thinking after the Ali-Frazier "Fight of the Century" that fans would clamor for a rematch, but that did not take place for quite some time. Frazier, angered by Ali's comments—that he was not black enough, that he was not the "People's Champion," that he was not smart, that he was ugly, that he was the white man's favorite—refused to get into the ring with Ali, and instead opted to fight a rising heavyweight by the name of George Foreman in Kingston, Jamaica, on January 22, 1973. Foreman won easily, knocking Frazier to the floor multiple times and winning by a technical knockout in the second round. Cosell, broadcasting for ABC, screamed: "Down goes Frazier! Down Goes Frazier!" If Ali was to fight for the title, it would have to be against the powerful young Foreman.

A few months later, however, hopes that this might happen seemed to be dashed. Ali had scheduled what he was treating as a warm-up match against an unheralded fighter named Ken Norton in San Diego for that March. Ali had fought ten bouts since his loss to Frazier, and he had won them all. Cosell was not concerned about Norton, but he did note that Ali looked heavy and out of shape. Nevertheless, he would remember Ali's trainer, Angelo Dundee, saying of Norton before the fight: "He's tailor-made for Ali. . . . He's wide open for a left, he has no right, kind of chops with it, his only good punch is a left hook to the belly, and he has an open stance and drags the one leg." The night before the bout, Cosell walked in and out of his hotel, and each time, until late into the night, he saw Ali entertaining crowds of fans in the coffee shop.[46] The next day, on his way into the ring, Ali showed Cosell his own prediction, written inside his boxing glove: a knockout in the third. Instead, Norton hurt Ali more than any fighter had done before. At some point during the bout he broke Ali's jaw, and for the second time since returning to the ring, Muhammad

Ali lost. It looked, for all practical purposes, as if Ali's career was over. Indeed, when Cosell wrote about the fight in his book *Cosell,* it was in the last of three chapters devoted to Ali, the one titled "The Fall."

Norton gave Ali a rematch that following September, enough time for Ali's jaw to heal. Ali had vowed never to return to the ring out of shape again, and this time he was able to defeat Norton, albeit by a split decision. Frazier, too, finally gave Ali a rematch on January 28, 1974. Four days before the bout, in the ABC studios in New York, the two fighters sat with Cosell to review the film of their first contest and to promote the upcoming one. Early in the broadcast they began to insult each other until Ali once again disparaged Frazier's intelligence. Frazier became incensed, rose to his feet, and challenged Ali to fight right there in the studio. The two scuffled, with representatives of each fighter rushing onto the set to break up the brawl. Frazier left the set, and Ali sullenly stayed to finish his commentary with Cosell. When the two did meet in the ring later that week, it was a fight that Dave Kindred describes as being "as dull as the first had been brilliant."[47] Ali won, which earned him a chance to fight Foreman and to regain the heavyweight title.

This, however, seemed to be a dubious honor. Foreman was a big, powerful fighter who had not just defeated his opponents; he had rarely had to go beyond the second round. The two fighters who had given Ali the greatest trouble—Frazier and Norton—had been finished off by Foreman in two rounds each. In March 1974 Ali witnessed Foreman (in the words of Cosell) reduce "Norton to boxing rubble" firsthand, sitting ringside with Cosell in Caracas, Venezuela.[48]

The fight with Foreman was set for October 30, 1974, in Kinshasa, Zaire. Ali told Cosell that the fight would be in the Congo, where Cosell would be "cooked." Not surprisingly, Foreman was the overwhelming favorite. Cosell went on the air himself to predict a Foreman victory, providing a virtual warning to Ali not to get into the ring. Certainly Ali's most recent fights did not say much for his abilities now at thirty-two, and Foreman had looked devastatingly strong in his last two victories. When Cosell went on the air to give audiences his prediction, he sounded more like a man delivering a eulogy than a fight analyst.

> The time may have come to say good-bye to Muhammad Ali,
> because very honestly, I don't think he can beat George
> Foreman. . . . Maybe he can pull off a miracle. But against George

Foreman? So young? So strong? So fearless? Against George Foreman, who does away with his opponents, one after another, in less than three rounds? It's hard for me to conjure with that. . . . After this fight, I suspect Ali will retire. And through all of the years, my own memories of him will be as a fighter, and as the strange and curious and gregarious and engaging and sometimes cruel, and sometimes family man that he is.[49]

Cosell's maudlin tone was an accurate expression of his feelings, as he no doubt harbored worries that Foreman could literally kill Ali in the ring. After all, Foreman had won forty fights in his career, thirty-seven by knockouts. Ali, however, was not cowed by Cosell's concerns. In fact, he fed off them, using Cosell's prediction as fodder for his own brand of brash humor.

> Howard Cosell, you told everybody I don't have a chance. You told them I don't have nothing but a prayer. Well, chump, all I need is a prayer, because if that prayer reaches the right man, not only will George Foreman fall, but mountains will fall. And you're always talking about, "Muhammad, you're not the same man you were ten years ago." Well, I asked your wife, and she told me you're not the same man you were two years ago. I'm going to let everybody know that that thing that you got on your head is a phony, and it comes from the tail of a pony [50]

Ali pronounced the fight the "Rumble in the Jungle" and claimed to have superior technique that would be more than enough to defeat Foreman's tremendous strength. Indeed, Ali pulled off perhaps the greatest upset in international sports history. In what proved to be a prescient observation, Cosell compared Foreman's pre-fight stare to that of Sonny Liston. Ali improvised a strategy against Foreman, drawing partly on his knowledge that his opponent had little experience carrying a fight into the late rounds. Abandoning his original, or at least his stated, strategy of dancing around the ring, Ali leaned against the ropes in the second round. Cosell, announcing the match, said as he observed:, "This would seem to be the most dangerous tactic that Ali could use. To give up movement and stay against the ropes."[51] Foreman punched at him continuously, but Ali stayed up, taunting his opponent to punch harder. Ali called it his "rope-a-dope" strategy.

Foreman, by the middle of the sixth round, was worn out. Toward the end of the eighth round, Ali attacked his opponent with a left-right combination and knocked him to the canvas. Foreman staggered to his feet by the end of the count, but the referee decided that he had had enough. Cosell cried into the microphone, "This is almost incredible!" Ali had regained his championship.

Less than a year later Ali once again took on his old rival Frazier, this time in the Philippine capital of Manila. In a brutal fight he won by a technical knockout in the fourteenth round. Yet unlike with Foreman, he did not train excessively for this bout. He also stooped to new lows when taunting Frazier, holding up a toy gorilla before the cameras: "This is the way he looks when you hit him. . . . Come on, gorilla, we're in Manila. Come on, gorilla, this is a thrilla."[52] Frazier was enraged by the time he entered the ring with Ali, and unlike Foreman, he had the stamina to last into the late rounds. By the twelfth Ali was able to counterpunch a rally, and he continued into the next round. "The mouthpiece went! You saw it fly out!" Cosell yelled as Ali's right struck Frazier in the face. Finally the fight was called a technical knockout, Frazier's face so bloody and swollen by now that he could barely see.[53]

Ali had also been damaged, however, and the rest of his career in the ring would betray signs of a steadily deteriorating fighter. He could no longer move around the ring the way he used to. He was heavy and was fighting often. In the twenty-three months following his brutal fight with Frazier, Ali had six bouts. In 1976 he barely defeated Ken Norton in a decision at Yankee Stadium, and in February 1978 he finally lost his title to a wild young fighter named Leon Spinks in a title bout in Las Vegas. They met for a rematch in New Orleans in September of that year. Once again Spinks came out wildly throwing punches, but this time Ali was able to establish control. Cosell noted during the tenth round that Ali was "in command of the fight," exclaiming: "What an extraordinary career. What an extraordinary man he has been!"[54]

Despite the calls from fans and sportswriters to retire, however, Ali continued to fight, losing to his old sparring partner Larry Holmes in October 1980 and to Trevor Berbick in a unanimous decision in 1981. It soon became apparent by the early 1980s that Ali's extensive fighting schedule and career had taken a serious toll on his health.

His speech had become slurred, and his hands trembled. Cosell was still on television, but it was clear that his longtime verbal sparring partner would no longer be able to sit by his side.

Reflecting on the relationship between Cosell and Ali, Dave Kindred writes, "As Cosell did not truly know Ali, Ali never knew Cosell." Kindred actually knew them both about as well as any sports journalist, and he makes the insightful observation that both were narcissists—"blind to the other's needs except as those need met their own." He notes in particular that Cosell never endorsed Ali's conversion to the Nation of Islam, even though Ali's religion, and his support for African nationalism, had become the core of Ali's identity. In fact, early on, Cosell did not even agree with Ali's position on the Vietnam War. This changed only when, in 1967, his daughter Hillary began organizing protests at her high school against U.S. involvement in Vietnam.[55]

If what Kindred says is true, then during the 1970s Cosell and Ali might seem to have gradually lost their need for each other. The Foreman fight in Zaire provides a good example. For Ali, the fight was in some ways the ultimate expression of his nationalist ideals. It was held in Africa. Don King was the promoter, the first African American to promote a major heavyweight title fight. He had won an unparalleled bid from Zaire's U.S. client dictator, Mobutu Sese Seko, to host the event, one in which both contestants were African American. As part of the festivities surrounding the boxing match, there would also be a musical celebration featuring James Brown, the Spinners, and B. B. King. Ali's opposition to the Vietnam War had made him a hero in Africa, and he in turn claimed that he considered Africa more his true home than America. In other words, the fight in Zaire was a celebration of black nationalism, one that did not require—indeed, was almost more authentic without—the support of a white television commentator like Cosell.

This does not mean that some prominent white people did not find it useful to identify with Ali during this bout. The historian Julio Rodriguez writes that, in fact, white liberals, who, during the 1970s post–Great Society era, were increasingly portrayed as social "elites," drew upon their identification with African American boxers to provide them with a sense of authenticity and connection to working-class America. As an example he cites the documentary by Leon Gast memorializing the Ali-Foreman fight, titled *When We Were Kings*. The film is ostensibly about the fight and the concert that accompanied it. But Rodriguez argues that in addition to drawing on images of primitivism to represent African culture and history, it also narrates the event not through the memories of Ali or Foreman but through those of Norman Mailer and George Plimpton. Rodriguez argues that the film thus becomes more about two white writers who attached themselves symbolically to Ali, than about the fight itself or even about Ali himself.[56]

Cosell was in a different position from Mailer and Plimpton. As we saw earlier, he did not share their commitment to liberal politics, nor did he feel the same level of attachment to Ali, even though he proclaimed himself to be a liberal and a defender of Ali's rights. While Mailer and Plimpton may have felt themselves beginning to fade from the cultural stage in the mid-1970s, Cosell was more of a presence than ever. If Ali had helped make him a celebrity in the 1960s, Cosell had firmly established himself without Ali by 1975. Unlike Mailer and Plimpton, Cosell did not come to Zaire following Ali's star; in fact he predicted Ali's defeat. David Halberstam, who was known for his investigative journalism on the Vietnam War, and who later went on to write critically acclaimed books on sports, identified with Ali in much the same way as Mailer and Plimpton, despite the boxer's affiliation with Cosell, whom he disliked. In 1980 he picked Ali to win his second-to-last fight, his ill-fated title defense against Larry Holmes, stating, "I remain faithful to him despite his too-considerable association with Howard Cosell.[57] Unlike in the 1960s, then, Ali was no longer a cause for Cosell. His prefight prediction is a telling one, not so much because it was incorrect, but because of the way Cosell portrayed Ali as an anachronism, a figure mired in the past, an athlete who might be nostalgically admired but was no longer taken seriously. For Ali's part, Cosell was more his foil than his ally, a motivation for winning rather than his most prominent defender in the court of public opinion.

———

Cosell may have been a constant source of offensive comments to women in the workplace, but he was also a defender of women's rights to equal opportunity. In fact, in his book *Like It Is,* he praises Betty Friedan and Gloria Steinem, albeit in order to diminish the social import of one particular female athlete by comparison. Writing about women's tennis champion Billie Jean King, he says that she was no Friedan or Steinem.

> They are the ones who have endured the years of work, the years of trying to educate people—not just men, but, almost tragically, women themselves—the years of recruitment, the years of grappling with ignorance and the years of suffering ridicule because of that ignorance. They are the ones who have been totally committed to the fight for equality for women: equality of opportunity, equality of pay, equality under the law. They are the ones who have sought the right to control their own bodies, to change ancient abortion laws, to eradicate the archaic sexual attitudes toward women. They, and some others, have been the intellectual and motivational core of the continuing growth of the women's rights movement in this country.[58]

This said in a book published by Playboy Press.

Nevertheless, by the late summer of 1973, King was set to play an aging tennis hustler named Bobby Riggs in a nationally televised event, known as the "Battle of the Sexes." Roone Arledge chose Cosell as his announcer. The King-Riggs match was a spectacle emblematic of the slow pace of change in attitudes toward female athletes at the time. King was thirty years old in 1973, and was one of the top three female tennis players that year, and arguably the most successful women's tennis player of her era. Riggs was a fifty-five-year-old retired professional who had been an excellent player in his day, ranking number one in the world in 1941, 1946, and 1947. He had won Wimbledon and the U.S. Open, but he was obviously long past the prime of his career. In the 1970s he had begun to earn a living by setting up matches against the top female tennis stars of the era, and making male chauvinist claims that any male tennis player was better than any female tennis player. In May 1973 he challenged the number-one women's tennis player, Margaret Court, to a match that was nationally televised. He beat her convincingly, winning a best-of-three set match, 6–2, 6–1. The next week he was pictured on the cover of *Sports Illustrated* leaning confidently against the post of a tennis net with the caption "Never Bet against This Man."[59] More significantly, female tennis players became the butt of jokes told by men around the United States. For

King, who had spent her career promoting women's tennis, the right of women to play as professionals, and women's sports more generally, Bobby Riggs was a disaster, and she took the first opportunity that she could to accept his challenge.

In the long buildup to the match, Cosell began to hang around with Riggs. He became somewhat enamored of him, enjoying his smart-aleck sense of humor and his tricky style of playing tennis. Former tennis players Gene Scott, Jack Kramer, and Billy Talbert, friends of Cosell's, all had predicted that Riggs would beat King. By the time of the match on September 20, 1973, Cosell was sure that Riggs would win. His certainty was all the more confirmed when, only weeks before the showdown, King forfeited a match against Julie Heldman at the U.S. Open, seemingly exhausted from the heat.

Like a boxing match, the "Battle of the Sexes" took on the aura of a dramatic spectacle, and the broadcast was to be structured accordingly. The promoter of the event, Jerry Perenchio, was in fact the promoter of the first Ali-Frazier fight. He chose ABC and Cosell to broadcast the match in order to highlight it as a mock-epic battle between women's liberation and male chauvinism. Arledge and Chuck Howard at ABC in turn created a broadcast booth in which there would be a male expert and a female expert, with Cosell as the moderator. Women's tennis professional Rosie Casals was to be the female commentator, and originally, Jack Kramer was chosen to represent the men. King objected to him, however, and persuaded ABC to change announcers. At the suggestion of Cosell, the network brought in Cosell's friend Gene Scott, a former top-ranked U.S. amateur and author of a popular book on tennis.

Before the match, the two players met in the Houston Astrodome. Riggs, sporting a bright yellow "Sugar Daddy" sport jacket, made his entrance in a chariot pulled by young women wearing T-shirts advertising the same sponsor; King was carried in on a throne wearing a white tennis dress with blue sequins. King dominated the contest from the very beginning, winning 6–4, 6–3, 6–3. The match was not even that close. King played the game cautiously; had she been more aggressive, she could have made it an even more lopsided victory. During the match, as it became increasingly apparent that Riggs's tactics would not work against King, Casals became increasingly excited and vocal in her support of King. In fact, this was what she had been instructed to do, and it was her comments, not Cosell's, that would cause audiences and sportswriters to respond with ire. Nevertheless, Cosell also spoke bluntly about what he was witnessing as Riggs went down. Late in the match, when Scott suggested that Riggs might be employing a new tactic, Cosell responded that the aging hustler just looked "dog tired."

The "Battle of the Sexes" drew entertainment value from the political struggles for women's equality. It took place only a year after Title IX of the Education Amendments of 1972 became law, a statute that would later be interpreted to protect equal access to educational opportunities for women and men, including within the realm of school sports. Yet the showdown between Riggs and King was also theater, and by the mid-1970s Cosell's career seemed to be drifting in a theatrical direction rather than toward the serious pursuits of which he saw himself more worthy. Early in the decade, in addition to his appearance in *Bananas,* he was a guest star, playing himself on the situation comedies *The Odd Couple* and *Nanny and the Professor.* He appeared on a number of Dean Martin celebrity roasts, performing in sketches and serving as the subject of verbal quips and clever impersonations. Shortly after he gave up on his dream of running for the United States Senate, ABC created a program for Cosell, the first show on television that would use the title *Saturday Night Live.* (Called *Saturday Night Live with Howard Cosell,* was also the first program on which future NBC *Saturday Night Live* performer Bill Murray had a regular spot.) In fact, the long promotional video for his show makes light of Cosell's political ambitions. Several celebrities, politicians, and newsmakers appear on the screen, commenting about Cosell and his upcoming show, including Barbara Walters, who says, "I hope everyone will watch Howard Cosell's new nighttime show, because if it's successful, he won't run for the Senate." [60]

In the promotional video Cosell makes light of himself as well, having fun with his own image and his well-established reputation for self-absorption. After a string of introductory insults by Senator Lowell Weicker, Woody Allen, Barbara Walters, Mike Wallace, and former New York mayor John Lindsay, Cosell responds:

> The people who you have just seen are throwing spitballs at a battleship. In 1975 and '76, the Sullivan Theater will be alive and well with Howard Cosell. We're not dealing with just an ordinary sports guy. In my time, I have sparred with Rickles, parried with

Carson, quipped with Hope, and flipped with Wilson. You talk
about Woody Allen: I made him a star in *Bananas*. [The video cuts
back to Allen shaking his head no.] I've hosted the Cavett, the
Frost, the Griffin, and the Douglas shows, and above all, I have
invaded prime time and won with *Monday Night Football*. Ask
Carol Burnett. They moved her to Saturday night. Ask Bill Cosby.
He's sent me a telegram of unconditional surrender. Ask NBC.
They had their last hurrah with the Monday night movies with
The Godfather. The Monday night movies will be elsewhere this
fall. Do you know what we're going to do? We're going to translate
to the world of entertainment the very same techniques that we
have brought to the wide world of sports, where ABC is an
unchallenged number one.[61]

Indeed, Cosell had hosted most of the big talk shows of the era, fill-
ing in as a guest host for Dick Cavett, David Frost, Merv Griffin, and
Mike Douglas. On these programs he got to do some of the serious
interviews with political leaders that he had long desired, but on *Saturday Night Live with Howard Cosell* he also got to play the role of
show business promoter. He tried, in vain, to get the Beatles back together for the show, then promoted a group called the Bay City Roll-
ers as the "next Beatles." He performed in sketches but told *TV Guide:*
"I am not going to do what I believe I don't do well. I am not going to
sit on a horse, pretending to be Cher, as I did on the Sonny Bono show."
As much as he tried to make fun of himself, however, his real sense of
alienation and bitterness come through. In the same article he told
Melvin Durslang of *TV Guide:* "The press tried for years to destroy
me, but it couldn't because I am too strong, too stable, too honest.
Well, it's all over now and I have won. The public believes me and
won't allow you [the press] to impeach my credibility. I have won
with the public because I am honest."[62]

In 1976 Cosell hosted a program called *Battle of the Network Stars,*
in which celebrities from ABC, CBS, and NBC competed in events
ranging from touch football to golf to tug-of-war to a track relay. He
maintained a tone of mock seriousness throughout, but he was once
again involved in an event that was purely about entertainment. That
same year he became one of the commentators for *Monday Night Baseball,* broadcasting a sport that he had long derided as anachronistic,

and whose promoters he had criticized for wrapping their game in a cloak of patriotism.

While Cosell may have willingly taken these assignments—Justin Cosell recalls that his grandfather thought *Battle of the Network Stars* was "hilarious"—his new ambition to engage in something more serious remained.[63] When Roone Arledge became the head of the news division at ABC in 1977, he brought Barbara Walters over from NBC, offering her a contract for what was then the outlandish sum of $1 million a year. For Cosell, however, this seemed a prime opportunity to move into a more substantive position in the network. He wanted Arledge to make him the anchor of the new ABC news program *World News Tonight,* alongside Jim McKay, with whom he had worked on broadcasts of *Wide World of Sports.* Arledge refused, a rejection that particularly hurt Cosell. As Arledge later wrote, "I'd won another black mark in his secret book of grievances."[64] This was not only Arledge's recollection. Justin Cosell remembers that his grandfather took the refusal to make him news anchor very hard, and believes that it was one of the things that soured Cosell's mood by the end of the 1970s.[65]

Instead of anchoring the network news, Cosell was reunited with Keith Jackson as a commentator on *Monday Night Baseball* beginning in the summer of 1976. His responsibilities included hosting the League Championship Series and the World Series. (ABC alternated with NBC, covering one or the other each year.) Despite his unhappiness at being passed over as a news analyst, the 1977 World Series provided Cosell with a platform for social commentary. The New York Yankees defeated the Los Angeles Dodgers in six games, the dramatic sixth game featuring Reggie Jackson hitting three home runs to cap off his first tumultuous year in pinstripes, playing for owner George Steinbrenner and volatile manager Billy Martin. Beyond baseball, however, the summer of 1977 had been a devastating one for New York City, marked by the hunt for the serial killer known as Son of Sam, and by a power blackout and subsequent riot that permanently scarred large sections of Brooklyn and the Bronx. During Game Two, ABC cameras captured a book depository burning beyond the outfield stands of Yankee Stadium. "There it is, ladies and gentlemen," Cosell said. "The Bronx is burning." Cosell's tired voice and cynical tone framed the image of the burning building in a way that was consistent with a more widespread disillusionment with urban life.[66]

Yet if Cosell was growing increasingly disillusioned, much of the rest of the country was also becoming increasingly fed up with Cosell. By the mid-1970s, newspapers and magazines were printing reader mail that was ever more critical of him. A letter from Paul Milkman of Brooklyn to the *New York Times* magazine in September 1974, for example, took exception to the idea that only racists and jingoistic patriots hated Howard Cosell:

> To set the record straight, Cosell was not the only figure in the sports world to support Ali. In the heart of cosmopolitan New York, it was very difficult *not* to support Ali. . . . Cosell's distinction was to turn his support for Ali into the sacrifice of the century. It provided him with an opportunity for moralistic posturing. Such posturing is what makes Cosell irritating. Particularly when it is joined by his characteristic ignorance. Never did a man who knows so little pretend to know so much. But none of this makes him worthy of hatred. That takes special talent.[67]

Milkman went on to criticize Cosell for engaging in "character assassination," particularly in the way he had criticized Stan Wright during the 1972 Olympics.

Lest anyone think that this represents only the opinions that appeared in the highbrow *New York Times* magazine, V. W. Russell of Sun City Center, Florida, sent a letter expressing a similar sentiment to the tabloid the *National Enquirer* in 1977. Unlike Milkman's letter, however, Russell's does not attempt to distance Cosell-hating from racism. The attention to Cosell's physical appearance and the accusation of network nepotism instead hint at the kind of anti-Semitic bias that Deford noted.

> By far the most nauseating and repulsive performer to grace, or rather, disgrace the tube, is the pompous, overbearing Howard Cosell. This little man is thrust upon the television equipped with colossal arrogance and an ego that has no limits. While purporting to be a sports announcer, Cosell delights in displaying his extensive vocabulary. Unlike Abraham Lincoln, he selects the largest possible words available to his pseudo-intelligence, attempting to dazzle the audience with his scholastic background. He has a nasal, droning and exceedingly boring voice that emanates from a rather homely,

pinched-in face, with two closely set, beady little eyes that glisten like raisins in the snow. This is all topped off by a ridiculously obvious hairpiece. This flabby, aging announcer surely must have a relative who owns ABC television. How else could he hold his job, much less be overpaid so extravagantly?[68]

Even some viewers purporting to be Cosell fans began to write letters displaying an increasingly critical tone. Horkey Turek of Petersburg, Virginia, wrote to ABC newscaster Frank Reynolds in 1980 that she enjoyed Cosell, "except for the times he is somewhat pompous as in 'the general public needs simple terms' and of course doesn't follow his guide line." Turek continued: "'T'was the night of the ALL-STAR GAME, 8 July 1980. The one and only Howard C. used the word 'ADJUSTABILITY.' Now I know he is popular and may well have written his own dictionary by now— (else it's one of those wrong words which have become proper since so many dumb people use them) —HOWSOMEEVER—methinks the noun is ADJUSTMENT. And yes, I have checked with much care!"[69]

Even the first mother of the United States, Lillian Carter, stated that she wished "he would be taken off the air." Perhaps the low point came in 1977, when *Philadelphia Daily News* sports columnist Stan Hochman alleged that Cosell had initiated an altercation as he boarded a plane from Los Angeles to New York. According to Hochman, he was seated when Cosell walked down the aisle. Hochman remembers sarcastically saying to Cosell, "What a pleasure." Cosell responded by unleashing a string of insults and finally slapping Hochman on the head repeatedly.[70] This was not the first time Cosell had expressed hostility toward a sportswriter, but like his meltdown in Minnesota earlier in the decade, it was a public display that betrayed a remarkable degree of frustration. By the end of the 1970s, Cosell's value to the network was finally being openly questioned, not so much at New York headquarters as it was among affiliate stations around the country. Jim Spence remembers an affiliates' meeting in which station managers suggested that Cosell be taken off the air.

> Roone and I attended the ABC affiliated stations board of governors meeting in Los Angeles in 1980. Kent Replogle, who ran our Kansas City station and was chairman of the affiliate sports committee, made a mini-speech [before all the top executives at ABC] about how many of our stations felt that we should take

Cosell off the air. I thought that we should respond. It quickly became clear that Roone was not going to say anything, so I stood up and did a little mini-speech back, saying how much Howard had contributed to our success and that CBS or NBC would hire him in a minute if we let him go. "Yes, he's controversial, stirs up comment, and is much criticized, but he's a positive force for us, and has been, is, and will continue to be." I sat down. There was no response, but the point of raising this story is that for the first time, we received negative commentary about Cosell from the ABC affiliate body.[71]

Replogle, the affiliate representative who objected to Cosell, was later named in a lawsuit by Christine Craft, an anchorwoman who alleged that she had been rejected for a position because of her age and gender. When she was thirty-eight years old, Replogle had told Craft that she was "too old, unattractive, and not deferential enough to men."[72] Replogle's objection to Cosell may very well have been inspired by similar prejudices, yet there is no doubt that by the end of the 1970s, he was echoed by many others who were tired of Cosell. Arledge's silence during the affiliates' meeting suggests that he was growing less enamored with Cosell himself. He kept Cosell on the air, however, and in an effort to appease him, allowed him to develop his own program, a show called *SportsBeat,* which proved to be one of the most critically acclaimed and least watched programs that Cosell created in his career.

7 Balancing Accounts

You know, I don't think anybody took fuller advantage of
his celebrity than Howard. He could get away with anything.
—Peter Mehlman, writer and producer for *SportsBeat*

In the late summer of 1981, ABC presented an entirely new
sports program called *SportsBeat.* It was created by and
starred Howard Cosell as a concession to him from the executives at ABC, who knew that he was getting tired of his
role and his position within ABC Sports. In fact the hard
feelings between Cosell and his employers seemed to be
mutual by this time, if they had not been for some years.

SportsBeat was an in-depth interview and investigative
journalism program. Those who worked on it recall it as being like the CBS newsmagazine *60 Minutes,* only focused on
sports. The one thing that made it different from other sports
programming at ABC was that it was not under the aegis of
ABC Sports. In fact, *SportsBeat* had its own floor at the network's New York offices. The separation was no accident. It
was a reflection of Cosell's own alienation from other sports
programming and from the network. During the first half of
the 1980s, Cosell would end his major contributions to television sports broadcasting. He covered his last game for
Monday Night Football in 1983, his last baseball game in 1985,
and his last boxing match in 1982. During these years, however, he considered *SportsBeat* to be his top priority and
hoped that it would become the crowning achievement of his
career.

SportsBeat won critical praise, but it also lacked a strong
viewership, and by 1985 it was off the air. Cosell, of course,
blamed the network, whose executives he accused of trying
to meddle in the content of the program. The executives, in
turn, claimed that *SportsBeat* was a financial drain that failed
to build an audience. Whatever the case, television—and

particularly sports television—was entering a new era. By the 1980s, the arrival of cable television and all-sports networks such as ESPN posed a variety of new challenges for the networks that would dramatically change sports programming. Cosell's decline at ABC coincided with these changes to the structure of television. No longer would a single voice like Cosell's be such a commanding presence as it was during the years when three networks, all centered in New York, dominated the medium in the United States.

In the early 1980s all three major networks promised to create programming that would combine television journalism with sports coverage. Cosell took the challenge posed by NBC seriously, largely because his daughter Hillary was now a producer for NBC Sports. After starting as a monthly program, *SportsBeat* began regular weekly broadcasts on February 7, 1982. Unlike *Saturday Night Live with Howard Cosell* or *Battle of the Network Stars*, *SportsBeat* promised to allow Cosell to develop a serious and critical exploration of the issues important to sports. It was billed as television's only regular show dedicated to sports journalism.[1] Indeed, the network provided Cosell with almost total freedom to shape it as he wished. He staffed it with young producers and writers, who not only were cheaper than more seasoned professionals but also would be less likely to take offense at his personality. Indeed, many who came to work for the program arrived having known Cosell as viewers and fans and had a kind of reverence for their new boss. Jimmy Roberts, now an author and anchor, reporter, and commentator for NBC Sports, worked on *SportsBeat*. "My impression of Howard before I met him," recalls Roberts, "was . . . [that] he was a larger-than-life figure. And after I met him, I realized he actually was a larger-than-life figure."[2]

In many respects, *SportsBeat* served as a metaphor for Cosell's position as the biggest name in sports and yet, simultaneously, the ultimate outsider to the sports establishment. Cosell headed the program as an independent operation, apart from the direction of ABC Sports, and it drew concern from company executives almost as soon as it went on the air. Predictably, Cosell felt in turn that the network was not giving *SportsBeat* the respect he thought it deserved. In an unidentified clipping in the collected papers of Roone Arledge, a short article about *SportsBeat* quotes an unnamed producer saying: "We're putting together a weekly half-hour show in three segments, with a staff of 12 people. That includes two secretaries!" The article continues: "By way of contrast, ABC's *20/20* broadcasts a weekly one-hour program with a staff of over 90. *SportsBeat* has been *busy*." A handwritten note attached to the clipping from Roone Arledge, addressed to "Howard," angrily dresses down the source of this quotation: "You might want to explain to this 'one producer' that we are all in the same family and that to praise his show it is unnecessary to compare it to other ABC shows. In addition to the basic bad taste it also invites other comparisons. . . . Roone."[3]

Yet despite the friction that it created with those who ranked above Cosell, those who worked below him on the program often were extremely loyal, looking at him with the perspective of a young family member relating to a quirky patriarch. *SportsBeat* employed a group of remarkably talented young sportswriters, including Roberts, Peter Mehlman (who later went on to write and produce for the television program *Seinfeld*), and the accomplished journalist and editor Peter Bonventre. Mehlman moved to ABC from a position as a sportswriter for the *Washington Post,* eventually gaining experience as a producer for *SportsBeat.* To Mehlman, Cosell was a pleasure to work for, someone who brought irreverence to sports journalism—as well as something he identifies as Cosell's "locker room sense of humor." Mehlman recalls: "He used to just come by my office and go, 'Petah, I'm going to go take a tinkle. Come on with me.'" He brought this wit to his relationships with those whom he interviewed on the program as well. Mehlman remembers that when interviewing African American athletes, Cosell would frequently add a final question: "At the end of an interview Howard would go, 'Okay, just one more question. Why is it that you hate the Jewish people?'" Most often, the interviewee would be caught off-guard for a few seconds and then break out in laughter.[4]

Like Mehlman, Jimmy Roberts has fond memories of working for Cosell. What others might identify as annoying egotism Roberts found endearing. For example, Cosell once summoned production assistant Kevin Granath into his office. "He would call him 'Kevster,'" recalls Roberts.

> "Come in here. I need you to go down to the corner to the hot dog stand, and get me two hot dogs, well done, tell him they're for me." Now, what you've got to understand if you've never had a hot dog from a vendor on the street in New York, number one, . . . the

stuff is cooking all day in lukewarm water. . . . And number two, I'm doubting whether the guy who was the hot dog man on the corner of Fifty-sixth and Sixth in those days . . . he might not have even spoken English. But the fact that Howard was so deluded [as] to think that the guy thought, like, "Oh, this hot dog is for Howard Cosell!" You know, he lived on another planet.

Roberts, however, does not tell this story as an example of Cosell's hubris. "He was the only one who could get away with this stuff," says Roberts. "I mean, it was very endearing. . . . I'm not saying this to poke fun at Howard."[5]

Indeed, as Roberts remembers, Cosell used to say that television was defined by the "three C's": Carson, Cronkite, and Cosell. Throughout his chaotic tenure on *Monday Night Football* and his continuing coverage of Ali, Frazier, and Foreman during the 1970s, Cosell had become a franchise. For better or worse, he was synonymous with the yellow blazer that symbolized ABC Sports, the single most recognizable personality on the network. Cosell, of course, was more than aware of this, and was never shy about reminding anyone who interviewed him of his status. Although even Cosell would admit that *SportsBeat* was not the program that elevated him into this category, he did at least have almost total control over its content, and the choice of topics that it addressed reflected his concerns.

In many respects, *SportsBeat* was a reprise of the 1960s for Cosell, a period when his documentary productions, news commentaries, and *Wide World of Sports* features addressed the social implications of sports in the United States. While the primary topic of interest for Cosell in the 1960s may have been civil rights, by the late 1970s he had become particularly disenchanted with the National Football League, and *SportsBeat* at times served as a continuing diatribe against the corruption that he associated with the league: team owners holding cities hostage for bigger stadiums; the league's partial antitrust exemption; the ability of the league to control its recruitment of new talent and its source of labor. It did not go unnoticed by executives within ABC that the NFL also provided the network with one of its most popular programs—the one that in many respects had created the network and helped Cosell build himself into a television icon.

This kind of contradiction was in many respects one of the most fascinating aspects of Cosell's career. For example, in August 1981, on the eve of the first *SportsBeat* broadcast, Ron Alridge of the *Chicago Tribune* wrote in a column that Cosell was contemplating a move to "pay TV," or what later became known as cable television. According to Alridge, an ally of Cosell's from the world of print sports journalism, "the 61-year-old Cosell, a fiercely loyal ABC employee, knows the future of television sports is in pay TV, and he'd like to get in on the action after he meets his commitment to help ABC cover the Olympics."[6] Indeed, Cosell was in most respects very loyal to ABC. He took assignments, like his contract to cover baseball, not because he loved the job or because he needed the money, but because he felt obligated to pull his weight for the network. He often wrote of how he always mingled with local advertisers and businesspeople at pregame receptions hosted by ABC in each *Monday Night Football* city, "a responsibility that both Gifford and Meredith usually shirked."[7] Yet at the same time, nobody could be more harshly critical of the franchises that were his network's bread and butter. Throughout his career, even before he accepted his position as a baseball color commentator, Cosell had been openly scornful of Major League Baseball; by the early 1980s he had become equally disgusted with boxing; and by the late 1970s he was thoroughly repulsed by the National Football League. *SportsBeat* provided him with a forum to express these sentiments as he never had before, yet he also continued to broadcast *Monday Night Football* during the 1981, 1982, and 1983 seasons; professional boxing until 1982 and amateur boxing through the 1984 Olympics; and baseball through the 1985 season. Ultimately, the conflict proved to be too much for either Cosell or the network to control.

Most problematically for the network, *SportsBeat,* by its very nature, upset what Cosell often decried as the unholy alliance between broadcasting companies and sports institutions. While networks might be in charge of covering sporting events journalistically, they were at the same time purchasing these same sporting events as commercial products. For Cosell, this was a gross conflict of interest, albeit one that he had built his own career exploiting. Nevertheless, *SportsBeat* allowed him to leave the broadcast booth and cover sports in a way that was not inhibited by the sense of obligation one might feel after schmoozing with local advertisers at a pregame Monday night cocktail party.

The ABC network did not immediately do its best to place the show at the forefront of its sports programming. From August 1981 through the end of the year, *SportsBeat* was a monthly program, and as such had difficulty building an audience. Cosell himself strained to maintain his obligations to cover events while at the same time producing *SportsBeat,* and some episodes were preempted. In 1982, however, the program got a weekly slot and was advertised along with the menu of Sunday afternoon programming on ABC beginning in February. Critics, even those who generally had a negative opinion of Cosell, gave it positive reviews almost from the start. William Taaffe of the *Washington Post* wrote after the first few months' worth of programs: "Unfortunately for Cosell loathers, the time has come to balance accounts. His new Sunday afternoon journalism show, 'ABC SportsBeat,' may be the best thing to happen to sports TV this year. It's lucid, intelligent and informative week after week." Taaffe added: "Somehow, Cosell has been coming across on this show not only as sufferable, but likable. Fans/victims of Cosell know his pompous, self-promoting side all too well. Would you now believe a compassionate, even tender side?"[8]

In distinguishing *SportsBeat* from the sports magazine program that was being offered at the same time on CBS, Cosell once again drew on his belief that network sportscasters were "shills" for the games they covered, not objective journalists. Commenting on the CBS program *Sports Saturday/Sunday,* which purported to provide the same kind of journalistic orientation as *SportsBeat,* Cosell said: "Very candidly, I don't see where CBS has done anything in sports journalism. I don't relate it to [CBS host] Brent Musburger personally. I just view him as sated with the jockocracy. . . . All they do is get up there with basketball schedules. They're a big hype. They're a joke. But that's their business, not mine."[9]

The topics that *SportsBeat* covered each week set the tone for a program that combined interviews, produced stories, and commentary by Cosell. Early shows addressed a lawsuit by Oakland Raiders owner Al Davis against the NFL, which at the time was attempting to prevent him from moving his team to Los Angeles. Cosell argued that Davis was legally right but morally wrong to move his team. He predicted that the NFL would lose the suit, and it did. The show took a critical look at the attempt by Pete Rozelle to gain an antitrust exemption for the NFL through federal legislation. Reporting that Senate Majority Leader Howard Baker, a Republican from Tennessee, had come out in favor of the law, Cosell told viewers, "It'll be interesting to see if the next expansion franchise in the NFL goes to Memphis. And who was it who said, 'Sports and politics don't mix?'"[10]

One segment examined the public image of Pittsburgh Pirates slugger Dave Parker, who had been criticized for his high salary and allegedly overconfident attitude. Another explored comments made by Notre Dame head basketball coach Digger Phelps, who had decried illegal recruiting in the college game. CBS sportscaster Billy Packer had criticized Phelps for making such allegations just before the outset of the NCAA basketball tournament, but Cosell noted that he had initially made the charges about half a year before, and they had been quoted by wire services distributed around the United States. In addition to these hard-hitting segments, *SportsBeat* included feature stories on topics such as former St. Louis Cardinal Ken Boyer's battle with cancer, golfer Jack Nicklaus's struggle with a losing streak, and Olympic hurdler Renaldo Nehemiah's move from track and field to football.[11]

Although *SportsBeat* was a critical success, it did not draw high ratings. During its first few months an average of only 3.4 percent of television households tuned in to watch the program. This may have been due in part to the fact that it was aired on Saturday or Sunday at three o'clock eastern and two o'clock central time—a logical slot for a sports program, but one that nevertheless made it difficult to build an audience. In addition, while most sportswriters found *SportsBeat* to be a refreshing injection of serious journalism into the coverage of sports, the show was not without its critics. Ira Berkow of the *New York Times,* for example, noted that *SportsBeat* did an excellent job of probing the issue of sports franchises moving from city to city, but he argued that the show did not do so in an evenhanded manner. Writing in May 1984, Berkow cited an episode that had profiled the Class AAA baseball team in Louisville, Kentucky, a farm team for the St. Louis Cardinals. The team drew large crowds for a minor league baseball franchise, but it had moved to Louisville from Springfield, Illinois, in 1982. Cosell, usually a critic of sports team owners' moving their teams from one city to another, praised the baseball team's owner, A. Ray Smith, in this case because he "did not leave Springfield, Illinois, the way the Colts left Baltimore. On the contrary, he paid the Mayor, in a settlement agreement, $300,000. The Mayor was delighted."[12]

Cosell was referring to the Baltimore NFL franchise's move to Indianapolis in 1984. That year, Colts owner Robert Irsay, unhappy with the team's home grounds in thirty-year-old Memorial Stadium, decided to relocate when the city of Baltimore failed to provide him with the kind of stadium deal he wanted. Infamously, he had the team headquarters packed up one night in the off-season and moved away under cover of darkness. According to Berkow, *SportsBeat*'s segment on this move was a "diatribe against Irsay and how the city [of Baltimore] had been 'raped'—Cosell's word—by the owner." Berkow went on to note that the segment did not provide a sufficiently fair account of Irsay's motivation, but instead slipped into "advocacy journalism; it is expected in editorial comment, as Cosell generally gives at the end of a segment, but when it pervades the story, it becomes in effect a witness for the prosecution."[13]

By contrast, according to Berkow, Cosell's treatment of A. Ray Smith was not only overly kind to him but also largely inaccurate. Berkow contacted the mayor of Springfield, Illinois, who reported that Smith had said he would sell the team to a local buyer and had denied that he was involved in any negotiations with Louisville. "I would not say I was 'delighted'" by the outcome, Mayor J. Michael Houston told Berkow. "We had a long, drawn-out situation in which the city of Springfield sued A. Ray Smith." What is more, the segment on the Colts also contrasted dramatically with one on the Raiders that Cosell had done earlier in the year. That piece had provided what Berkow described as an evenhanded exploration of the efforts of the Oakland franchise to move to Los Angeles, concluding with a measured editorial comment at the end, in which Cosell said: "What is needed is a Federal law that would protect both team and city. A law based on the rule of reason. It would provide that after good faith negotiation between city and franchise, the sports franchise could remove itself from that city only after having proved that it had suffered undue financial distress over a prescribed period of time, or upon abridgement of the lease by the landlord." Berkow concluded his column by accusing Cosell of posturing and hyperbole.[14]

Indeed, posturing and hyperbole had long been Cosell's style. They were what made him entertaining to watch, but as Berkow's column illustrates, his tendency to engage in such rhetoric also opened him up to accusations of being too cozy with his friends and too cruel to his enemies. *SportsBeat*—from its choice of topics to the editorial comments by Cosell at the end of each segment—was not an "objective" program. For that matter, no program on television is. All reflect biases in the selection of topics, the way a topic is covered, the choice of whom to interview, the angles and video images chosen, and the amount of time devoted to a particular issue. Clearly, however, *Sports-Beat's* biases were Cosell's more than they were the biases of advertisers, the network, a sports league, or a team owner. In the spring of 1983, for example, Cosell presented a profile of Larry Little, who had been named head football coach at the historically black Bethune-Cookman College in Daytona Beach, Florida. The *New Pittsburgh Courier* took note of the profile for its largely African American readership, stating: "The exposure will be the most Bethune-Cookman has ever received. Like most other small colleges, the Wildcats have never been featured on national television." The reporter, Barry Cooper, aptly noted, "It is good to have friends in high places."[15]

Within ABC, however, Cosell was losing some of those friends and exasperating others. In part his problems within the network were due to events that were taking place outside the realm of *SportsBeat* and within his role as an event broadcaster. The first came in November 1982, when he was assigned to call the World Boxing Council fight between heavyweight champion Larry Holmes and Randall "Tex" Cobb. By this time Cosell had grown disillusioned with boxing. He saw the sport as being supported by three corrupt institutions that benefited from a brutal competition, which he did not think was adequately regulated. The first were the television networks, which profited from prizefights; the second were the fight promoters; and the third were the print journalists and other reporters, whom he saw as turning a blind eye to the problems within the sport. In 1972 Cosell had testified before Congress in favor of creating a federally controlled boxing commission to regulate these aspects of the sport. Congress had not done so, however, and in the intervening years Cosell had become increasingly disenchanted.

In the month before the fight between Cobb and Holmes, there were two other championship bouts that further shook Cosell's faith in the sport. The first was between World Boxing Association lightweight champion Ray "Boom Boom" Mancini and a Korean fighter named Duk Koo Kim. Mancini brutally knocked out Kim, who slipped into a coma and never woke up. He died shortly after the fight. Then Aaron Pryor and Alexis Arguello met for the junior welterweight title, and once again the challenger was severely beaten. Arguello did not wake up for several minutes after being knocked out in the fourteenth round. So when Cobb and Holmes met in the Houston Astrodome on November 26, 1982, Cosell was already predisposed to take a hard look at a sport that was deeply in need of reform.

The fight turned out to be one of the biggest mismatches that Cosell had ever broadcast. In the ninth round alone, Holmes delivered twenty-six consecutive unanswered blows to Cobb. Despite being punished in every round, and despite Holmes's opening up cuts on his face, Cobb did not fall to the canvas, and the referee refused to stop the fight. The champion won all fifteen rounds unanimously. By the middle of round twelve, Cosell simply went silent at ringside. For a full minute he said nothing. Holmes continued to land jabs and rights on Cobb's face, and Cobb's punches continued to fall short. Cosell ended the round saying, "This kind of savagery doesn't deserve commentation [sic]." He continued, as the fighters were cleaned up in their corners between rounds, "I'll tell you something, my friend Don Chevrier [who was announcing the fight at ringside with Cosell], this is as brutal a mismatch as I think I've ever seen." Chevrier agreed with Cosell, suggesting that if the eight-second standing count that was mandatory in amateur boxing were part of the professional sport, the fight would have been over many rounds earlier. "That's a good point. Also, optional headgear . . . ," then Cosell stopped himself and shook his head as if it were pointless to say anything further. "I've been through it, I've testified before the Congress any number of times."[16]

Cosell and Chevrier were both particularly critical of the fight referee, Steve Crosson. "I don't understand his judgment or thinking," Cosell wearily said at the beginning of round thirteen, questioning why the fight had not been stopped. "What is achieved by letting this man take this kind of beating for fifteen rounds?" In reference to the recent death of Duk Koo Kim and the brutal knockout of Arguello, Cosell observed at the conclusion of the round, "From the point of view of boxing, which is under fire, and deservedly so, this fight could not have come at worse time." Yet the fight continued, and Cosell's commentary, such as it was, remained focused on the futility of the fight rather than on the technical aspects of the match itself. "Obviously, this referee has no intention of stopping this fight," Cosell said, breaking a long silence during the fourteenth round, noting that there was "blood all over Cobb's face now." After another hard right by Holmes to the side of Cobb's head, Cosell said, "I wonder if that referee understands that he is constructing an advertisement for the abolition of the very sport that he is a part of." At the end of the fight, as Holmes hit Cobb with one final flurry of punches, Cosell exclaimed: "I can't believe this referee. It's outrageous!" After the final bell, as the camera focused on Cobb's swollen, bloody face, Cosell remarked sadly "What is achieved by such as this?"[17]

In his book *I Never Played the Game,* Cosell reveals that he received an order through his headset from Jim Spence in New York, by way of producer Chet Forte, to interview referee Steve Crosson, but he had refused. As the ring became crowded with reporters and trainers entering from ringside, Cosell told viewers that there would be no interviews: "I think what you have seen tonight speaks for itself." The next morning he decided that he would never broadcast another professional fight. The decision violated his contract at ABC, which obligated him to cover all championship fights aired by the network. He let the public know of his decision a few days later, when he sat down for an interview with Dave Kindred of the *Washington Post* while in Tampa preparing for a *Monday Night Football* telecast. He told Kindred that the recent events had constituted boxing's "two weeks of disgust." He qualified his decision, however, by saying that he would still be willing to cover amateur boxing. "I love amateur boxing, and if the company wants me to, I would do Olympics boxing. But professional, no. I have walked away from it. I don't want to be party to the hypocrisy, the sleaziness. . . . I'm worn out by it." Cosell ended with a call for federal intervention.

> I would declare a moratorium on boxing until some form of legislation was passed to, 1: protect the men who fight with the strictest rules for safety and medical examinations, 2: create an honest system of ratings and records, and, 3: create one federal government group to administer boxing. The print media should support such legislation instead of, by saying the federal government has no business in sports, vilifying those who suggest it. There should be licensing of promoters, and there should be an accounting of money [spent] on every fight. It has to be in all

50 states under the administration of one group. Either that, or abolish the quote-sport-unquote.[18]

Cosell later wrote that his attitude toward boxing had begun to change even before the Holmes-Cobb fight. In 1977 ABC had partnered with Don King to air a tournament called the United States Boxing Championships. Soon after it began, the tournament came under scrutiny as accusations began to fly of rigged matches and erroneous records meant to prop up particular fighters. Cosell called himself a "minor principal" in the event, but he was the public face of the tournament. Although no criminal charges were filed, he still felt sullied by what he called an "unholy mess." Furthermore, he had simply tired of a sport in which "the objective is chillingly simple: one man purposefully endeavors to inflict bodily harm on another man." He had seen Benny Paret, Willie Classen, and Cleveland Denny die in the ring, had witnessed serious eye injuries to Ernie Shavers and Sugar Ray Leonard, and had seen Ali deteriorate from a quick-witted young man to a slow-moving, slow-talking shadow of himself in only a few short years.[19]

According to Cosell, Roone Arledge called him in Tampa on the morning Kindred's article appeared in the *Washington Post* and told him: "I think you've done the right thing. Congratulations and have a good game tonight."[20] Echoing Jim Spence, however, Arledge writes that Cosell's decision to quit boxing was part of a larger personal disintegration. Cosell was angry at not being made anchor of *World News Tonight*, "bored with an occupation he felt—maybe rightly—was beneath him." Arledge understands Cosell's decision as little more than an act of petty vindictiveness. Cosell's critiques of baseball and the National Football League were, he feels, rooted in the same kind of sentiment. Arledge had been the single most important figure in building Howard Cosell's television career. He had risked his own career, and in many ways the fate of ABC, on the gamble that Cosell could become a franchise personality. To his credit, Cosell came through, but from Arledge's perspective, ABC had also been more than fair to Cosell. Now Cosell was forsaking the sports institutions, the advertisers, and the network that had made him rich and famous.[21]

Almost a year after the Holmes-Cobb fight, Cosell became embroiled in another incident, this one largely of his own making. September 5,

1983, the opening night of the *Monday Night Football* season, featured the Dallas Cowboys at the Washington Redskins. Late in the second quarter Redskins receiver Alvin Garrett broke through for a long gain. Garrett had been something of a journeyman in the NFL, and had won a position with head coach Joe Gibbs's squad only after being cut by two other teams. Referring to this, Cosell said, "Gibbs wanted to get this kid and that little monkey gets loose, doesn't he?"[22] Almost immediately phones at the network began to light up with calls from viewers offended by what sounded like a racial slur.[23] At halftime Cosell was informed of his slip and was asked to make an apology at the start of the second half. Instead of apologizing outright, he said: "According to the reporters, they were told that I called Alvin Garrett a 'little monkey.' Nothing of the sort, and you fellows know it. No man respects Alvin Garrett more than I do. I talked about that man's ability to be so elusive despite the smallness of his size."[24]

After the game, the Reverend Joseph Lowery, leader of the Southern Christian Leadership Conference, sent a telegram demanding an apology from Cosell. His initial statement, however critical, was also relatively measured. "As a sportsman," Lowery said to the press, "I would urge him to issue an apology. He said it. If he doesn't remember saying it he ought to check the tape. I heard it, and then I started getting telephone calls. That many people can't be wrong. While he may not have meant it as disparaging, it is offensive to many people." For his part, Garrett, immediately after the game, attempted to play down the significance of the remark, although he did seem to be somewhat insulted by it. "It doesn't offend me," said Garrett to reporters, "because Howard is always shooting off his mouth. Half the time he doesn't know what he's talking about. I think he looks like a monkey. I guess it would bother me if I heard it in person, but that's Howard." Cosell, however, still refused to admit that he had made the statement. "I definitely did not call him a monkey," Cosell said after the game. "If I used that phrase I may have said he moved like a monkey. It was obviously meant as a compliment to his talent." In addition, he told Leonard Shapiro of the *Washington Post,* "I don't remember saying that. I was being complimentary to the man all night." Referring to those who were critical of the racial stereotyped implied by the comment, Cosell lashed out: "Where were they when I fought for Muhammad Ali's rights? Where were they when I created the Jackie Robinson Foundation? This is the cheapest kind of trash in the world. My record as far as race relations is supreme." Irv Bodsky, an ABC spokesperson, also backed up Cosell's claim, saying that network operations people in New York reported that Cosell never made the statement. Yet both the *Washington Post* and the Associated Press had almost immediately reviewed tapes of the game, which showed conclusively that Cosell had in fact used the term.[25]

Those who knew Cosell tend to find the criticism that he received following this incident unfair, citing his own strong commitment to civil rights and the fact that he had used the same term in 1972 to describe Mike Adamle, a small white player. Indeed, throughout his career Cosell had made the defense of civil rights a core part of his life's work. It drove him in ways that even the money and fame of television did not. To suggest as some detractors have that he supported black athletes only to enhance his own portfolio ignores how much he risked, and often how little he got in return, for defending people like Tommie Smith and John Carlos. Devoting an entire chapter to this incident in *I Never Played the Game,* Cosell offers a powerful argument that his "little monkey" comment was blown out of proportion, and that it would be absurd to cast him as a racist for making it. Indeed, in the days following the incident, Cosell received support from a wide array of prominent African American leaders in both civil rights and sports, including Arthur Ashe, Jesse Jackson, Ralph Abernathy, John Thompson, and Harry Edwards.[26]

For his part, Cosell saw the whole episode as the creation of Joseph Lowery and willing co-conspirators in the print media who turned a "single, innocent crack" into a "national furor."[27] In particular among reporters he blamed Leonard Shapiro of the *Washington Post.* Cosell was clearly stung by the accusation that he had said something that was racially insensitive, but in many respects he did not help himself with the defensive manner in which he responded to it. Many were more outraged by Cosell's denial that he had ever made the statement in the first place, and by his continued assertions of his own credentials as a civil rights champion. The denial, issued in very strong terms, effectively cast doubt on the judgment and perception of those who had—correctly—heard him say "little monkey." Furthermore, by lauding his own history as a champion of African Americans, he appeared to demand indulgence even if he had made the remark, and further appeared to be stating that black people were not sufficiently grateful to him for all he had done for them.

Cosell's denials "stunned" Joseph Lowery, who issued another statement a few days later. Instead of focusing on Cosell, Lowery took the opportunity to point out how such a comment might reflect an overall problem in the network's coverage of professional football itself. "The unfortunate and offensive remark by Howard Cosell on Monday night's football game referring to Washington Redskin receiver Alvin Garrett as 'a little monkey,'" Lowery wrote in a telegram to Roone Arledge, "gives occasion not only to ask for an apology, but to point out the disparity between Blacks on the playing field and the absence of Blacks as fulltime members of the crew that broadcasts the event, seen weekly by millions of television viewers."[28]

While Lowery was a constant source of criticism, and Shapiro did keep the "little monkey" story alive in the *Washington Post,* Cosell's comment created a storm of attention that went beyond these two individuals. For example, the statement particularly angered some journalists for newspapers that were published primarily for African American readers, and they used it as a springboard to express resentment toward what they perceived as an image of Cosell as a white savior of black people. Brad Pye Jr. of the *Los Angeles Sentinel* wrote a number of columns sharply critical of Cosell. Initially he joked that the sportscaster was afflicted with "foot in mouth disease."[29] In a later column he called Cosell "that great so-called liberal and alleged defender of Black athletes" and concluded by saying: "Cosell has used Blacks to promote Howard Cosell. No, it's not enough for Howard Cosell to apologize to Rev. Joseph Lowery. He should apologize to the nation and the world on *Monday Night Football,* which this week will be carried on Thursday night. Cosell may be the best known sportscaster in the world but that's not what they call him on Crenshaw Blvd. and in a whole lot of other non-Black communities around the world."[30]

A. S. "Doc" Young, also of the *Los Angeles Sentinel,* suggested that "we Black people take up a collection and pay Howard Cosell for whatever he has done for us and dare him ever to mention us again in life!"[31] Eddie Jefferies of the *New Pittsburgh Courier,* a paper that only a few months earlier had celebrated the profile of Bethune-Cookman on *SportsBeat,* wrote, "All the inimitable (and the term is used looseley [sic] here) 'Voice of the Wasteland' did that evening was refer to Washington Redskin receiver Alvin Garrett as 'that little monkey,' then deny that he ever said it ('and I have the tapes to prove it,' he pompously stated afterwards), before subsequently apologizing the following day to, of all people, The Rev. Joseph Lowery of the Southern Christian Leadership Conference, an act tantamount to the Soviet Union apologizing to Japan for shooting an unarmed Korean plane from the sky." Like Pye, Jefferies cast doubt on the motivation for Cosell's positive record in his treatment of African American athletes. "Down through the years he has attached himself to many of sportdom's brightest black stars, and, as his custom, has taken credit for the subsequent publicity they have generated." Jefferies concludes by saying that he would not call Cosell a racist. "What I would call Howard, if he were here, is sesquipedalian. And as such he could have used such terms as capuchin, titi, tamarind, macaque, langur, loris or marmoset. But, in any respect, it's nice to see Howard Cosell squirm!"[32]

Even columnists in the mainstream press struck a similar note. Dorothy Gilliam of the *Washington Post* did not go so far as to say that Cosell had deliberately defended black athletes only to exploit their glory. She did argue, however, that Cosell's commitment to civil rights illustrated how dependent African Americans were on white allies within the broadcast media, and how such dependence signaled a continued paternalistic relationship between whites and blacks. "Howard Cosell is great because he championed black athletes. You have to respect this. But the fact that we do reflects the scarcity of blacks in sports broadcasting in the first place. The plantation mentality is alive and well when millions of black American viewers must be content with the anxious hope that the networks find a good white savior to protect their image and interests."[33]

Others journalists for newspapers that addressed black audiences defended Cosell, albeit in a much more muted fashion. Les Matthews of the *New York Amsterdam News* wrote at the end of his column on September 10: "Howard Cosell, sportscaster, apologized for his recent description, on ABC-TV, of Washington Redskins' Alvin Garrett as 'that little monkey.' Cosell is not a racist and has fought for the Black man's cause in sports. Remember how he carried the banner for Muhammad Ali?"[34]

Garrett himself continued to dismiss the comment after the game. He was quoted by William Cotterell of United Press International as saying: "Howard Cosell is just great. I did not, and do not, take exception to anything he said about me in the broadcast last night. Matter of

fact, I am pleased that he singled me out for such favorable attention."
Yet Cosell's own critique of "sportsworld" should lead one to take this
forgiveness with a grain of salt. In the same article that quotes Garrett
speaking in such glowing terms about Cosell, Redskins owner Jack Kent
Cooke says that he was "flabbergasted at the furor raised over Howard
Cosell's comment. To our certain knowledge, Howard Cosell did not
intend, nor mean, to impugn Alvin Garrett's race, size or character,
when he referred to him as he did in a manner that can be described,
at least, as affectionate."[35] One can only imagine how flabbergasted
Cooke would have been if Garrett had criticized Cosell. Given that he
had barely made the team after preseason training camp, Garrett's
comments would seem to have been a prudent choice for someone
wishing to keep his job.

In fact, a little over a week after the incident, the *Washington Post*
published a follow-up piece on Garrett which suggested that the fall-
out generated by the Cosell controversy continued to land on him, often in ways that were quite degrading. He reported that neighbors had
taken to shouting, "How's the little monkey?" as he left his house each
day, and almost daily someone would put a banana in his locker or in
an article of his clothing. He once again repeated that he did not think
Cosell had meant anything racist by the comment, but pointed out that
it nevertheless had created an untenable situation for him that needed
to be addressed: "What will clean up all this would be for Howard Cosell, on our next Monday night game to just apologize to me in front of
all those people. I'd like him to say it to me in person, on camera. That
would end it for both of us." Garrett added, "I just want it to end. No
more bananas."[36]

When the "little monkey" incident finally ended for Garrett is unclear. For Cosell, however, the comment was the beginning of the end
of his career on *Monday Night Football.* It raises an important question
as to why such a seemingly minor error made by someone who had devoted so much of his career to African American rights, and to what was
often an astonishingly strong analysis of race and racism in sports and
society, would cause such a reaction. In writing about the incident, few
of even his sharpest critics ever called him a racist. One might blame
the response on Cosell's own reaction. But Cosell always responded
defensively to criticism; this was nothing new. Yet neither was the
power of the term "monkey" and its connotations for depicting African
Americans as subhuman. Just as Cosell's status as a defender of civil

rights was elevated by his acknowledging Muhammad Ali's name, now that same status had been shattered by the thoughtless use of an equally powerful moniker. As Frank Gifford remembers it, this moment seemed to signal the end of Cosell's career.

Howard was the least racist person you'd ever meet in your life. But when he said that, I almost croaked because I'd been around television long enough to know what was going to happen. Boy did it happen, too. He was never the same again. I think he was slipping physically at the time, too. Howard had never exercised in his life. He was a heavy smoker and heavy drinker. He lived a tough life. And I don't know how old he would have been at that time, but he certainly hadn't taken very good care of himself, and he just wasn't physically strong enough to take all of the things that came when people were beginning to really get very critical of everything he did and everything he said.[37]

Cosell missed three *Monday Night Football* broadcasts following the fateful opening game. He returned to finish the rest of the 1983 season. But after the Olympics in Los Angeles the following summer, he announced to Roone Arledge that he was quitting *Monday Night Football*. Arledge had heard such threats before, and had successfully talked Cosell into staying on the show. This time, however, he had decided not to do so. Cosell had caused too much personal stress for Arledge. Moreover, his penchant for generating controversy was no longer seen as an asset to the network, as it had been in the 1960s and 1970s. For the 1984 season Cosell's close friend O. J. Simpson replaced him in the booth with Gifford and Meredith. In November 1984 Roger Stanton, editor of *Football News–Basketball Weekly,* called on Arledge to make the "dramatic move" of rehiring Cosell for the remainder of the season. He reported that 56 percent of the publication's readers wanted him to return. Cosell never did come back to *Monday Night Football*.[38]

Despite calling his last *Monday Night Football* game in 1983, Cosell continued to work on *SportsBeat* for two more years, until the program was canceled in 1985. With nothing to lose—and, according to Arledge, a tremendous grudge against the NFL—*SportsBeat* continued to provide hard-edged stories about corruption in professional and college sports. In April 1985 Michael Katz praised Cosell in the

New York Times for his report on a "point shaving" scandal that had been exposed among the Tulane University basketball team.[39] Katz writes that Cosell not only addressed the scandal but also, more centrally, brought up the "perversions of values surrounding big-time college athletics: the exploitation of athletes without educating them, recruiting violations, under-the-table payments and emphasis on winning." He favorably compared Cosell's treatment of this topic to a profile done by Ted Koppel on ABC's *Nightline* that, according to Katz, had struggled to address the core issues of the story.[40]

Yet ratings for the program continued to fall. Cosell publicly complained about the scheduling of the program, telling the *Washington Post* in 1985: "When *SportsBeat* was on three years ago on Sundays at 5:30, it consistently killed the opposition. The solution would be [to put the show back] where we were originally. But we can't get the time back." The article quotes Jim Spence's response: "Howard's correct. In certain other time periods, the show might do better. But you can't look at *SportsBeat* in a vacuum. There is a relatively limited audience for this type of programming."[41] Spence's reply aside, the poor ratings for *SportsBeat*—only 2 to 4 percent of viewing households in the United States were watching—were in large measure the result of scheduling. In 1985 the network made the decision to feed the program at the same time as its Sunday public affairs show *This Week with David Brinkley*. Most stations in major markets chose to air the latter, including the ABC affiliate in Washington, D.C. Much of the country never even got the chance to watch *SportsBeat* regardless of the time it was scheduled.

From the perspective of ABC's top executives, there was good reason to hide the program in the network schedule. Early in its run Roone Arledge wrote to network president Fred Pierce, "I think it is true that 'SportsBeat' is hurting the programs that follow it."[42] Perhaps of even greater concern, *SportsBeat*'s programs on the NFL were beginning to upset this all-important client of the network. They also came at a very sensitive time for both bodies, as during the spring of 1983 ABC had begun broadcasting games of the upstart United States Football League (USFL). *SportsBeat* produced a number of stories that involved the new league, and later, while testifying in the lawsuit the USFL had brought against the NFL, Cosell claimed that Jim Spence had tried to censor them. Spence denies this, although he does admit that he "called a few times to make certain we were being fair and presenting both sides of an issue." Indeed, a memo that Spence sent to Roone

Arledge confirms his description of his communications with *Sports-Beat*. His memo reads: "I spoke today with [*SportsBeat* managing editor] Ed Silverman concerning the necessity—the requirement—that both you and I be kept up-to-date weekly on the content of ABC *Sports-Beat*. I also said—and emphasized that I was not speaking about censorship in any way, shape, or form—that segments such as the USFL piece which aired last Saturday should be discussed with management of ABC Sports prior to air." Whether or not Spence and Arledge were pressuring Cosell, it is clear that they were concerned about the content of the program.[43]

For his part, Cosell was concerned that ABC was working to sabotage *SportsBeat,* not necessarily through outright censorship but by burying the program in unfavorable scheduling. In March 1983, for example, he fired off a rambling three-page single-spaced memo to Jim Spence, angrily complaining that ABC had ignored a breaking news interview with USFL commissioner Chet Simmons about quarterback Steve Young, who had just signed to play in the USFL, which had aired on *SportsBeat*. Cosell wrote, "It was as if there was a deliberate attempt to ignore journalistic exclusivity that benefitted our company." Spence replied to Cosell that, indeed, the network probably made a mistake, but it had to do with a complex series of events out of anyone's control. He ended his memo, widely circulated throughout ABC, by saying: "In the future, I would ask that you please involve only responsible ABC Sports management in ABC Sports business. To involve the top management of the company in matters of this kind is unnecessary."[44]

By early 1985 Cosell was nevertheless complaining to ABC executives about *SportsBeat*'s scheduling, writing that the program was not being allowed to develop an audience that would appreciate the quality of its programming. Directing a memo straight to ABC president Fred Pierce, Cosell stated: "I am taking the liberty of writing you directly because I feel so strongly about ABC *SportsBeat* and its importance to this company. It is in no sense intended as a self-serving statement, but only as a factual recital. From the beginning, ABC *SportsBeat* has been a quality show bringing pride and distinction to this company and winning Emmys in sports journalism every year." He went on to cite recent programs that dealt with "carpetbagging" professional sports franchises, an interview with *Time* magazine "Man of the Year" Peter Ueberroth (who had been the chair of the Los Angeles Olympic

Organizing Committee), and exclusive interviews with Doug Flutie and Donald Trump.[45]

By that spring, however, it was clear that *SportsBeat* would be canceled, and Arledge was beginning to ask serious questions about Cosell's role within ABC Sports. At the time, Cosell had a guaranteed minimum salary of $500,000 per year. He earned an additional $20,000 per game for covering baseball. In 1985, if Cosell were to broadcast eleven baseball games, he would earn $195,000 over his minimum. On a memo from Bob Apter, ABC's director of administration and financial controls, dated April 2, 1985, Arledge wrote, "Howard may be too expensive for our B.B. package." On a memo detailing the salaries for *SportsBeat* staff dated two days later Arledge scribbled: "Something *must* be done. We are currently at more than a million $ loss."[46]

In the fall of 1985 the William Morrow publishing company released to the press Cosell's third book, *I Never Played the Game.* Excerpts were subsequently published in *TV Guide.* The volume almost immediately made headlines, as Cosell attacked in it some of the people with whom he worked most closely on *Monday Night Football:* he criticized Don Meredith for being lazy, Frank Gifford for being incapable of doing play-by-play, O. J. Simpson for his inability to pronounce words correctly on the air. All were castigated for being "jocks." Yet the book was also his clearest articulation of the problems that he associated with sports—the "unholy alliance" between networks and leagues. Reactions to the book varied. Shirley Povich of the *Washington Post,* long a harsh critic of Cosell's, praised the inside story that the book provided about the NFL and said that he enjoyed the chapter on the Cobb-Holmes fight. Yet he felt that the positive aspects of the book were undermined by Cosell's "brutish trashing" of his colleagues on *Monday Night Football.*[47] Tony Kornheiser, also of the *Post,* found more to admire in the book. He criticized what he called Cosell's "pedantic" tone—though writing, "What were you expecting from him, something subtle, something tame, something in a discreetly muted plaid?"—but he also praised him for addressing with journalistic rigor topics such as NFL franchise removal.[48]

Its admirers notwithstanding, Cosell's book was clearly the last straw for the network. If loyalty to "the company" had been Cosell's last ace, he no longer held even that. On October 19, a few weeks after news of *I Never Played the Game*'s publication, ABC announced that it had canceled *SportsBeat.*[49] Cosell began to ponder his future on television. He told the *New York Times:* "I'll be 68 in March. I guess I reached a point in time where it was a relief to have it terminated."[50] A month later ABC announced that Cosell had quit. He maintained his daily radio commentaries, *Speaking of Sports,* but his career as a television broadcaster was over.

8 Public Trust

Sports were very important to him, obviously, but I think the social
picture was just as important. . . . He was much more interested in the
Curt Flood–type stories. The injustices of the games. Sports the arena
and a sign of . . . what's wrong with America.

—Justin Cosell on his grandfather

In March 1985 a little-known company called Capital Cities—
a media conglomerate that owned thirty-six weekly newspapers, ten daily newspapers, ninety radio stations, two
hundred network-affiliated television stations, and several
magazines—announced that it was purchasing the ABC
broadcasting network. The $3.5 billion deal was at the time
the largest merger in the history of the United States, apart
from the oil industry. John Morton, a media analyst for the
Washington, D.C., firm of Lynch, Jones and Ryan, told the
New York Times, "We're a long way from the day when a
handful of companies will control all of the media, but not
far away from the day when a handful will control most of
it."[1] Capital Cities/ABC took a step toward the first of these
two scenarios in 1996, when Disney purchased the network.
Yet even the 1986 deal consolidated a significant array of
media companies, including one of particular significance
to sports broadcasting, the cable sports network ESPN. Capital Cities owned 85 percent of ESPN at the time of the
merger, effectively grafting ABC onto it.[2]

One might expect Howard Cosell to have condemned
this development. After all, it meant a consolidation of media resources and power, reduced competition, and an even
stronger relationship between sports institutions and the
media outlets that bring games to the public. One might even
argue that the corporate consolidation of media industries
made it decreasingly likely that there would ever be another
Howard Cosell on mainstream television. Yet at least in

terms of Cosell's opinion of the merger, the contrary was true. In his 1991 book *What's Wrong with Sports,* Cosell praises the Capital Cities takeover for bringing ESPN to ABC. In one passage he congratulates "my dear friend Herbie Granath" for turning the cable network into a profitable enterprise. In another he accuses Jim Spence of having tried to censor his *SportsBeat* programs, writing gleefully, "Then Cap Cities took over ABC and blew Jim Spence to oblivion."[3]

The Capital Cities/ABC deal ushered in a new era of media mergers. Soon after, NBC merged with General Electric; in 1995 CBS merged with Westinghouse, and in 1999 the "Tiffany Network" was acquired again by its former syndication arm, Viacom. It is hard to imagine that, his praise for Capital Cities notwithstanding, Cosell would have been able to stomach the corporate culture that arose from these mergers and acquisitions. Yet as one might well imagine, Cosell did not leave his career peacefully. Shortly after leaving ABC, he took a position as a columnist at the *New York Daily News,* accepting a job that moved him into the realm of the print journalists he had disparaged throughout most of his career. His radio commentaries went on, now from the study of his Upper East Side apartment, as always unscripted, spontaneously spoken, and timed to the second. The most distinctive voice on the airwaves—"to voices what the Grand Canyon is to ditches," Dave Kindred writes—Cosell kept up his show until January 1992.[4] He continued to testify to Congress on corruption in the ranks of professional sports (particularly with regard to the NFL), and he enthusiastically served as a witness for the USFL in its lawsuit against the NFL in 1986. Cosell even taught courses at a third college, Brown University. And until the end, he held onto his friendship with Muhammad Ali, publicly praising his verbal sparring partner as late as the boxer's fiftieth birthday celebration, broadcast in 1992.

For Roone Arledge, the Capital Cities takeover was a disaster. The key personalities who had been central to building ABC Sports were driven away within a year of the merger: Chet Forte, Chuck Howard, and Jim Spence. Arledge himself had the word "sports" removed from his title within the company. The sports division now worked under a Capital Cities executive named Dennis Swanson, a former marine who ran the network like a drill sergeant: urine tests, no swearing in the control booth, dress codes, balanced budgets. Swanson, who had been in charge of affiliate stations, had himself been something of a trailblazer, having provided Oprah Winfrey with her first opportunity as a talk show host in Chicago. Few of the divisions in the network were making money when he arrived. He was ready to clean house, and that meant virtually dismantling the ABC Sports structure that Arledge had built over the course of twenty years.[5]

Perhaps to a greater degree than Cosell could have imagined, the new era of media consolidation put more emphasis on profit than ever before. The *Arkansas Democrat-Gazette* opined in December 1986 that the media mergers heralded a new era, one dominated by a "business school mentality that looked at the world through Vuarnet-colored glasses and viewed every aspect of life with a sort of 'bottom line' brutality engendered by biz school types who conditioned a whole young generation to think like Ivan Boesky and T. Boone Pickens."[6] What made these media mergers possible were changes in the Federal Communications Commission rules, effective April 1, 1986, which expanded the ability of companies to dominate markets, now allowing single entities to own up to twelve television stations (an increase from seven) in markets comprising up to 25 percent of the country's population.[7]

This consolidation caused much chagrin to media activists, who had long spoken of the dangers that emerge when broadcasting network ownership is overly centralized. In fact, the idea that broadcasting should be decentralized was nothing new. It was written into law in the 1934 act of Congress that created the Federal Communications Commission in the first place. Central to that act, and to the 1927 Radio Act which preceded it, is the idea that the airwaves belong to the public and cannot be owned by any private enterprise. Broadcasting networks are therefore companies that are held in public trust.[8]

In his memoir Arledge addresses this issue very briefly. When the takeover came, he happened to be in South Africa, and was summoned back to New York to receive the news, not knowing what it would be and wondering what was so important that he had to leave a production crew preparing an interview with Winnie Mandela. The possibility that ABC might be the subject of a corporate takeover crossed his mind. He thought it unlikely, though. "Television networks were more than corporate commodities," he writes; "they were 'public trusts,' in the FCC definition." By placing the term "public trusts" in quotation marks and attributing the term to a government agency, Arledge signaled that he did not take the idea very seriously. For him, being a public trust was simply a bureaucratic obstacle, a term written in red tape. In fact, even though as an executive he clearly was not happy about the Capital Cities takeover of ABC, he initially was pleased to see the value of his stock options balloon enough to make him "modestly rich," and credited Ronald Reagan's deregulation of the broadcasting industry, a move that effectively weakened public oversight of media concentration, with boosting his stock portfolio.[9]

Cosell, by contrast, always took seriously the notion that the media are a public trust. As with many of his other principles, his application of this one was not always even. His career was filled with as many, if not more, examples of schlock as of distinguished journalism. For every story about Grambling College or about NFL corruption, one can find several Dean Martin celebrity roasts and episodes of *Battle of the Network Stars*. His very job on *Monday Night Football*—as an analyst in the booth working for a network with a vested interest in the client it was supposed to be covering—often turned him into precisely the kind of "shill" he had always sworn he would not become. Yet no matter what one's opinion is of Cosell, he understood that the mass media are a public trust in a way Arledge did not.

Throughout much of his career he was driven to be successful, to make money, to show that he had made the right decision by choosing broadcasting. As his grandson Justin puts it, "He was just a little Jewish kid in Brooklyn who wanted to keep the damn lights on."[10] By the time he quit ABC, however, he had little left to lose. He began to focus more exclusively on issues pertaining to the relationship between sports and what he saw as the public interest. In particular, he took aim at the NFL, and his vehicle for doing so was the league that was attempting to turn itself into a rival to the more established organization of professional football teams: the United States Football League. The USFL played a spring season, so it did not compete directly with the more established NFL. By the mid-1980s, however, its owners had decided to challenge the NFL for professional football's top players. In May 1986 the USFL brought an antitrust suit against the NFL, and Cosell was called to testify as the USFL's final witness.

ABC had broadcast games for both leagues. It would not have been surprising if NFL commissioner Pete Rozelle had preferred that ABC maintain an exclusive deal with the NFL. Cosell's testimony addressed this conflict. In three and a half hours on the witness stand, Cosell's most incriminating statement was his claim that Rozelle had pressured the network to drop coverage of the USFL. "Arledge told me, 'Pete's all over me on the grounds that I'm sustaining the USFL with the spring [television] contract,'" said Cosell, who told the court he was so shocked by the statement that he called his *SportsBeat* staff and repeated it to them.[11]

Cosell's testimony may have implicated the NFL, but it made more headlines for its entertainment value. Newspaper reports described him as going off on tangents and playing to the courtroom audience, which often responded to his statements with loud laughter. A headline in the *San Francisco Chronicle* called him the "Court Jester at USFL Trial" and reported that his testimony was "overshadowed by what became 'the Howard Cosell Show.' Throughout his 3 1/2 hours on the stand, the first 39 minutes of which Cosell spent talking about himself, he used some of the words, phrases and figures of speech that made him an institution on ABC's *Monday Night Football* telecasts. 'I'm telling it like it is,' Cosell said half a dozen times."[12]

Cosell did not reserve his attacks on the NFL for the courtroom. He repeatedly launched barbs at the league's monopoly over professional football, sometimes on a weekly basis in his nationally syndicated *Daily News* columns. In his July 24, 1986, column he accused the NFL witnesses of perjury.[13] On July 27 he chided television executives for their lack of courage in failing to take on the NFL and share what they knew with the jury.[14] When the jury ended their deliberations on July 29, they found the NFL guilty of violating antitrust law in trying to prevent a rival league from establishing itself. They ended up deadlocked, however, over whether the NFL had prevented the USFL from getting a television contract, and in the end decided to award the USFL one dollar. After the trial ended, one jurist, Miriam Sanchez, told reporters that the instructions to the jury had confused her. She said that she wanted to award the USFL $300 million, but had agreed to the one-dollar figure in the belief that the judge could amend the settlement.[15] Nevertheless, the award effectively killed the USFL and seemed to vindicate the NFL, even though it had been found guilty of holding a monopoly.

Cosell, however, did not give up. He continued to use both his column and his radio show to rail against the NFL. He disparaged the quality of play in the NFL and noted how many USFL players had made a successful transfer to the NFL. And he accused the NFL of conspiring to keep Heisman Trophy winner Doug Flutie out of the league. Flutie had played for the USFL's New Jersey Generals, a team owned by Donald Trump, who many NFL owners thought had encouraged the USFL suit only to put himself in a position to gain an NFL franchise. Cosell wrote:

> The Heisman Trophy winner sits and waits in disbelief as the Los Angeles Rams, who have the NFL rights to Flutie, make public statements about their lack of interest in him. This is, of course, because they have such stellar athletes at quarterback, no doubt. After all, wouldn't you prefer Dieter Brock to Flutie? A quarterback brought down from Canada to lead the Rams last year—a man who drew snickers from knowing ones all over the league? A quarterback with a knee injury who just underwent arthroscopic surgery and will miss at least four to six weeks' play and probably more? A quarterback whose entire offense was [to] run [running back Eric] Dickerson right, run Dickerson left, the dullest and most stereotypical offense in the league?[16]

As far as Jim Spence was concerned, Cosell's stance on the USFL was merely posturing and bluster. He accused Cosell of taking a stand against the NFL only out of bitter and self-serving vindictiveness. "The minute Howard joined the newspaper fraternity," Spence writes, "he began to take pot shots at the NFL. It figured. He could no longer suppress his deep resentment of the league and its commissioner."[17]

As angry as Cosell's words may have been, the settlement in the USFL case perhaps served as a metaphor for Cosell's declining influence. In 1987 he decided that he wanted to return to television. He announced that he was to host a weekly syndicated talk show, produced by Don Ohlmeyer and Ohlmeyer Communications. Borrowing from his weekly radio program, it was titled *Howard Cosell: Speaking of Everything*. He told reporters, "[I] still had things I wanted to say."[18] The program went on the air in 1988 but lasted only three months before Ohlmeyer, feeling as if he was not being listened to, told Cosell, "I can't do this anymore."[19]

The biggest blow to Cosell came on November 18, 1990, three days after he had finished the manuscript of his last book, *What's Wrong with Sports*. He was away on a speaking engagement in Kansas City when Emmy, his wife of more than forty-six years, died suddenly of a heart attack. Cosell wrote in the postscript to his last book: "I've always said that I couldn't go on without her. But being the fighter that she was, she would, I know, want me to go on." Her memorial service was at All Souls Unitarian Church in Manhattan, "a fitting service," Cosell wrote, "honoring a Presbyterian, a WASP who for forty-six and a half years had lived a wonderful life with a Jew."[20]

"They might as well have put Howard in a box when she died," says Frank Deford. "I mean, he was finished then. . . . He was declining anyhow, but when she died, he lost everything."[21] Cosell continued his daily radio broadcast until January 1992. That same year he taped a short segment on a television gala honoring Muhammad Ali. The show featured a montage of moments the two shared during their careers, including outtakes, celebrity roasts, and comedy acts onstage. The segment ended with Cosell speaking from his apartment in New York City. "It's hard to believe," he said. "All the years. Everything that's passed between us. It's so hard to believe. And so memorable. And now, it's time to say to you Muhammad, God bless you, and happy birthday to you. You're fifty years old. I never thought that could happen. Not to you, but it has. And you know something? You are exactly who you said you are. You never wavered. You are free to be who you want to be. I love you. . . . Happy birthday."[22]

During the last portion of Cosell's speech, tears welled up in his eyes and his voice broke. This was to be one of his last appearances on television. The year before he had had a cancerous tumor removed from his chest, and his health was failing. He spent most of the next few years in his Manhattan apartment, where his daughters Jill and Hillary took care of him. Howard Cosell died on April 22, 1995.

———

The final years of Cosell's life were lonely ones. Friends would only occasionally stop by to talk or say hello. Cosell now had difficulty carrying on conversations or walking from place to place. His memory was failing him. By the early 1990s it had been almost a decade since he had dominated the media spotlight. For someone who had once been one of the most recognized public figures in the United States, he was now almost unknown to a growing number of young people.

Frank Gifford remembers Cosell's physical decline as being emblematic of his life. "He kind of held everything in contempt that he didn't really know anything about," says Gifford. "It never ever bothered me, but he was just so negative about so many things. In the last years, when he was being attacked so viciously, I don't know how he held it all together. And then he didn't. He just came apart." Gifford feels that Cosell confronted the emptiness of his celebrity at the end of his life, and paints a picture of someone who was so pathetically self-obsessed that he never had any real friendships. He recalls: "I went to see him several times right before he died. I remember seeing him when he could hardly talk . . . just a whisper of a voice. I remember him saying to me, 'Frank, it really hurts.' It really broke me up. I felt very sad for him. He was all alone, and all these people who were fans, or who were half-assed friends, none of them were there. I saw him several times." Gifford added, "He died very lonely."

For Gifford, these final, wasted years are what we should learn from Cosell's life—a kind of moral lesson on the tragedy of narcissism. Gifford may be right. Perhaps any remembrance of Cosell should address his egotism, or the people he hurt during his career, or even more generally the shallowness of fame. But even Cosell's critics would have to acknowledge that he was an unusual celebrity, perhaps a tragic one, but also a television star whose significance is much more complex than a simple narrative of decline might suggest.[23]

Why was Cosell so important? This question might sound like another way of saying, What was so important about Howard Cosell? This is not what I mean. That Cosell was important is a given. A look at popular culture of the 1960s and 1970s should prove to even the most casual observer that Howard Cosell was a franchise, a big deal, someone who mattered. As sports columnist Robert Lipsyte wrote when Cosell died, any accurate historical account of him would show that he was more of a celebrity than most of the people he interviewed.[24] In an era when television made celebrity more important than ever in the United States, Cosell was one of the biggest celebrities of all.

The question, however, is why? As any commentator on the man has noted, he was not good-looking, he remained in many ways a Jewish boy from Brooklyn, and he had a voice that was distinctive for its ability to irritate. He was brilliant, but this is usually not considered a qualification for becoming a sportscaster. His overblown recall of obscure dictionary entries and his use of complex and convoluted sentence structure certainly made him unique but also left him open to ridicule.

Yet by the 1970s he had become glamorous—the type of celebrity who appeared on television often, who sat alongside Sammy Davis

Jr., Cary Grant, and Jimmy Stewart at a Dean Martin celebrity roast.
When Roone Arledge had a major event to cover, from a prizefight
to the Riggs-King "Battle of the Sexes," Cosell's presence as the announcer either was called for by the significance of the event or signaled that the event was important—or both. To his critics, he was
much like other celebrities, someone famous for being famous. Yet a
long view of Cosell's life and career reveals depth. He was someone
who was interested in and contributed to serious civic discussion.

But by the mid-1980s, when he turned his attention to a program
devoted to high-quality sports journalism, he was—to quote Cosell's
own words describing running back Leroy Kelly during the opening
game of *Monday Night Football*—"not a factor." In the 1960s he had
risen quickly to emerge from his larva-like state as a local New York
City sportscaster and ABC radio commentator, but within twenty
years his star was steadily fading.

Robert Lipsyte wrote in 1992 upon the airing of Cosell's last radio
commentary that Cosell had been like a grain of sand in an oyster—an
irritant that turned into a pearl. And he'd been to Roone Arledge the
"spice in his stew." Howard Cosell was "a living mixed metaphor. And
he was a symbol, know-it-all uncle, stern coach, comic relief. He was
even a dichotomy: Who else could lure us into the SportsWorld tent
with promises of jockomamie delights, then, once inside, berate us for
wasting our time at such foolish entertainments. Cosell always hated
the dichotomy line."[25]

Cosell may have hated the dichotomy line, but it fit. What detractors
often disliked about Cosell were his inconsistencies. His harshest critics called them hypocrisies. Ira Berkow pointedly noted such failings in
his article about the *SportsBeat* feature in which Cosell let a Triple-A
baseball team owner off the hook for moving his team while condemning Robert Irsay for doing the same in Baltimore. Jim Spence took a
similar shot at Cosell for his testimony on behalf of the USFL: "Just as
boxing wasn't corrupt until the Cosell coffers were full, the National
Football League was sacrosanct as long as he was in the broadcast
booth on Monday nights."[26] There is no way of getting around Cosell's
contradictions.

But some embraced them. In a way, in fact, his striking contradictions were what made Cosell. He was the ultimate company man, but
he would bite the hand that fed him when it was least expected. He
called himself a liberal and privately railed against Richard Nixon

and Ronald Reagan, yet he numbered staunch Republicans such as George Steinbrenner and Rudy Giuliani among his closest friends. He was a union loyalist who wrote an open letter condemning strike-breaking professional football players during the 1987 players' strike, yet he refused to represent a television writers' union when one of its leaders pleaded the Fifth Amendment before HUAC. He was "born of Jewish parents" and had a school of physical fitness named after him at Hebrew University in Jerusalem, yet he spent some of the final moments of his life with John Cardinal O'Connor.

Cosell famously complained that he was too smart for sports. In fact, as Bob Costas noted toward the end of Cosell's career, most of his work was light entertainment—or to use a Yiddish term, schlock. Costas made the point that if one listed the top ten pieces of quality sports journalism of Cosell's era, Cosell's name would be next to at least five of them. Yet if one listed the bottom ten moments in television sports of Cosell's era, Cosell's name would be next to half of them as well. Both go into making Cosell who he was.

In other words, Cosell without the schlock was nothing special. What allowed him to reach so many people was his ability to play himself—to create a character that was part company man, part shill, part crank, part windbag, part moral crusader. It was a role that, ultimately, he had too much pride to continue to play any longer.

———

To put Cosell in context, one need look no further back than 2005, when journalist Jonathan Mahler used Cosell's words as the title for his book about the New York Yankees, New York City, and the year 1977. Cosell's description of a burning building that he could see from the press box of Yankee Stadium during that year's World Series—"Ladies and gentlemen, the Bronx is burning"—still echoes hauntingly today. His tone suggested that he may very well have thought of himself as Virgil describing the incineration of Troy.

The cable network ESPN did a miniseries based on Mahler's book shortly after it was published, but instead of using actors to play Cosell and the other ABC broadcasters of that World Series, it used the actual tapes from the telecast. It captures brilliantly the kind of multiple personalities that Cosell embodied. Despite Cosell's obvious disaffection, in Game Six he joked with play-by-play announcer Keith Jackson, jocularly wishing him a happy birthday during the pregame introductions. Mahler's story is superbly written and weaves together politics, sports, and urban life in an engaging fashion. While it does not provide in-depth history, it does offer some historical context that helps readers understand how the borough became populated predominantly by African Americans, how many of its neighborhoods became impoverished, and what the Bronx was like before the transformations of the 1960s.

Cosell may not have gone into these issues in any depth either, but he was, by virtue of his very personality, a concrete link to this history. What nagged people about Cosell, in a real sense, is what nagged many about the United States and its past: he reminded them of its inequalities, its injustices, its unmet ideals, and its racism. Cosell never let people forget these things, and the personal history that he brought with him—a history written into his Brooklyn Jewish accent and a vocabulary that betrayed his culture's reverence for education; a history that he recalled in his endless defenses of Ali and of civil rights; a history that made him part of the transformation of generations—gave him the credentials he needed to keep reminding them.

As long as he was on TV, as long as he was a big deal, that history was in evidence. But as soon as he fell off the air—especially as soon as he left *Monday Night Football* and boxing—he no longer mattered. His *SportsBeat* work may have been the most politically potent sports journalism ever seen on network television, but it was in some respects less political than his work a decade earlier, when he was yukking it up with Robert Conrad on *Battle of the Network Stars*.

Of course, Cosell's concern for social justice was not pure. Some critics, both white and African American, accused him of exploiting civil rights to advance his career. This is a dubious claim. Cosell was very lucky to have worked for a network with an iconoclast like Arledge who recognized the value of controversy. It is unlikely that Cosell could have predicted that his defense of Ali or of Smith and Carlos would actually have turned out to be a good career move. Nevertheless, Cosell did, in the words of *Ebony*'s Bill Rhoden, present himself as "somewhat of an expert on the black mind (as if there is such a collective) and its social-political consciousness."[27] One senses that Cosell was not entirely joking when he said that he "made" Ali. As with his reaction to the "little monkey" comment at the end of his career, Cosell expected gratitude. It is not unreasonable for black audiences to recoil from a white public figure who acts as if he has "rescued" African Americans from injustices that never should have happened in the first place.

As much as Cosell's relationship with African Americans was a complex and contradictory one, *Monday Night Football* was really at the heart of Cosell's celebrity and the tensions that went along with it. While his ongoing relationship with Ali was also important, it was his national exposure every week in the fall that truly made Cosell a constant presence in people's homes across the United States, and it was on that program that most audiences developed an understanding of Cosell as a character type. The Cosell-Meredith duo was central to this understanding. Cosell was "old," Meredith was young. Cosell was educated and formal in speech. Meredith was folksy and casual, approaching his job with an informal glibness. Cosell's accent was eastern, from a city whose glory days, by the 1970s, seemed to be in the past. Meredith's accent was Texas, the booming Sunbelt, the future.

George Lipsitz writes that during the 1950s, a new social order was being sold to Americans on television, a new ideal based on the values of consumer culture. The foundations of these ideals—from individualistic acquisition to spending on credit—were sold by drawing on representations of the recent past: the ethnic neighborhoods and extended family networks that were vanishing with urban renewal and suburban development.[28] Just as was true in the 1950s, a new reality was being sold to the country in the 1970s. It was a post-progressive reality, one that rejected the idealism of democratic, egalitarian society nurtured during the New Deal and Great Society eras. The emerging ethic of the 1970s embraced values that promoted the concentration of wealth and corporate power. No form of popular entertainment better embodied this change than the NFL.

Already on the rise as the most popular sport in America by the early 1970s, football had been established as an almost sacred institution by the end of the decade. The NFL had created a business model that was different from that governing other sports, a model in which the wealth generated by television revenue was shared far more among the owners. It was like socialism for the rich, foreshadowing policies to the same effect that would become instituted on a federal level in the 1980s. Teams became cultural hubs for corporate networking and advertising. The NFL even created its own holiday, a celebration of corporate wealth called the Super Bowl, a spectacle so overwhelming in scope that it has grown almost to obliterate the significance of the actual game being played.

As much as anyone else, Cosell sharply criticized this new corporate order in sports. Yet he also, ironically, was as responsible as anyone else for helping to bring it about. His presence on *Monday Night Football* effectively made the new corporate order consistent with the past, just as television in the 1950s made the new consumer culture consistent with values and lessons learned in the past. Even when Cosell was critical of the NFL, his presence as the resident crank in the broadcast booth served the interests of a corporate order just fine. When reading about Cosell in books like Kindred's *Sound and Fury* or Mahler's *Bronx Is Burning,* it is easy to forget that many people *hated* Cosell. Polls that showed him among both the most and least liked media figures of the decade notwithstanding, more hated Cosell than loved him, and with far more passion. The past evoked by Cosell was not sold as a time to which one might nostalgically long to return. It was a past from which one fled. And when Cosell critiqued the new corporate order emerging in the 1970s, his own critics could easily dismiss him as a hypocrite who fed at the corporate trough until full and then complained about the cooking.

Even with all of this being said, his passing from the sports scene was like a final victory for the corporate interests who ascended to power during the 1970s and 1980s. At least while he was a weekly presence in American homes, his history came with him as if it were his luggage. Listening to some of what he said on the air—from his defense of Tommie Smith and John Carlos to his condemnation of boxing in 1982—is almost jolting. It is hard to imagine a network television commentator from any realm of the medium today—whether sports, music, news, or entertainment—expressing that level of genuine, heartfelt, articulate criticism.

More than fifteen years after his death, Cosell has become a new kind of television celebrity—on YouTube. For someone so hated while he was alive, it is easy to find clips from his career posted by fans, and hit tallies show that at least computer users voluntarily continue to watch him. There is even a YouTube Cosell impersonator called "Mr. C" who dons aviator sunglasses and a yellow *ABC Wide World of Sports* blazer while intoning Cosell's distinctive cadences. Presenting himself as Cosell come down from heaven, he interviews former athletes and current sportscasters. Why is there a renewed interest in Cosell?

To use a term that bubbled up from the streets of Cosell's Jewish Brooklyn, Cosell had chutzpah, a Yiddish term that roughly translates as "audacity" or even "insolence." It took chutzpah for a gangly, awkward Jewish kid from Brooklyn, someone with no discernible background in sports, to think that he could become a sports broadcaster. It took chutzpah to leave a thriving law practice in the 1950s, purchase an expensive tape recorder, and invade the sanctified space of a professional athlete's locker room. It took chutzpah to pursue this career, even after being shunned by the television network, to call Muhammad Ali by his chosen name, to defend Tommie Smith and John Carlos, to broadcast *Monday Night Football,* to condemn boxing, and to create *SportsBeat.* Anybody who tuned in to watch him, whether one wanted it or not, received a healthy serving of chutzpah. Maybe not, at times, enough, but certainly a lot more than just about anybody else who has appeared on television before or since has offered.

At times Cosell was a crusading journalist, but he was much more as well, for there have been a great many crusading journalists who have slipped under the radar. He also loved the limelight, and knew how to grab it. He understood that society and history and culture were not distractions from sports but were the very things that made sports, and entertainment in general, meaningful. Perhaps, after all is said and done, despite all of his bombast and ego and pomposity and even meanness, this is why it is easier for many to miss Cosell than to hate him.

Notes

Introduction

1. Jesse Lemisch, "If Howard Cosell Can Teach at Yale, Why Can't Herbert Aptheker?" *Newsletter of the Radical Historians Caucus* 22 (May 1976): 1–9.
2. Howard Cosell with Mickey Herskowitz, *Cosell* (Chicago: Playboy Press, 1973), 119.

1. Poor, Jewish, and from Brooklyn

1. Cosell and Herskowitz, *Cosell,* 120.
2. See Jewish Virtual Library, *Contemporary Authors,* www.jewishvirtualli brary.org/jsource/biography/Cosell.html (accessed May 24, 2010).
3. HeritageQuest Online Census Image, Fourteenth Census of the United States: 1920–Population, Borough of Brooklyn (ProQuest LLC), www.heri tagequestonline (accessed June 1, 2007).
4. Cosell and Herskowitz, *Cosell,* 119.
5. Ibid., 120; HeritageQuest Online Census.
6. Dave Kindred, *Sound and Fury: Two Powerful Lives, One Fateful Friendship* (New York: Free Press, 2006), 15.
7. Howard Cosell, interview by Elli Wohlgelernter, July 31, 1981, for the American Jewish Committee, William E. Wiener Oral History Library, New York Public Library, 43. Once again, there is a discrepancy with the census records with regard to the country of Isadore Cohen's birth. The census recorder wrote "Russia," although Cosell recalls that it was Poland. This can be explained by the fact that a portion of what is today Poland had been acquired by the Russian Empire in 1855.
8. Kindred, *Sound and Fury,* 15.
9. Ibid.
10. Cosell, interview by Wohlgelernter, 44.
11. Howard Cosell, *Like It Is* (Chicago: Playboy Press, 1974); Wendell Pritchett, *Brownsville, Brooklyn: Blacks, Jews, and the Changing Face of the Ghetto* (Chicago: University of Chicago Press, 2002).
12. Cosell and Herskowitz, *Cosell,* 120.
13. Cosell, *Like It Is,* 290.
14. Cosell, interview by Wohgelernter, I53.
15. Cosell, *Like It Is,* 269.
16. Ibid., 285.

17. Howard Cosell (Howard William Cohen) Curriculum Vitae, Howard Cosell Folder, Biographical Collection, University Archives, New York University.
18. Ibid.; Leonard Shapiro, "Cosell Dies at 77," *Washington Post,* April 24, 1995.
19. Cohen, Howard, SN: 12057393/01944643, National Personnel Records Center, St. Louis; Howard Cosell biography file.
20. "Marriages That Work: Howard and Emmy Cosell," *Family Circle,* December 13, 1977, 224.
21. Kindred, *Sound and Fury,* 20.
22. Cosell and Herskowitz, *Cosell,* 124.
23. "Dorothy Farley Renz Is Bride of Media Man in Nuptials at Lutheran Church in Norwood," *Chester Times,* March 15, 1947; *Chester Times,* June 3, 1950; "Ridley Twp. Civic Group Plan for Halloween Party," *Chester Times,* October 26, 1951.
24. "County Native May Get P.O. Post," *Chester Times,* March 24, 1953.
25. Kindred, *Sound and Fury,* 22.
26. "Paid Notice: Deaths—Pomper, Lewis," *New York Times,* March 10, 2000.
27. Cosell and Herskowitz, *Cosell,* 127.
28. Kindred, *Sound and Fury,* 22; Howard Cosell Curriculum Vitae.
29. Cosell, interview by Wohlgelernter, 45.
30. Ibid., 46.
31. Ibid., 45.
32. Cosell, *Like It Is,* 281.
33. Ibid., 275.
34. Ibid., 281.
35. Whitfield writes that Jews who, like Cosell, have stood up for African American athletes have done so out of a desire to compensate for their own stereotypical weakness in sports by fixating on the conversely stereotypical strength of African American athletes. He writes: "The Jew's mind has been among the glories of Western civilization, a testament to soaring spiritual and intellectual grandeur. The Jew's body has long been portrayed as feeble and inferior. Over-endowed with brains (according to his enemies), the Jew has not been quite virile enough. In the climactic fight that [Bernard] Malamud stages in *The Tenants* (1971), the blocked black writer Willie Spearmint aims at the groin of Harry Lesser with a saber, as though picking the site where the Jew is least impressive and most vulnerable. By contrast, the blocked Jewish writer puts an ax to the skull of his opponent, targeting the attribute where the Jew has long felt superior." Yet the historical realities of Jewish participation in sports, even into the 1950s, when Jews dominated the 1950–51 championship City College basketball team, contradict any simple understanding of Jews as not athletic. See Stephen J. Whitfield, "Unath-

letic Department," in *Jews, Sports, and the Rites of Citizenship,* ed. Jack Kugelmass (Chicago: University of Illinois Press, 2007), 51; Gena Caponi-Tabery, "Jump for Joy: Blues, Dance, and Basketball in 1930's African America," in *Sports Matters: Race, Recreation, and Culture,* ed. John Bloom and Michael Willard (New York: New York University Press, 2002), 45.

36. Cosell, *Like It Is,* 293–94.

37. Ibid., 272.

38. Cosell, interview by Wohlgelernter, 37.

39. Ibid., 47.

40. Cosell and Herskowitz, *Cosell,* 126.

41. Ibid., 127.

42. Kindred, *Sound and Fury,* 21.

43. Cosell, interview by Wohlgelernter, 44.

44. Kindred, *Sound and Fury,* 21.

45. Cosell and Herskowitz, *Cosell,* 121.

46. Ibid., 121–23.

47. Cosell, *Like It Is,* 303.

48. Ibid.

49. Ibid.

50. Jill Cosell, telephone interview with the author, July 26, 2006.

51. Riv-Ellen Prell, *Fighting to Become Americans: Assimilation and the Trouble between Jewish Women and Men* (Boston: Beacon Press, 1999), 67–68.

52. Ibid., 69–70.

53. Cosell and Herskowitz, *Cosell,* 121.

54. Ibid., 125.

55. Michael Denning, *The Cultural Front: The Laboring of American Culture in the Twentieth Century* (New York: Verso, 1996), 107–8. Writing in *American Mercury* in 1939, Farrell disparaged the "cultural front," calling them "hastily enlisted commercial writers, high-priced Hollywood scenarists, a motley assortment of mystery-plot mechanics, humorists, newspaper columnists, stripteasers, band leaders, glamour girls, actors, press agents, Broadway producers, aging wives with thwarted literary ambitions, and other such ornaments of American culture." He goes on: "A large proportion of the literary talent of America is now diverted to Hollywood and to radio writing. . . . This is a positive and incalculable social loss. . . . [C]onsider how many lives, how much labor power, how much talent, how much of social goods is poured not only into Hollywood but into American commercial culture as a whole. The social cost is fabulous." James T. Farrell, "The End of a Literary Decade," *American Mercury* 48 (1939), quoted in Denning, *Cultural Front,* 108.

56. Denning, *Cultural Front,* 251–54.

57. Cosell and Herskowitz, *Cosell,* 125–26.

58. Prell, *Fighting to Become Americans,* 125. Also see Leonard Dinnerstein, *Anti-Semitism in America* (New York: Oxford University Press, 1994); and Charles Stember, *Jews in the Mind of America* (New York: American Jewish Congress, 1966).

59. Cosell, *Like It Is,* 265–66.

60. Cosell and Herskowitz, *Cosell,* 125.

61. Cosell, *Like It Is,* 273–74.

62. See Denning, *The Cultural Front.*

63. "Conversations with Scholars of American Popular Culture—Featured Guest: George Lipsitz," *Americana: The Journal of American Popular Culture: 1900–Present* (Spring 2002), www.americanpopularculture.com/journal/articles/spring_2002/lipsitz.htm (accessed May 24, 2010).

64. Cosell, *Like It Is,* 277.

65. Ibid., 284–85.

66. Ibid., 285.

67. "Conversations with Scholars of American Popular Culture—Featured Guest: George Lipsitz."

68. Kindred, *Sound and Fury,* 24.

69. Cosell and Herskowitz, *Cosell,* 127.

2. From the Law Office to the Broadcast Booth

1. Howard Cosell with Mickey Herskowitz, *Cosell* (Chicago: Playboy Press, 1973), 129.

2. From compact disc accompanying Ted Patterson, *The Golden Voices of Football,* (Champaign, Ill.: Sports Publishing, 2004), track 59.

3. Patterson, *Golden Voices of Football,* 139.

4. Cosell and Herskowitz *Cosell,* 127.

5. Dave Kindred, *Sound and Fury: Two Powerful Lives, One Fateful Friendship* (New York: Free Press, 2006), 22.

6. "Voorloper," *New Yorker,* June 11, 1958, 28–29.

7. "Sportscaster Howard Cosell: In the Right Place, at the Right Time with the Right Questions," ABC Radio Network Press Release, August 29, 1958, Howard Cosell microform file, Museum of Television and Radio, New York.

8. "Voorloper," 29.

9. "Sportscaster Howard Cosell: In the Right Place, at the Right Time with the Right Questions."

10. Richard F. Shepard, "2 Feature Films Bought by WOR-TV," *New York Times,* June 16, 1956.

11. Kindred, *Sound and Fury,* 26.

12. Cosell and Herskowitz, *Cosell,* 128.

13. Kindred, *Sound and Fury,* 27.

14. Frank Gifford, telephone interview with the author, June 4, 2009.

15. Cosell and Herskowitz, *Cosell,* 128.

16. Ibid.

17. Gifford, interview with the author.

18. Kindred, *Sound and Fury,* 28.

19. "Union Musicians Ask 15% Pay Rise," *New York Times,* January 15, 1954.

20. Michael Denning, *The Cultural Front: The Laboring of American Culture in the Twentieth Century* (New York: Verso, 1996), 47.

21. Ibid., 49.

22. Paul Buhle and Dave Wagner, *Hide in Plain Sight: The Hollywood Blacklistees in Film and Television, 1950–2002* (New York: Palgrave, 2003), 58–59.

23. See interview with Dick Powell in Paul Buhle, *From the Knights of Labor to the New World Order: Essays on Labor and Culture* (New York: Garland Publishing, 1997), 242–45. A more conservative faction of writers in radio and film, living mostly on the West Coast, formed a rival union, the Screen Writers Guild. This second group worked mostly in film and in non-live television.

24. Patrick McGulligan and Paul Buhle, *Tender Comrades: A Backstory of the Hollywood Blacklist* (New York: St. Martin's Press, 1999), 593. Joan LaCour's real name is Joan Scott, though I continue to refer to her as LaCour in the text.

25. "We Are for TWA" circular, 1953, American Business Consultants, Counterattack: Research Files, ser. 13: Communist Party Influenced Trade Unions, box 23, folder 13–68, Robert F. Wagner Labor Archives, Tamiment Library, New York University.

26. Ibid.

27. McGulligan and Buhle, *Tender Comrades,* 593.

28. Buhle, *From the Knights of Labor to the New World Order,* 242.

29. Martin Berkeley, "Reds in Your Living Room," *American Mercury,* August 1953, 55.

30. Ibid., 59–60.

31. McGilligan and Buhle, *Tender Comrades,* 593.

32. At the time, the willingness to betray even one's closest friends to HUAC was all that prevented a witness who had been identified as a communist from being blacklisted from a profession. See Victor Navasky, *Naming Names* (New York: Penguin, 1980).

33. McGilligan and Buhle, *Tender Comrades,* 593.

34. Joan Scott, telephone interview with the author, May 30, 2007.

35. "East Union Head Quits TV Writers," *New York Times,* January 14, 1954.

36. Jill Cosell, telephone interview with author, July 26, 2006.

37. Ibid.

38. Buhle, *From the Knights of Labor to the New World Order,* 242–43.

39. Scott, telephone interview with the author.

40. Berkeley, "Reds in Your Living Room," 56. Also see John Cogley and Merle Miller, *Blacklisting: Two Key Documents* (New York: Arno Press and the *New York Times,* 1971), 47.

41. *The Relation of the Writer to Television: A Discussion by Robert Alan Aurthur, Rod Serling, Irve Tunick, and Others* (Santa Barbara, Calif.: Center for the Study of Democratic Institutions/Fund for the Republic, 1960), 13.

42. Ibid., 8.

43. Ibid., 9.

44. Buhle and Wagner, *Hide in Plain Sight,* 26.

45. *Relation of the Writer to Television,* 10–12.

46. Paul Buhle, *From the Lower East Side to Hollywood: Jews in American Popular Culture* (New York: Verso, 2004), 9.

47. Denning, *The Cultural Front,* 9.

48. Cosell and Herskowitz, *Cosell,* 124–25.

49. Ibid., 126.

50. Howard Cosell, *Like It Is* (Chicago: Playboy Press, 1974), 277–78.

3. On the Network "Blacklist"

1. Howard Cosell with Mickey Herskowitz, *Cosell* (Chicago: Playboy Press, 1973), 141.

2. Howard Cosell file, "Sportscaster Howard Cosell: In the Right Place, at the Right Time with the Right Questions," August 29, 1958, Museum of Television and Radio, New York.

3. "Howard Cosell," *Contemporary Authors Online* (Thomson Gale, 2004), galenet.galegroup.com (accessed May 24, 2010); Val Adams, "NBC Continues Sunday Program," *New York Times,* May 24, 1957.

4. Jim Kensil, "Solons, Judges in Sports News with Athletes," *Lima (Ohio) News,* May 26, 1957.

5. Dave Kindred, *Sound and Fury: Two Powerful Lives, One Fateful Friendship* (New York: Free Press, 2006), 28; John Barrington, "Discovers Athletes 'Human,'" *Hammond (Ind.) Times,* February 11, 1957.

6. Cosell and Herskowitz, *Cosell,* 135.

7. Bert Sugar, *"The Thrill of Victory": The Inside Story of ABC Sports* (New York: Hawthorn Books, 1978), 4–5. Also see Jim Spence with Dave Diles, *Up*

Close and Personal: The Inside Story of Network Television Sports (New York: Atheneum Publishers, 1988), 51–55.

8. Roone Arledge, *Roone: A Memoir* (New York: HarperCollins, 2003), 18.

9. Sugar, *"The Thrill of Victory,"* 40–41.

10. Cosell and Herskowitz, *Cosell,* 137.

11. Dennis Hevesi, "Tom Moore, President of ABC Television in '60's, Dies at 88," *New York Times,* April 4, 2007.

12. Sugar, *"The Thrill of Victory,"* 42; Cosell and Herskowitz, *Cosell,* 137–38.

13. Cosell and Herskowitz, *Cosell,* 139.

14. John P. Shanley, "T.V.: A Look behind Babe Ruth Legend," *New York Times,* August 16, 1963.

15. Cosell and Herskowitz, *Cosell,* 141.

16. Arthur Daley, "Sports of the Times: In Fond Farewell," *New York Times,* April 15, 1964.

17. "T.V.–Radio Backtalk," *Washington Post,* September 27, 1959.

18. Jack Gould, "Radio TV: Test of Senses," *New York Times,* June 22, 1960.

19. Robert Slater, *Great Jews in Sports* (New York: Jonathan David Publishers, 2005), 60.

20. Howard Cosell, interview by Elli Wohlgelernter, June 3, 1981, for the American Jewish Committee, William E. Wiener Oral History Library, New York Public Library.

21. Red Smith, "Oh, Those Mets," *Washington Post,* May 10, 1962.

22. Arthur Daley, "Sports of the Times," *New York Times,* August 26, 1963.

23. Helen Spiro, "Cosell Calls 'Em as He Sees 'Em," *Daily Argus* (Mount Vernon, N.Y.), August 8, 1964.

24. Jack Gould, "TV: A Sports Interview with Hard-Hitting Candor," *New York Times,* November 30, 1964.

25. Sugar, *"The Thrill of Victory,"* xvii.

26. Arledge, *Roone,* 91–93.

27. Ibid., 92–93.

28. Cosell and Herskowitz, *Cosell,* 142.

29. Arledge, *Roone,* 92.

30. Jackie Robinson, *Chicago Daily Defender,* June 29, 1960.

31. Jackie Robinson, *Chicago Daily Defender,* June 30, 1960.

32. Ibid.

33. *Los Angeles Sentinel,* May 9, 1963.

34. *Chicago Daily Defender,* February 4, 1964.

35. "Patterson Irked over Segregation," *New York Times,* February 15, 1961.

36. "Red Smith's Column," *Washington Post,* February 1, 1961.

37. Cosell and Herskowitz, *Cosell,* 156–67.

4. Telling It Like It Was in the Era of Civil Rights

1. Dave Kindred, *Sound and Fury: Two Powerful Lives, One Fateful Friendship* (New York: Free Press, 2006), 113–16.

2. Quoted ibid. George Kimball has disputed this account, having tracked down Pete Hamill, who said he was not at the Greenwich Village meeting. Jack Newfield, however, writes in his 2002 memoir *Somebody's Gotta Tell It:* "A writers' committee seeking Ali's reinstatement was led by Norman Mailer, George Plimpton, and Pete Hamill. Howard Cosell declined to join this small faction of writers in Ali's corner when asked by Plimpton, although years later Cosell acted as if he had joined." See George Kimball, "Cosell, Ali, Kindred, and Me," www.thesweetscience.com/boxing-article/3520/cosell-ali-kindred (accessed May 24, 2010); Jack Newfield, *Somebody's Gotta Tell It: The Upbeat Memoir of a Working-Class Journalist* (New York: Macmillan, 2002), 89.

3. Jim Spence with Dave Diles, *Up Close and Personal: The Inside Story of Network Television Sports* (New York: Atheneum, 1988), 3–4.

4. Roone Arledge, *Roone: A Memoir* (New York: HarperCollins, 2003), 94–95.

5. Bert Sugar, *"The Thrill of Victory": The Inside Story of ABC Sports* (New York: Hawthorn Books, 1978), 186–87.

6. Kindred, *Sound and Fury,* 94.

7. Ibid., 94–95.

8. *Muhammad Ali Retrospective* (ESPN Video, 1999).

9. Howard Cosell with Mickey Herskowitz, *Cosell* (Chicago: Playboy Press, 1973), 181.

10. Kindred, *Sound and Fury,* 11–13.

11. Cosell and Herskowitz, *Cosell,* 182.

12. Quoted in Kindred, *Sound and Fury,* 95–96.

13. Ibid., 98.

14. Interview originally broadcast on *ABC's Wide World of Sports* (accessed on YouTube March 12, 2010; no longer available).

15. Sugar, *"The Thrill of Victory,"* 187–89.

16. Cosell and Herskowitz, *Cosell,* 191–92.

17. Ibid., 90.

18. From *Wide World of Sports,* as seen on ESPN Classic, *Classic Ali* (accessed on YouTube June 3, 2008; no longer available).

19. Cosell and Herskowitz, *Cosell,* 90.

20. Ibid., 207.

21. Cosell and Herskowitz, *Cosell,* 90, 281.

22. Sugar, *"The Thrill of Victory,"* 192.

23. Arledge, *Roone,* 92.

24. Kindred, *Sound and Fury,* 6.

25. Frank Deford, telephone interview with the author, May 30, 2006.
26. Ibid.
27. Kindred, *Sound and Fury,* 140–41.
28. Deford, telephone interview with the author.
29. Dick Young, column from *New York Post,* August 25, 1983, in Roone Arledge Papers, box 34, folder 3, ser. 4 (ms. no. 1423), "General Administrative Records, 1977–1986," Columbia University Rare Book and Manuscript Library.
30. Ron Briley, "Not So 'Young Ideas' on the Barricades in 1968," *Nine* 15, no. 1 (Fall 2006): 46.
31. Ibid., 48.
32. Ibid., 49.
33. Ibid., 52.
34. Dick Young column, Roone Arledge Papers.
35. Frank Gifford echoed these sentiments in his phone interview with the author. When asked if he thought Cosell's interest in civil rights was genuine or an act of self-promotion, Gifford responded: "I wouldn't want to be that judgmental. I think a lot of it was self-promoting. Howard would do almost anything to move up. Howard would be a shrink's delight. He wanted to be loved, he wanted to be accepted, he wanted it all. And it was all so personal." Keith Jackson gave a different answer in his phone interview. When asked if he thought Cosell's promotion of civil rights was genuine, he answered: "Well, I would think that you would have to be; if you're going to go as far as he did with civil rights, you're going to have to believe it. And whether his family history had anything to do with it, I don't know." Frank Gifford, telephone interview with the author, June 4, 2009; Keith Jackson, telephone interview with the author, June 4, 2009.
36. Sugar, *"The Thrill of Victory,"* 191.
37. Bert Randolph Sugar, telephone interview with the author, February 2, 2006. Neilsen is the survey company that compiles viewership figures for the networks.
38. Cosell and Herskowitz, *Cosell,* 198.
39. Sugar, interview with the author.
40. Howard Cosell microfiche file, "Howard Cosell Named Sports Editor for ABC-TV's Expanded 'Peter Jennings with the News' Program," ABC News Press Release, January 6, 1967, Paley Center for Media, Museum of Television and Radio New York.
41. "Baseball/Comeback Try/Massachusetts," ABC Evening News, August 16, 1968, record no. 1331, Vanderbilt University Television News Archive.
42. Commentary (Super Bowl), ABC Evening News, January 10, 1969, record no. 2051, Vanderbilt University Television News Archive.

43. Commentary (New York Jets' win), ABC Evening News, January 13, 1969, record no. 2093, Vanderbilt University Television News Archive.

44. Commentary (Olympics), ABC Evening News, October 18, 1968, record no. 147, Vanderbilt University Television News Archive.

45. Commentary (Olympics), ABC Evening News, October 25, 1968, record no. 262, Vanderbilt University Television News Archive.

46. Harry Edwards, *The Revolt of the Black Athlete* (New York: Free Press, 1970).

47. Harry Edwards, telephone interview with the author, July 13, 2006.

48. Ibid.

49. Chris Elzey, "American Jews and the Summer Olympics," in *Jews and American Popular Culture,* vol. 3, *Sports and Popular Culture,* ed. Paul Buhle (Westport, Conn.: Praeger, 2007), 51–70; also see Marty Glickman, *The Fastest Kid on the Block: The Marty Glickman Story* (Syracuse: Syracuse University Press, 1996), 60–61.

50. Douglas Hartmann, *Race, Culture, and the Revolt of the Black Athlete: The 1968 Olympic Protests and Their Aftermath* (Chicago: University of Chicago Press, 2003), 95–96.

51. Arledge, *Roone,* 90–91; Sugar, *"The Thrill of Victory,"* 216.

52. Arledge, *Roone,* 96–97.

53. Jim Spence, telephone interview with the author, April 5, 2005. Also see Spence and Diles, *Up Close and Personal,* 284.

54. Cosell and Herskowitz, *Cosell,* 50.

55. Ernie Kreiling, "A Closer Look," *Van Nuys (California) News,* November 8, 1968.

56. Cosell and Herskowitz, *Cosell,* 49.

57. Eric Zolov, "Harmonizing the Nation: Mexico and the 1968 Olympics," in *In the Game: Race, Identity, and Sports in the 20th Century,* ed. Amy Bass (New York: Palgrave Macmillan, 2005), 191–217.

58. Amy Bass, *Not the Triumph but the Struggle: The 1968 Olympics and the Making of the Black Athlete* (Minneapolis: University of Minnesota Press, 2002), 112–14.

59. Cosell and Herskowitz, *Cosell,* 56.

60. Edwards, telephone interview with the author.

61. Bass, *Not the Triumph but the Struggle,* 298–300.

5. Bigger than the Game

1. Roone Arledge to Pete Rozelle, box 34, folder 12, ser. 4 (ms. no. 1423), "NFL General, 1967–1971," Roone Arledge Papers, Columbia University Rare Manuscript Collection.

2. Howard Cosell with Mickey Herskowitz, *Cosell* (Chicago: Playboy Press, 1973), 341.

3. *Bananas*, DVD, directed by Woody Allen (United Artists/MGM Home Entertainment, 1971).

4. Cosell and Herskowitz, *Cosell*, 346.

5. Ibid.

6. "Keith Jackson and Howard Cosell Named to Broadcast Team for 'NFL Monday Night Football' on ABC Television Network," July 8, 1970, press release, ABC Sports, Howard Cosell biography microfiche file, Museum of Television and Radio, New York.

7. Roone Arledge, *Roone: A Memoir* (New York: HarperCollins, 2003), 113.

8. Frank Gifford, telephone interview with the author, June 4, 2009.

9. Arledge, *Roone,* 109.

10. Keith Jackson, telephone interview with the author, June 4, 2009.

11. Dan Jenkins to Roone Arledge, box 34, folder 12, ser. 4 (ms. no. 1423), "NFL General, 1967–1971," Roone Arledge Papers, Columbia University Rare Manuscript Collection.

12. Roone Arledge to Dan Jenkins, box 34, folder 12, ser. 4 (ms. no. 1423), "NFL General, 1967–1971," Roone Arledge Papers, Columbia University Rare Manuscript Collection.

13. Box 34, folder 12, ser. 4 (ms. no. 1423), "NFL General, 1967–1971," Roone Arledge Papers, Columbia University Rare Manuscript Collection.

14. "The Man Says the Gals Will Love It," *Los Angeles Times* and *Washington Post* News Service, *Victoria (Texas) Advocate,* July 15, 1970.

15. Ibid.

16. "Football Wins First Monday Ratings Fight," *Daily Mail* (Charleston, W.Va.), September 24, 1970.

17. Arledge, *Roone,* 113.

18. Jack Gould, "TV Review: ABC Football Draws 33% of the Audience," *New York Times,* September 23, 1970.

19. Roone Arledge to Joe Namath, box 34, folder 12, ser. 4 (ms. no. 1423), "NFL General, 1967–1971," Roone Arledge Papers, Columbia University Rare Manuscript Collection.

20. Loel Schrader, "Eyes and Ears on Sports," *Independent/Press-Telegram* (Long Beach, Calif.), September 25, 1970.

21. Cynthia Lowry, "The Young Lawyers," *Gallup (New Mexico) Independent,* September 23, 1970.

22. Paul Ernst, "Sports Shorts" *Columbus (Nebraska) Telegram,* September 25, 1970.

23. Chuck Dell, "Sports Scope," *Lima (Ohio) News,* September 24, 1970.

24. Jim Murray, "An Insult to the Game," *Los Angeles Times,* October 9, 1970.

25. Cosell and Herskowitz, *Cosell,* 294.

26. Ibid., 287.

27. "Meredith New 'Dimension,'" *San Antonio Light,* November 20, 1970.

28. Quoted in Leonard H. Goldenson with Marvin J. Wolf, *Beating the Odds: The Untold Story behind the Rise of ABC: The Stars, Struggles, and Egos that Transformed Network Television by the Man Who Made It Happen* (New York: Scribners, 1991), 210.

29. Gould, "TV Review."

30. Goldenson and Wolf, *Beating the Odds,* 204.

31. Cosell and Herskowitz, *Cosell,* 295.

32. Goldenson and Wolf, *Beating the Odds,* 210.

33. Ibid., 210–11.

34. "Editor's Note," *Courier News* (Blytheville, Arkansas), November 20, 1970.

35. Ibid.

36. "The Don and Howard Show," *Time,* December 14, 1970, 59.

37. Cosell and Herskowitz, *Cosell,* 309.

38. Ibid., 312–13.

39. Arledge, *Roone,* 115.

40. Ibid.

41. Cosell and Herskowitz, *Cosell,* 315.

42. Arledge, *Roone,* 115.

43. Accounts of Cosell's drinking appear in Dave Kindred, *Sound and Fury: Two Powerful Lives, One Fateful Friendship* (New York: Free Press, 2006); and in Jim Spence with Dave Diles, *Up Close and Personal: The Inside Story of Network Television Sports* (New York: Atheneum, 1988).

44. Nielsen ratings for *Monday Night Football,* box 34, folder 12, ser. 4 (ms. no. 1423), "NFL General, 1967–1971," Roone Arledge Papers, Columbia University Rare Manuscript Collection.

45. Howard Cosell with Peter Bonventre, *I Never Played the Game* (New York: William Morrow, 1985), 129–30.

46. Cosell and Herskowitz, *Cosell,* 89; Kindred, *Sound and Fury,* 181.

47. Mark Dollinger, "The Other War: American Jews, Lyndon Johnson, and the Great Society," *American Jewish History* 89, no. 4 (2001): 458–60; Karen Brodkin, *How Jews Became White Folks and What That Says about Race in America* (New Brunswick, N.J.: Rutgers University Press, 1998), 175; George Lipsitz, *The Possessive Investment in Whiteness* (Philadelphia: Temple University Press, 1998).

48. Kameel Nasr, *Arab and Israeli Terrorism* (Jefferson, N.C.: McFarland, 2007), 58–59.

49. Ibid., 58.
50. Cosell and Herskowitz, *Cosell*, 2.
51. Ibid., 9.
52. Kindred, *Sound and Fury*, 184–85; Nasr, *Arab and Israeli Terrorism*, 60.
53. Cosell and Herskowitz, *Cosell*, 10.
54. Frank Litsky, "Stan Wright, a U.S. Olympic Track Coach, Is Dead at 78," *New York Times*, November 8, 1998. Nine days after the disqualification, Hart did get some measure of revenge as he anchored the 4×100 relay team to a world record–setting time of 38.19 seconds. Hart and his teammates beat a Soviet team featuring Valery Borzov, who had won the gold in the 100 meters in Hart's absence. See Jeff Faraudo, "Hart Not Bitter about Olympics," *Oakland Tribune*, November 7, 2007.
55. Cosell and Herskowitz, *Cosell*, 22–23.
56. Ibid., 25–26. Mark Spitz won seven gold medals in swimming for the United States in 1972, an Olympic record for any individual that lasted until 2008, when swimmer Michael Phelps won eight gold medals.
57. Litsky, "Stan Wright, a U.S. Olympic Track Coach, Is Dead at 78."
58. "Sound Off, Sports Fans," *Chicago Tribune*, September 7, 1972.
59. "Sound Off, Sports Fans," *Chicago Tribune*, September 8, 1972.
60. John Henry Auran, "Cosell on the Griddle," *New York Times*, September 10, 1972.
61. Dave Wimbish, "Tenth Inning," *Arizona Daily Sun*, September 4, 1972.
62. Norm Unis, "Morning Line," *Times-Standard* (Eureka, California), September 6, 1972.
63. Jim Spence, telephone interview with the author, April 5, 2005.
64. "Games of the XX Olympiad," Paley Center for the Media, Museum of Television and Radio, New York.
65. Ibid.
66. Douglas Hartmann, *Race, Culture, and the Revolt of the Black Athlete* (Chicago: University of Chicago Press, 2003), 241–42.
67. George Soloman, "Howard Cosell's Wonderful World of Sports, Etc.," *Pacific Stars and Stripes*, October 3, 1972.
68. Ibid.
69. Allen Guttmann, *The Games Must Go On: Avery Brundage and the Olympic Movement* (New York: Columbia University Press, 1984), 254.
70. Cosell and Herskowitz, *Cosell*, 14.
71. Howard Cosell, interview with Elli Wohlgelernter, June 3, 1981, for the American Jewish Committee, William E. Wiener Oral History Library, New York Public Library, 61.

72. Melani McAlister, "One Black Allah: The Middle East in the Cultural Politics of African American Liberation, 1955–1970," *American Quarterly* 51, no. 3 (1999): 622–56.

73. Howard Cosell, interview with Wohlgelernter, 54.

6. Essential Contradictions

1. Lawrence Laurent, "Producer Forte Makes ABC Go on Monday Night," *Washington Post,* November 26, 1972.

2. Ibid.

3. "Marriages That Work: Howard and Emmy Cosell," *Family Circle,* December 13, 1977, 224.

4. "Another Side of Howard Cosell," *Salisbury (Maryland) Daily Times,* May 1, 1973.

5. Jill Cosell, telephone interview with author, July 26, 2006.

6. Ferdie Pacheco, *Blood in My Coffee: The Life of the Fight Doctor* (Chicago: Sports Publishing, 2005), 111.

7. Roone Arledge, *Roone: A Memoir* (New York: HarperCollins, 2003), 93.

8. Jim Spence with Dave Diles, *Up Close and Personal: The Inside Story of Network Television Sports* (New York: Atheneum, 1988), 6.

9. See Eleanor Sanger Papers, box 5, Sophia Smith Collection, Smith College, Northampton, Mass.

10. It is important to remember that by the 1970s, many women did in fact bring lawsuits against employers for tolerating harassment and creating a hostile working environment. See Laura W. Stein, *Sexual Harassment: A Documentary History* (Westport, Conn.: Greenwood Press, 1999).

11. Spence and Diles, *Up Close and Personal,* 6. In an e-mail message after reviewing this manuscript, Spence noted that he was not actually in the elevator when this incident allegedly happened.

12. Arledge, *Roone,* 119–20; Dave Kindred, *Sound and Fury: Two Powerful Lives, One Fateful Friendship* (New York: Free Press, 2006), 176–77.

13. Keith Jackson, telephone interview with the author, June 4, 2009.

14. Howard Cosell with Peter Bonventre, *I Never Played the Game* (New York: William Morrow, 1985), 152.

15. Frank Deford, telephone interview with the author, May 30, 2006.

16. Gerald Nachman, "Speaking of Howard Cosell," *New York Post,* May 14, 1966.

17. Myron Cope, "Would You Let This Man Interview You?" *Sports Illustrated,* March 13, 1967, 70–85.

18. Ibid., 85.

19. William Gildea, "Cosell Backs Federal Clout," *Washington Post,* March 20, 1973.

20. Christopher Lehmann-Haupt, "People Who Have Known Me," *New York Times,* October 17, 1973.

21. "Buckley Accepts Cosell Challenge," *New York Times,* April 22, 1974.

22. Unidentified news article, biographical files, Library of American Broadcasting, University of Maryland, College Park.

23. Sydney H. Schanberg, "Carey and Cosell," *New York Times,* November 21, 1981.

24. Justin Cosell, telephone interview with the author, May 22, 2006.

25. Cope, "Would You Let This Man Interview You?" 78.

26. Justin Cosell, telephone interview with the author.

27. Deford, telephone interview with the author.

28. Frank Gifford, telephone interview with the author, June 4, 2009.

29. Justin Cosell, telephone interview with the author.

30. Ibid.

31. William Leggett, "He Was a Jolly Good Fellow," *Sports Illustrated,* June 21, 1976, 42.

32. Alden Whitman, "Historians, Confident about the Past, Unsure about Their Future as They Open Annual Meeting," *New York Times,* April 7, 1976.

33. Jesse Lemisch, "If Howard Cosell Can Teach at Yale, Why Can't Herbert Aptheker?" *Newsletter of the Radical Historians Caucus* 22 (1976): 1–9; also see Jesse Lemisch, "If Howard Cosell Can Teach at Yale, Why Can't Herbert Aptheker?" *Radical History Review* 3 (Spring 1976): 46–48; George F. Will, "Yale, Aptheker and the 'Cosell Criterion,'" *Washington Post,* September 2, 1976; Jim O'Brien, "'Be Realistic, Demand the Impossible': Staughton Lynd, Jesse Lemisch, and a Committed History," *Radical History Review* 82 (2002): 65–99; "Faculty Reversal Awards Aptheker a Seminar at Yale," *New York Times,* April 30, 1976.

34. Leggett, "He Was a Jolly Good Fellow," 42.

35. Howard Cosell file, New York University Archives.

36. Ibid.

37. Howard Cosell, *Great Moments in Sport: A Sport Magazine Anthology* (New York: MacFadden-Bartell, 1964).

38. Cosell file, New York University Archives.

39. Ibid.

40. Ibid.

41. John Byrd, "200 Crowd to See Cosell," *Washington Square News,* February 6, 1978, ibid.

42. Ibid.

43. Mitchell Seidel, e-mail correspondence with author, January 6, 2010.

44. John Byrd, "Cosell to Stay On," *Washington Square Times,* February 22, 1978; Daniel Aquilante, "Student Disrupts Cosell Class," *Washington Square Times,*

April 3, 1978; Daniel Aquilante, "Cosell Resigns from Class," *Washington Square Times,* April 10, 1978, all in Howard Cosell Folder, Biographical Collection, University Archives, New York University.

45. Howard Cosell with Mickey Herskowitz, *Cosell* (Chicago: Playboy Press, 1973), 225.

46. Ibid., 230.

47. Kindred, *Sound and Fury,* 190.

48. Cosell, *Like It Is,* 28.

49. *When We Were Kings: The Untold Story of the Rumble in the Jungle,* DVD, directed by Leon Gast (Gramercy Pictures/Polygram Video, 1996).

50. Ibid.

51. *Muhammad Ali Retrospective* (ESPN Video, 1999).

52. Kindred, *Sound and Fury,* 207.

53. Ibid., 209.

54. ABC Broadcast of Muhammad Ali vs. Leon Spinks, September 15, 1978, www.youtube.com/watch?v=Dca9E3EipqY (accessed May 24, 2010).

55. Kindred, *Sound and Fury,* 156–57.

56. Julio Rodriguez, "Documenting Myth: Racial Representation in Leon Gast's *When We Were Kings,*" in *Sports Matters: Race, Recreation, and Culture,* ed. John Bloom and Micheal Nevin Willard (New York: New York University Press, 2002), 209–21.

57. Quoted in "Views of Sport: Some Views of Ali-Holmes Fight: Sentiment Favors Ali," *New York Times,* September 28, 1980.

58. Howard Cosell, *Like It Is* (Chicago: Playboy Press, 1974), 50.

59. *Sports Illustrated,* May 21, 1973.

60. Howard Cosell file, B:27111 018008, Paley Center for Media, Museum of Television and Radio, New York City.

61. Ibid.

62. Advertisement from *TV Guide,* reprinted in *New York Times,* October 1, 1975.

63. Justin Cosell, telephone interview with the author.

64. Arledge, *Roone,* 189.

65. Justin Cosell, telephone interview with the author.

66. See Jonathan Mahler, *Ladies and Gentlemen, the Bronx Is Burning: 1977, Baseball, Politics, and the Battle for the Soul of a City* (New York: Macmillan, 2006).

67. Letter to the editor, *New York Times Magazine,* September 22, 1974, 71.

68. "TV Stars You Love to Hate," *National Enquirer,* September 27, 1977.

69. Horkey Turek to Frank Reynolds, July 14, 1980, Frank Reynolds Papers, box 6, folder 34, Georgetown University Special Collections.

70. Thomas Boswell, "Writer Says Cosell Slapped Him on Plane, Threatens to File Suit," *Washington Post,* October 12, 1977.
71. Jim Spence, telephone interview with the author, April 5, 2005.
72. William Henry III, "Requiem for TV's Gender Gap?" *Time,* August 22, 1983.

7. Balancing Accounts

1. "Cosell to Host New Sunday Sports Show," *Broadcasting,* May 11, 1981.
2. Jimmy Roberts, telephone interview with the author, April 11, 2006.
3. Roone Arledge Papers, 1953–2002, box 16, folder 5, ser. 2.2 (ms. no. 1423), Rare Book and Manuscript Library, Columbia University.
4. Peter Mehlman, telephone interview with the author, March 21, 2006.
5. Roberts, telephone interview with the author.
6. Ron Alridge, "Pay TV May Be in Cosell's Future," *Chicago Tribune,* August 7, 1981.
7. Howard Cosell with Peter Bonventre, *I Never Played the Game* (New York: Morrow, 1985), 130.
8. William Taaffe, "Telling It Like It Is: Cosell a Breath of Fresh Air on 'Sports-Beat,'" *Washington Post,* April 23, 1982.
9. Ibid.
10. Ibid.
11. Ron Alridge, "Tempo: 'SportsBeat' Begins to Show Cosell's Real Nose for News," *Chicago Tribune,* May 11, 1982.
12. Ira Berkow, "Cosell and 'SportsBeat,' *New York Times,* May 1, 1984.
13. Ibid.
14. Ibid.
15. Barry Cooper, "Black College Sports," *New Pittsburgh Courier,* April 9, 1983.
16. Larry Holmes vs. Randall "Tex" Cobb (1982), ABC Sports (accessed on You-Tube July 22, 2008; no longer available).
17. Ibid.
18. Dave Kindred, "Fighting Mad, Cosell Walks Away from Sport Turned Spectacle," *Washington Post,* December 2, 1982.
19. Cosell and Bonventre, *I Never Played the Game,* 183–84.
20. Ibid., 191.
21. Roone Arledge, *Roone: A Memoir* (New York: HarperCollins, 2003), 284–87.
22. Ibid., 286.
23. It has long seemed ironic to me that this one remark would draw such attention when Washington's franchise name is in fact an extremely offensive racial slur in and of itself.
24. Leonard Shapiro, "Cosell's Remark Raises Ire," *Washington Post,* September 6, 1983.

25. Ibid.; "Remark Stirs Dispute," *New York Times,* September 6, 1983.

26. Cosell and Bonventre, *I Never Played the Game,* 330–47.

27. Ibid., 331.

28. "Lowery Hits Cosell," *Atlanta Daily World,* September 8, 1983.

29. Brad Pye, "Cosell Is Crass, Forgetful," *Los Angeles Sentinel,* September 8, 1983.

30. Brad Pye, "What Has Cosell Done to Promote Blacks?" *Los Angeles Sentinel,* September 8, 1983.

31. A. S. Doc Young, "Nobody Asked Me, But," *Los Angeles Sentinel,* September 29, 1983.

32. Eddie Jefferies, "Sports Spectrum," *New Pittsburgh Courier,* September 24, 1983.

33. Dorothy Gilliam, "White Domain," *Washington Post,* September 10, 1983.

34. Les Matthews, "Sports Briefs," *New York Amsterdam News,* September 10, 1983.

35. William Cotterell, "Howard Cosell Apologizes for Monkeying Around," *Atlanta Daily World,* September 13, 1983.

36. Leonard Shapiro, "Alvin Garrett: Cosell's Words Still Carry Sting," *Washington Post,* September 14, 1983.

37. Frank Gifford, telephone interview with the author, June 4, 1009.

38. Roone Arledge Papers, 1953–2002, box 11, folder 3, ser. 2.2 (ms. no. 1423), "Incoming," Columbia University Rare Book and Manuscript Library.

39. "Point shaving" occurs when gamblers illegally pay athletes to deliberately avoid scoring points during victories in order to keep the score within the "point spread."

40. Michael Katz, "Cosell Shines in Point-Shaving Report," *New York Times,* April 2, 1985.

41. Norman Chad, "He Still Is the One Telling It Like It Is," *Washington Post,* May 21, 1985.

42. Roone Arledge Papers, box 16, folder 5, ser. 2.2 (ms. no. 1423), Columbia University Rare Book and Manuscript Library.

43. Jim Spence with Dave Diles, *Up Close and Personal: The Inside Story of Network Television Sports* (New York: Atheneum, 1988), 170–71; Roone Arledge Papers, box 8, folder 7 ser. 2 (ms. no. 1423), "Correspondence, 1954–2002—Howard Cosell," Columbia University Rare Book and Manuscript Library.

44. Roone Arledge Papers, box 8, folder 7, ser. 2 (ms. no. 1423), "Correspondence, 1954–2002—Howard Cosell," Columbia University Rare Book and Manuscript Library.

45. Ibid.

46. Ibid.

47. Shirley Povich, "Cosell: What's a Low Punch among Friends?" *Washington Post,* October 11, 1985.

48. Tony Kornheiser, "Cosell's Book: Many Targets, Many Direct Hits," *Washington Post,* October 5, 1985.

49. "Cosell SportsBeat Show Is Cancelled by ABC," *New York Times,* October 20, 1985.

50. Michael Goodwin, "A Familiar Voice Expounds," *New York Times,* November 19, 1985.

8. Public Trust

1. Alex S. Jones, "And Now, the Media Mega-Merger," *New York Times,* March 24, 1985.

2. Randy Minkoff, "TV Sports: ESPN Has Become Major TV Force," United Press International, November 5, 1986.

3. Howard Cosell with Shelby Whitfield, *What's Wrong with Sports: America's Most Uninhibited Sports Critic Takes Aim at the Scandalous State of Sports Today* (New York: Simon and Schuster, 1991), 319, 172.

4. Dave Kindred, *Sound and Fury: Two Powerful Lives, One Fateful Friendship* (New York: Free Press, 2006), 263, 284.

5. Roone Arledge, *Roone: A Memoir* (New York: HarperCollins, 2003), 316–17.

6. "Business Takes Control," *Arkansas Democrat-Gazette,* December 17, 1986.

7. Jones, "And Now, the Media Mega-Merger."

8. Robert W. McChesney, *Telecommunications, Mass Media, and Democracy: The Battle for Control of U.S. Broadcasting, 1928–1935* (New York: Oxford University Press, 1993).

9. Arledge, *Roone,* 299.

10. Justin Cosell, telephone interview with the author, May 22, 2006.

11. Jack Craig, "Cosell Says Arledge 'Buckled'; USFL's Final Witness Claims Rozelle Applied Pressure to ABC Head," *Boston Globe,* June 26, 1986.

12. "Cosell: The Court Jester at USFL Trial," *San Francisco Chronicle,* June 26, 1986.

13. Howard Cosell, "Did Power Produce Perjury in USFL Trial?" *Minneapolis Star and Tribune,* July 24, 1986.

14. Howard Cosell, "Few in TV Displayed Any Courage at USFL Trial," *Minneapolis Star and Tribune,* July 27, 1986.

15. Ezra Bowen, "Sacked!" *Time,* August 11, 1986.

16. Howard Cosell, "Flutie Plays as NFL Tries to Punish Trump, USFL," *Minneapolis Star and Tribune,* August 17, 1986.

17. Jim Spence with Dave Diles, *Up Close and Personal: The Inside Story of Network Television Sports* (New York: Atheneum Publishers, 1988), 168.

18. "Howard Cosell Planning a Return to Television," *New York Times,* September 2, 1987.

19. Kindred, *Sound and Fury,* 262.

20. Cosell and Whitfield, *What's Wrong with Sports,* 331–32.

21. Frank Deford, telephone interview with the author, May 30, 2006.

22. *Muhammad Ali's 50th Birthday Celebration,* ABC, March 1, 1992, www .youtube.com/watch?v=ZsK8QU-EAW0 (accessed May 24, 2010).

23. Frank Gifford, interview with the author, June 4, 2009.

24. Robert Lipsyte, "A Doff of the Cap to Cosell," *New York Times,* January 31, 1992.

25. Ibid.

26. Spence and Diles, *Up Close and Personal,* 168.

27. Bill Rhoden, "Howard Cosell Tells It Like It Is," *Ebony,* December, 1976, 76–84.

28. George Lipsitz, *Time Passages: Collective Memory and American Popular Culture* (Minneapolis: University of Minnesota Press, 1990), 39–76.

Index